MURDERERS, ROBBERS
& HIGHWAYMEN

MURDERERS, ROBBERS & HIGHWAYMEN

True Tales of Crime and Punishment in Eighteenth-Century England

Edited and Introduced by

Stephen Brennan

SKYHORSE PUBLISHING

Skyhorse Publishing books may be purchased in bulk at special discounts for sales promotion, corporate gifts, fund-raising, or educational purposes. Special editions can also be created to specifications. For details, contact the Special Sales Department, Skyhorse Publishing, 307 West 36th Street, 11th Floor, New York, NY 10018 or info@skyhorsepublishing.com.

Skyhorse® and Skyhorse Publishing® are registered trademarks of Skyhorse Publishing, Inc.®, a Delaware corporation.

www.skyhorsepublishing.com

10 9 8 7 6 5 4 3 2 1

Library of Congress Cataloging-in-Publication Data is available on file.

ISBN: 978-1-62636-044-0

Printed in the United States of America

Table of Contents

Thomas Lympus
Executed for Robbing the Mail

Jonathan Bradford
Executed for a Supposed Murder

Elizabeth and Mary Branch
Executed for Murder

Martha Tracy
Executed for a Street Robbery

Henry Simms
Executed for Highway Robbery

William York
Convicted of Child Murder

Benjamin Tapner, and Others
Executed for Murder

John Mills
Executed for Murder

Captain Clarke, R. N.
Convicted of Murder

John Everett, alias George Anderson
Executed for Robbery

Introduction

"To make the punishment fit the crime,
The punishment fit the crime"

—*W. S. Gilbert*

OH, but we do love crime. Now, now, it's no good denying it. Our fascination, especially with *true* crime, easily rises to the level of a compulsion. Stop and think about it. When we hear of some atrocity, do we ignore it and go on our way? Not a chance, we sprint to the newsstand on the corner, we turn to our TVs, our laptops and cell phones, and, desperate for information, fairly revel in every gory little detail. Should we witness some misdeed, do we avert our gaze and turn away? No, we do not. The boldest among us may attempt to intervene, while the less . . . dauntless merely bang the tocsin and raise a hue and cry. Most of us simply stand there stunned, transfixed, mesmerized by the all-too-human drama enacted before our eyes. And though murder, rapine, and robbery angers and outrages us, it titillates us, too. Wickedness has a charm all its own, and no swami with his horn ever better charmed the cobra than we are . . . charmed—that is the word—by even the most monstrous and deplorable criminality. Why is this? Why should it be so? Each of us, in his (or her) own life knows something of what it is to be the victim of a fraud, or a theft of one kind or another, or of violence, or of some other abuse. You'd think then that all our sympathies would be with the victim, but they are not—not always. Which of us has not occasionally discovered herself in "sympathy with the devil"—and identifying with the predator? But what are the wages of sin?

Crime and punishment are inexorably linked, and always have been, even in our earliest stories. Adam and

Eve disobey the Lord—a crime if ever there was one—and they are punished. Cain kills brother Abel and he is sanctioned, banished from the society of his own kind. (Please note the absence of capital punishment, even for this, the very first murder.) In our Civil society, where law must be upheld and order be maintained, we recognize that it is not always expedient to wait upon the action of the Deity, and so we, who believe ourselves made in God's image—this is what we claim—take it upon ourselves, corporately, to render God's retribution. When an abomination is committed, the wicked are punished. We call this Justice. This has always been the paradigm. Crime and punishment—two sides of the same coin; we rarely think of one without the other. And in our long and deep fascination with these often horrific, sometimes humorous, always interesting stories, the one has always modified the other. They are best understood together, one without the other being only half the tale, and we have always craved the whole story.

In eighteenth-century Great Britain—the Georgian years—we have a society in flux. With the advent of the Industrial Revolution, vast numbers of people deserted village and shire to take up work in the mills and foundries of the big cities. Their populations, particularly in London, grew exponentially, as did the physical and geographic reach of the city. For the first time we see the rise of something resembling a true urban middle class; also a thriving professional class as lawyers and doctors set themselves up to cater to the press of new inhabitants. A sprawling and well-founded Empire abroad required profound adjustments at home, as the teeming city streets filled up with "strangers" just off the boat from every corner of the Domain. The plague had abated, the birth rate was up, John Bull had never seen such prosperity, but at the same time, poverty was widespread and crime was everywhere. A great urban stew then, unlike anything seen before. It is Hogarth's

London, city of *A Rake's Progress*, and *A Harlot's Progress*, *Marriage a-la-Mode*, and *Gin Lane*. The forces of law and order soon discovered themselves ill equipped to meet the challenges of this new order. They responded with an exacting hierarchy of brutal punishments.

This book is a collection and an adaptation of excerpts, stories, and reports that are in themselves adaptations of earlier accounts. Largely taken from the *Newgate Calendar*, these tales of true crime and punishment were compiled by the attorneys Knapp and Baldwin, and though published in the years 1824–28, this sampling includes examples throughout the eighteenth century. These chronicles of horrific crime and bloody punishment began as ha-penny broadsheets sold on the occasion of a hanging, pillorying, or other public chastisement. Eventually they were collected into something like a pulp or penny-dreadful magazine format, then re-edited and eventually issued as bound volumes. At each stage the stories were re-written, embellished and edited for the various publications, so as to better reflect or to speak to the particular time in which they were issued. Thus, the *Newgate Calendar* per se was not a specific publication, but rather a generic term for this type of publication, much like our True Crime magazines of the 1930s and '40s. The illustrations are all contemporaneous, and taken from the Knapp and Baldwin version. I especially enjoy the high-minded tone of this reportage, the kind of superior, moral certainty that so often attempts to excuse the necessity for ferocious punishment. As Knapp and Baldwin tell us: "More offences were made capital during the single reign of George III, than during the reigns of all the Plantagenets, Tudors, and Stuarts, put together."

Look ye, reader, we have here, on offer, tales of every imaginable felonious outrage. There's murder, premeditated and accidental; spouse-killing, parricide, and matricide, and child-murder; manslaughter and assassination;

adultery and bigamy and assault; torture and rape; sodomy and all manner of bestiality. There's kidnapping, slavery, sacrilege, blasphemy, piracy, and arson; perjury, sedition, riot, and treason, robbery and burglary and fraud. And as to judicial chastisement, the list is not so long, but what it lacks in variety, it more than makes up in savage and disproportionately rigorous punishment, often for little more than a misdemeanor. An eighteenth-century, Georgian perp faced fine and imprisonment, branding, public humiliation, transportation, and of course execution; to that end, the pillory and the block, the gallows, scaffold, and the stake.

So step right up! View the whole catalogue of horribles. They're delicious—true crime and punishment, old-style. Enjoy them.

Stephen Brennan
West Cornwall, Connecticut
2013

MORGRIDGE KILLING LIEUTENANT COPE.

JOHN MORGRIDGE

Executed for murder.

———

W E now present a dreadful instance of the effects of intoxication. This unfortunate man, who, through indulgence in this vice, met an untimely fate, was a native of Canterbury, whose ancestors had served the crown for upwards of two hundred years. He had been kettle-drummer to the first troop of horse-guards for a considerable time, and would have been promoted, had it not been for the following unfortunate quarrel:—A Mr. Cope, having obtained the rank of lieutenant in the army, invited several officers to dine with him at the Dolphin Tavern, in Tower

Street; and one of the parties invited Morgridge likewise to go, assuring him that he would be made welcome on the part of Mr. Cope.

When dinner was over, Cope paid the reckoning, and then, each man depositing half-a-crown, Morgridge and others adjourned to the guard-room, to which place more liquor was sent. They had not been long there before a woman of the town came in a coach, and asked for Captain Cope. Being introduced, she remained a short time, and then said, 'Who will pay for my coach?' Morgridge said 'I will'; and, having done so, he advanced to salute her; but she pushed him from her in a disdainful manner, and spoke to him in very abusive terms, which induced him to treat her with the same kind of language.

Morgridge's rudeness was resented by Cope, who took the woman's part, and a violent quarrel ensued between Cope and Morgridge, both of whom were intoxicated. This contest increased to such a degree, that they threw the bottles at each other; till at length Morgridge, inflamed with passion, drew his sword, and stabbed Cope, who instantly expired.

Morgridge, being taken into custody, was tried at the Old Bailey, July 5, 1706; but a doubt arising in the breast of the jury, whether he was guilty of murder or manslaughter, they brought in a special verdict, and the affair was left to be determined by the twelve judges.

The judges having consequently met at Serjeants' Inn, the case was argued before them by counsel; when they gave a unanimous opinion that he was guilty of wilful murder, because he did not kill Cope with the weapons he was originally using, but arose from his seat, and drew his sword, which was deemed to imply a malicious intention.

Morgridge, in the interim, made his escape from the Marshalsea Prison, and went into Flanders, where he remained about two years; but, being uneasy to revisit his native country, he imprudently came back to England, and, being apprehended, received sentence of death, and suffered along with William Gregg, at Tyburn, on the 28th of April, 1708.

After conviction he was truly sensible of the crime of which he had been guilty, acknowledged the justice of his sentence, and submitted to his fate with a devout wish that his misfortune might have its proper effect, in preventing similar destruction happening to others.

This is but one instance of several that we shall have occasion to record of the fatal consequences arising from a connexion with women of abandoned characters: but for a woman of this cast, the two men who were thus sacrificed, the one to the impetuosity of passion, the other to the rigour of the law, might have lived, a credit to themselves, and an advantage to the community.

On this occasion it may not be improper to reflect on the horrid crime of seduction. The man who is guilty of seducing a modest young woman from the paths of virtue is, in some degree, an accessory to every crime she may thereafter commit.

Women in general are of natures more gentle, of dispositions more harmless, than men; yet, when the mind of a woman is once contaminated, she commonly becomes more vicious even than a man of bad character; and the amiable softness of the sex seems to be totally eradicated.

If a youth is tempted to a criminal connexion with a woman already debauched by another, let him reflect that he is but seeking to perpetuate that infamy she has acquired, and to render still baser a mind already contaminated. One would imagine that a slight degree of thought would be sufficient to restrain youth from connexions of this nature; but, unhappily, the passions are more prevalent than reason, and the connexion is made before the youth has given himself time to think of its criminality.

May the case of Morgridge be an instructive one; and may those who are tempted to a commission of the crimes we would reprobate receive a timely warning therefrom.

DUEL BETWEEN THE DUKE OF HAMILTON AND LORD MOHUN.

COLONEL JOHN HAMILTON

*Convicted of manslaughter, as a second in a duel
between the Duke of Hamilton and Lord Mohun.*

———

No occurrence, short of a national misfortune, at this
time engaged the public equal to the memorable duel
between the Duke of Hamilton and Lord Mohun; and no
crime of this nature was ever committed with more sanguinary dispositions. The principals murdered each other, and
Mr. Hamilton was one of the seconds.

John Hamilton, Esq. of St. Martin's in the Fields, was
indicted at the sessions held at the Old Bailey on the 11th

of September, 1712, for the murder of Charles Lord Mohun, Baron of Oakhampton, on the 10th of November preceding; and at the same time he was indicted for abetting Charles Lord Mohun, and George Macartney, Esq. in the murder of James Duke of Hamilton and Brandon; and having pleaded 'not guilty' to these indictments, the evidence proceeded; to give their testimony, in substance as follows:—

Rice Williams, footman to Lord Mohun, proved that his master having met the Duke of Hamilton at the chambers of a master in chancery, on Thursday the 13th of November, a misunderstanding arose between them respecting the testimony of an evidence. That when his lord came home at night, he ordered that no person should be admitted to speak with him the next morning except Mr. Macartney. That on the Saturday morning, about seven o'clock, this evidence, having some suspicion that mischief would ensue, went towards Hyde Park, and, seeing the Duke of Hamilton's coach going that way, he got over the Park-wall; but, just as he arrived at the place where the duellists were engaged, he saw both the noblemen fall, and two gentlemen near them, whom he took to be the seconds; one of whom he knew to be Mr. Macartney, and the other (but he could not swear it was the prisoner) said 'We have made a fine piece of work of it.'

The waiters at two different taverns proved that the deceased noblemen and their seconds had been at those taverns; and, from what could be collected from their behaviour, it appeared that a quarrel had taken place, and that a duel was in agitation; and some of the duke's servants and other witnesses deposed to a variety of particulars, all which tended to the same conclusion.

But the evidence who saw most of the transaction was William Morris, a groom, who deposed that, 'as he was walking his horses towards Hyde Park, he followed a hackney-coach with two gentlemen in it, whom he saw alight by the Lodge, and walk together towards the left part of the ring, where they were about a quarter of an hour, when he saw two other gentlemen come to them; that, after having saluted each other, one of them, who he was since told was the Duke of Hamilton, threw off his cloak, and one of the other two, who he now understands was Lord Mohun, his surtout coat, and all immediately drew; that the duke and lord pushed at each other but a very little while, when the duke closed, and took the lord by the collar, who fell down and groaned, and the duke fell upon him; that just as Lord Mohun was dropping, he saw him lay hold of the duke's sword, but could not tell whether the sword was at that time in his body; nor did he see any wound given after the closing, and was sure Lord Mohun did not shorten his sword. He declared he did not see the seconds fight, but they had their swords in their hands, assisting their lords.'

Paul Boussier, a surgeon, swore that, on opening the body of the Duke of Hamilton, he found a wound between the second and third ribs, which entered into the body, inclining to the right side, which could not be given but by some push from above.

Henry Amie, a surgeon, swore that he found the Duke of Hamilton had received a wound by a push, which had cut the artery and small tendon of his right arm; another very large one in his right leg; a small one in his left leg, near the instep; and a fourth in his left side, between the second and third ribs, which ran down into his body most forward, having pierced the skirt of his midriff, and gone through his caul; but that the wound in his arm caused his so speedy death; and that he might have lived two or three days with the wound in his breast, which wound could not be given but by an arm that reached over, or was above him.

He further deposed, that he also viewed the Lord Mohun's body, and found that he had a wound between the short ribs, quite through his belly, and another about three inches deep in the upper part of his thigh; a large wound, about four inches wide, in his groin, a little higher, which was the cause of his immediate death; and another small wound on his left side; and that the fingers of his left hand were cut.

The defence made by the prisoner was, that 'the duke called him to go abroad with him, but he knew not any thing of the matter till he came into the field.'

Some Scottish noblemen, and other gentlemen of rank, gave Mr. Hamilton a very advantageous character, asserting that he was brave, honest, and inoffensive; and the jury, having considered of the affair, gave a verdict of 'manslaughter;' in consequence of which the prisoner prayed the benefit of the statute, which was allowed him.

At the time the lives of the above-mentioned noblemen were thus unfortunately sacrificed, many persons thought they fell by the hands of the seconds; and some late writers on the same opinion: but nothing appears in the written or printed accounts of the transaction, nor did any thing arise on the trial, to warrant so ungenerous a suspicion; it is therefore but justice to the memory of all the parties to discredit such insinuations.

But here a reflection will naturally arise, that we hope may be of service to our readers of superior rank. If all duellists are, as common sense seems to intimate, murderers, in what light are we to consider their seconds? Certainly in no other than as accessories before the fact. The law says, and with great justice, that accessories in case of murder shall be deemed principals.

With regard to the particular case in question, if we believe the plea of the prisoner, we cannot consider him as an accessory, because he was ignorant of the intention of the duke.

Be this as it may, it is much to be lamented that we have not laws of force sufficient to put an effectual stop to the horrid practice of duelling—a practice which had its rise in the ferocious manners of the most barbarous ages, and is a disgrace to any people that pretend to be polished or refined. Honour is made the vile pretence; and murder, real or intended, is always the consequence.

Men ought to consider that their great Creator has intrusted them with life for more valuable purposes than to put it to the hazard on every frivolous occasion. One would imagine that the reflection of a moment would teach any man in his senses that the determination to rush into the presence of his Maker with the crime of murder on his head was sufficient to ensure his perdition!

Happy are those, who have been thus tempted to imbrue their hands in the blood of their fellow-creatures, if they escape the murdering award or pistol, and have time allotted them to repent of their misdeeds and surely a whole life of penitence is short enough to atone for the intentional murder of a fellow-creature.

SPURLING, A TURNKEY, SHOT BY JOHNSON, IN THE OLD BAILEY.

WILLIAM JOHNSON and JANE HOUSDEN

Executed for the murder of Mr. Spurling.

———

THROUGHOUT the whole annals of our Criminal chronology, though the denial of culprits condemned on the clearest evidence of their guilt is by far too frequently recorded, we cannot adduce an instance similar to the following dying declarations of innocence:

William Johnson, one of these unrelenting sinners, was a native of Northamptonshire, where he served his time to a butcher, and, removing to London, opened a shop in

Newport Market; but, business not succeeding to his expectation, he took a house in Long Acre, and commenced corn-chandler: in this business he was likewise unsuccessful, on which he sold his stock in trade, and took a public house near Christ Church, in Surrey. Being equally unsuccessful as a victualler, he sailed to Gibraltar, where he was appointed a mate to one of the surgeons of the garrison; in short, he appears to have possessed a genius suited to a variety of employments. Having saved some money at Gibraltar, he came back to his native country, where he soon spent it, and then had recourse to the highway for a supply. Being apprehended in consequence of one of his robberies, he was convicted, but received a pardon. Previous to this he had been acquainted with one Jane Housden, the other hardened wretch, who had been tried and convicted of coining, but also obtained a pardon. It was not long after this pardon (which was procured by great interest) before Housden was again in custody for a similar offence. On the day that she was to be tried, and just as she was brought down to the bar of the Old Bailey, Johnson called to see her; but Mr. Spurling, the head turnkey, telling him that he could not speak to her till her trial was ended, he instantly drew a pistol, and shot Spurling dead on the spot, in the presence of the court, and all the persons attending to hear the trials; Mrs. Housden at the same time encouraging him in the perpetration of this singular murder. The event had no sooner happened than the judges, thinking it unnecessary to proceed on the trial of the woman for coining, ordered both the parties to be tried for the murder; and there being such a number of witnesses to the deed, they were almost immediately convicted, and received sentence of death. From this time to that of their execution, which took place September 19th, 1712, and even at the place of their death, they behaved as if they were wholly insensible of the enormity of the crime which they had committed; and, notwithstanding the publicity of their offence, to which there were so many witnesses, they had the confidence to deny it to the last moment of their lives: nor did they show any signs of compunction for their former sins. After hanging the usual time, Johnson was hung in chains near Holloway, between Islington and Highgate.

DOUGLAS KILLING HIS SHIPMATE

THOMAS DOUGLAS

Executed for murder.

———

Thomas Douglas was indicted at the Old Bailey, for the murder of William Sparks, a seaman, at a public house in Wapping.

It appeared, in the course of the evidence, that the parties had been drinking together, till they were inflamed with liquor, when the prisoner took up a knife, and stabbed the other in such a manner that he died on the spot. The atrociousness of the offence was such that Douglas was immediately taken into custody, and, being convicted on the clearest evidence, received sentence of death.

This criminal was born in the county of Berwick, in Scotland, and, having been educated by his parents according to the strictly religious plan prevailing in that country, he was bound apprentice to a sea-faring person at Berwick; and, when he was out of his time, he entered on board a ship in the royal navy, and in this station acquired the character of an expert and valiant seaman.

Having served Queen Anne during several engagements in the Mediterranean and other seas, he returned to England, with Sparks, who was his shipmate, on whom he committed the murder we have mentioned.

After conviction, it was a difficult matter to make Douglas sensible of the enormity of the crime that he had committed; for he supposed that, as he was drunk when he perpetrated the fact, he ought to be considered in the same light as a man who was a lunatic.

This unhappy malefactor suffered at Tyburn, on the 27th of October 1714.

From his fate and sentiments we may learn the following useful instructions. We see that drunkenness is a crime of a very high nature, since it may lead to the commission of the highest. If this man had not been in a state of intoxication, he would probably never have been guilty of murder. We should remember that the bounties of Providence were sent for our use and sustenance, not to be abused. It is a judicious observations of the ingenious authors of the Spectator, that 'If a man commits murder when he is drunk, he must be hanged for it when he is sober. It is no excuse for any one to say he was guilty of a crime when drunk, because drunkenness itself is a crime; and what he may deem an excuse is only an aggravation of his offence; since it is acknowledging that he has been guilty of two crimes instead of one.'

The conclusion to be drawn from this sad story is, that temperance is a capital virtue; and that drunkenness, as it debauches the understanding, reduces a man below the level of the 'beasts that perish.' The offender before us acknowledged, in his last moments, that it was but the fore-runner of other crimes: and, as what happened to him may be the case with others, as drunkenness produces quar-rels, and quarrels lead to murder, we hope the case of this unhappy man will impress on the minds of our readers the great importance of temperance and sobriety. We see that Douglas had received a very religious education; yet even this was inadequate to preserve him from the fatal effects of a casual intoxication! When men drink too much, and in consequence thereof assault and wound their companions, we may say, in the words of the poet, that

'Death is in the bowl.'

MARQUIS DE PALEOTTI STABBING HIS SERVANT.

THE MARQUIS DE PALEOTTI

Executed for the murder of his servant.

———

THIS rash man was the head of a noble family in Italy, and, like Colonel Hamilton, was brought to a disgraceful death, through the vice of gaming, with all the aggravated horrors of suffering in a strange country; thus doubly disgracing the honours of his house.

Ferdinando Marquis de Paleotti was born at Bologna, in Italy, and in the reign of Queen Anne was a colonel in the Imperial army.

The cause of his coming to England arose from the following circumstance:—The Duke of Shrewsbury, being at Rome in the latter end of King William's reign, fell in love with, and paid his addresses to, the sister of Paleotti; and the lady following the Duke to Augsburgh in Germany, they were there married, after she had first renounced the Roman Catholic religion. The duchess residing with her husband in England, and the marquis having quitted the Imperial army on the peace of Utrecht, he came to this country to see his sister.

Being fond of an extravagant course of life, and attached to gaming, he soon ran in debt for considerable sums. His sister paid his debts for some time, till she found it would be a burdensome and endless task. Though she declined to assist him as usual, he continued his former course of life till he was imprisoned for debt; but his sister privately procured his liberty, and he was discharged without knowing who had conferred the favour on him.

After his enlargement, he adopted his old plan of extravagance; and, being one day walking in the street, he directed his servant, an Italian, to go and borrow some money. The servant, having met with frequent denials, declined going: on which the Marquis drew his sword, and killed him on the spot.

Being instantly apprehended, he was committed to prison, tried at the next sessions, and, being convicted on full evidence, he received sentence of death. The Duke of Shrewsbury being dead, and his duchess having little interest or no aquaintance in England, it appears as if no endeavours were used to save the marquis, who suffered at Tyburn on the 17th of March, 1718.

Italian pride had taken deep root in the mind of this man. He declared it to be disgraceful to this country to put a nobleman to death like a common malefactor, for killing his servant; and lamented that our churches, as in Italy, did not afford a sanctuary for murderers. Englishmen, however, are thankful that neither of this marquis's desires prevail in their country, where the law makes no distinction in offenders. To his last moment this pride of aristocracy was predominant in his mind. He petitioned the sheriffs that his body should not be defiled by touching the unhappy Englishmen doomed to suffer with him, and that he might die before them, and alone. The sheriffs, in courtesy to a stranger, granted this request, and thus, in his last struggle, he maintained the superiority of his rank.—Vain man! of what avail were his titles in the presence of the Almighty?

CLARKE, WHILST IN THE ACT OF EMBRACING A YOUNG WOMAN, CUTS HER THROAT.

MATTHEW CLARKE

Executed for murder.

———

THIS offender was the son of poor persons at St. Albans, and brought up as a plough-boy; but, being too idle to follow his business, he sauntered about the country, and committed frequent robberies, spending among women the money he obtained in this illegal manner.

Clarke had art enough to engage the affections of a number of young women, to some of whom he promised marriage; and he seems to have intended to have kept his word with one of them, and went with her to London to tie the nuptial knot; but, going into a goldsmith's shop to buy the ring, he said he had forgot to supply himself with money, but would go into the country and fetch it.

The young woman stayed in town while he went to Wilsden Green, with a view to commit a robbery, that he might replenish his pocket. As it was now the season of hay-making, he met a man, who, wondering that he should be idle, gave him employment. Besides the business of farming, his employer kept a public house, and had a servant maid, whom Clarke had formerly courted.

The villain, leaving his fellow-labourers in the field, went to the house, and, finding only the girl at home, conversed with her some time; but, having determined to rob his employer, he thought he could not do it securely without murdering her; and, while she was gone to draw him some beer, he pulled out his knife for this horrid purpose; and, when she entered the room, he got up to kiss her, thinking to have then perpetrated the deed, but his conscience prevented him: on this he sat down, and talked with her some time longer; when he got up, and, again kissing her, cut her throat in the same instant.

Hereupon she fell down, and attempted to crawl to the door, while the blood streamed from her throat; on which the villain cut her neck to the bone, and, robbing the house of a small sum, ran off towards London, under all the agonizing tortures of a wounded conscience.

Tyburn being in his way to town, he was so terrified at the sight of the gallows, that he went back a considerable distance, till, meeting a waggon, he offered his service in driving, thinking that his being in employment might prevent his being suspected in case of a pursuit. But he had not gone far before some persons rode up, and asked him if he had seen a man who might be suspected of a murder. He seemed so terrified by the question that the parties could not help noticing his agitation, and, on a close inspection, they found some congealed blood on his clothes, to account for which he said he had quarrelled and fought with a soldier on the road.

Being taken into custody, he soon acknowledged his crime, and, being carried before a magistrate, he was committed to Newgate; and, when brought to trial, he pleaded guilty: in consequence of which he was executed at Tyburn on the 28th of July, 1721, and then hung in chains near the spot where he committed the murder.

There is something dreadfully enormous in the crime for which this man suffered. When under sentence of death he was one of the most miserable wretches that ever endured a situation so calamitous. Nor is this to be wondered at; for the murder he committed was one of the most unprovoked imaginable. It is probable, from the affection the poor girl had for him, that she would have lent him a greater sum than he obtained by cutting her throat.

His terrors at the sight of the gallows should teach those who are prompted to iniquity to avoid all crimes that may lead to a fatal end. The wicked can never be happy; and it is only by a life of integrity, virtue, and piety, that we can hope for the blessing of God, the applause of a good conscience, and 'that peace of mind which passeth all understanding.'

HARTLEY AND REEVES ROBBING A JOURNEYMAN TAILOR NEAR HARROW.

JOHN HARTLEY and THOMAS REEVES

Footpads, executed for robbery.

———

THESE offenders were tried for stopping a journeyman tailor, in the fields near Harrow, and robbing him of two pence and his clothes; and, because he had no more money, they beat him most inhumanly, stripped, and bound him to a tree.

While he was in this wretched situation, some persons coming by unbound him, and took him to an alehouse, where he told the particulars of the robbery, mentioned the colour of his clothes, and described the persons of the robbers to the best of his power.

These circumstances were heard by a fiddler, who, going next day into a public house in Fore Street saw the fellows offering to sell the tailor's coat. The fiddler immediately proposed to be the purchaser gave earnest for it, and, pretending he had not money enough, said he would fetch the difference; instead of which he brought the party robbed, who, knowing the footpads, they were taken into custody.

The evidence on their trial was so plain that the jury could not hesitate to find them guilty; in consequence of which they received sentence of death.

After conviction their behaviour was unbecoming persons in their unhappy circumstances. That of Reeves was particularly hardened: he would sing and swear while the other convicts were at prayers; yet he told the Ordinary that he was certain of going to heaven.

The most curious circumstance arising from the detection of these offenders was the singular method that Hartley took to save his life. He procured six young women, dressed in white, to go to St. James's, and present a petition in his behalf. The singularity of their appearance gained them admission; when they delivered their petition, and told the king that, if he extended the royal mercy to the offender, they would cast lots which should be his wife, but his Majesty said that he was more deserving of the gallows than a wife, and accordingly refused their request.

As they were going to execution the Ordinary asked Reeves if his wife had been concerned with him in any robberies. 'No,' said he; 'she is a worthy woman, whose first husband happening to be hanged, I married her, that she might not reproach me by a repetition of his virtues.'

At the fatal tree Reeves behaved in the most hardened manner, affected to despise death, and said he believed he might go to heaven from the gallows as safely as from his bed.

These offenders suffered at Tyburn on the 4th of May, 1722.

We see, in the instance of these malefactors, from what a casual circumstance their detection arose. A man hears a description of them in a public house; the next day he goes accidentally into another alehouse, where he sees them offering the stolen goods for sale; and, by an honest deception, procures their being taken into custody. The poor fiddler had no interest in their detection but what arose from his abhorrence of vice; yet he was so regardful of what he had heard, that he became the immediate instrument of bringing them to justice.

Hence let us learn to admire the inscrutable mysteries of the providence of God, which, as they surpass our finite comprehension, should excite our wonder and our gratitude. Nothing can be hid from the all-seeing eye of Heaven; and the man that commits a crime with the hope of concealing it does but treasure up a fund of uneasiness for his own mind: for, even if the crime should be concealed from the public, he will be perpetually harassed with the corroding stings of a guilty conscience, and at all times carry with him a hell in his own bosom!

Brinsden killing his Wife in a Quarrel.

BRINSDEN KILLING HIS WIFE IN A QUARREL.

MATTHIAS BRINSDEN

Executed for killing his wife.

———

THIS offender served his time to a cloth-drawer, in Blackfriars, named Beech, who, dying, was succeeded by Mr. Byfield, who left his business to Brinsden, who married Byfield's widow; but how long she lived with him is uncertain.

After the death of this wife, he married a second, by whom he had ten children, some of the elder of whom were brought up to work at his business. At length he was seized with a fever so violent that it distracted him, so that he fell down to his bed. This misfortune occasioned such a decay in his trade, that on his recovery he carried news papers, and did any other business he could, to support his family.

Going home about nine o'clock one evening, his wife, who was sitting on a bed, suckling a young child, asked him what he should have for supper. To which he answered, 'Bread and cheese; can't you eat that as well as the children?' She replied, 'No, I want a bit of meat.' 'But (said he) I have no money to buy you any.' In answer to which she said, 'You know I have had but little to-day'; and, some farther words arising between them, he stabbed her under her left breast with a knife.

The deed was no sooner perpetrated than one of the daughters snatched the infant from the mother's breast, and another cried out, 'O Lord! father, you have killed my mother.' The prisoner now sent for some basilicon and sugar, which he applied to the wound, and then made his escape.

A surgeon, being sent for, found that the wound was mortal, and the poor woman died soon after he came, and within half an hour of the time the wound was given.

In the interim the murderer had retreated to the house of Mr. King, a barber, at shad well; whence, on the following day, he sent a letter to one of his daughters, and another to a woman of his acquaintance; and in consequence of these letters he was discovered, taken into custody, carried before a magistrate, and committed to take his trial for the murder.

When on trial, he urged, in his defence, that his wife was in some degree intoxicated, that she wanted to go out and drink with her companions, and that, while he endeavoured to hinder her, she threw herself against the knife, and received an accidental wound.

However, the evidence against him was so clear, that his allegations had no weight, and he received sentence of death. After conviction he became serious and resigned; and being visited by one of his daughters, who had given evidence against him, he took her in his arms, and said, 'God forgive me, I have robbed you of your mother: be a good child, and rather die than steal: never be in a passion; but curb your anger, and honour your mistress: she will be as a father and mother to you. Farewell, my dear child; pray for your father, and think of him as favourably as you can.'

On his way to the place of execution, the daughter above mentioned was permitted to go into the cart, to take her last farewell of him,—a scene that was greatly affecting to the spectators.

As some reports very unfavourable to this malefactor had been propagated during his confinement, he desired the Ordinary of Newgate to read the following speech just before he was launched into eternity.

'I was born of kind parents, who gave me learning: I went apprentice to a fine-drawer. I had often jars, which might increase a natural waspishness in my temper. I fell in love with Hannah, my last wife, and after much difficulty won her, she having five suitors courting her at the same time. We had ten children (half of them dead), and I believe we loved each other dearly; but often quarrelled and fought.

'Pray, good people, mind, I had no malice against her, nor thought to kill her two minutes before the deed; but I designed only to make her obey me thoroughly, which the Scripture says all wives should do. This I thought I had done when I cut her skull on Monday, but she was the same again by Tuesday.

'Good people, I request you to observe, that the world has spitefully given out, that I carnally and incestuously lay with my eldest daughter I here solemnly declare, as I am entering into the presence of God, I never knew whether she was a man or a woman since she was a babe. I have often taken her in my arms, often kissed her, sometimes given her a cake or a pie, when she did any particular service beyond what came to her share; but never lay with

her, or carnally knew her, much less had a child by her.
But when a man is in calamities, and is haled like me, the
women will make surmises be certainties.

'Good Christians, pray for me! I deserve death: I am
willing to die; for, though my sins are great, God's mercies
are greater.'

He was executed at Tyburn, on the 24th of September,
1722.

If any credit is to be given to Brinsden's last solemn declaration, his wife, as well as himself, seems to have been of
an unhappy disposition, since they could not refrain from
quarrelling, though they had a sincere regard for each
other. We fear this is but too commonly the case in the married state; but it is a lamentable consideration that those
who have engaged to be the mutual comfort and support of
each other, through life, should render the rugged path still
more difficult by their mutual contentions and animosities.

It is the part of a husband to protect his wife from every
injury and insult; to be at once a father and a guardian to
her; and, so far from ill-treating her himself, he ought to be
particularly watchful that she be not ill used by others: the
tenderer sex have a natural claim to the protection of the
more robust. Indeed it would appear that one reason for
Providence bestowing superior strength on the man, was
for the defence and protection of the woman.

On the other hand women should be grateful for this
protection; and, in the emphatical words of St. Paul, wives
should learn to be 'obedient to their husbands in all things.'

> Such duty as the subject owes the prince,
> Ev'n such a woman oweth to her husband;
> And when she's froward, peevish, sullen, sour,
> What is she but a foul contending rebel,
> And graceless traitor to her loving lord?
>   SHAKESPEARE.

It is a very unfortunate circumstance when persons of opposite sentiments happen to be united in wedlock: but, even in this case, people of sense and humanity will learn to bear with the failings of each other, considering that much allowance is to be made for their own faults. They will endeavour to make the lot which has befallen them more supportable than it otherwise would be; and, in time, by the constant wish to please, they may even conciliate the affections of each other, and mutual happiness may arise where it is least expected.

In general, however, a coincidence of temper and a purity of manners, added to a sacred regard to religious duties, are the greatest security for happiness in the married state. Beautiful are the lines of the poet:

> Two kindest souls alone should meet,
> 'Tis friendship makes their bondage sweet,
> And feeds their mutual loves:
> Bright Venus, on her rolling throne,
> Is drawn by gentlest birds alone,
> And Cupids yoke the doves.

SARAH PRIDDON STABBING A GENTLEMAN IN A BAGNIO.

SARAH PRIDDON, alias SALLY SALISBURY

Convicted of an assault in which murder was attempted.

———

THERE is no state in human nature so wretched as that of the prostitute, Seduced, abandoned to fate, the unhappy female falls a prey to want; or she must purchase existence at a price degrading, in the last degree, to the mind of sensibility. Subject to the lust and debauchery of every thoughtless blockhead, she becomes hardened in shame. Hence modesty is put to the blush by the obscenity of those, once pure as our own darling daughters. Every public place swarms with this miserable set of beings, so that parents dread to indulge their children with even the sight of a moral stage performance. The unhappy prostitute, heated by drink, acquires false spirits, in order to inveigle men to her purpose; and, in so doing, she too often takes apparent satisfaction in annoying, by looks and gestures, often by indecent words, the virtuous part of the audience. The law, while it assumes the guardianship 'Of youth by suppressing immorality,' still permits these wantons to rove, uncontrolled, among the virtuous as well as the profligate. There ought, in public at least, some bounds to be set— some check to the pernicious example. They may surely be restrained, at least to the outward show of decency, when in mixed company.

Yet, says the philanthropist, they demand our pity. They do indeed! The cause, while nature progresses, cannot be removed; but the legislature might do more to regulate the evil than is done in this country. It is by some held a necessary evil, tending, in its utmost extent, even to the benefit of the yet virtuous female; but a mind once formed by precept and good example will ever repel a liberty attempted by a profligate man; they are cowards when reproved by virtuous indignation.

We can only accord our tribute of pity to them, though about to give the effects of prostitution in its greatest extent, by quoting the words of the poet, as applied to the miseries of the unhappy Jane Shore:

> 'When she was mine, no arm came ever near her;
> I thought the gentlest breath of heaven
> Tue rough to blow upon her.
> Now, sad and shelterless, perhaps she wanders,
> And the rain drops from some penthouse
> On her wretched head, drenches her locks,
> And kills her with cold.'

On the 24th of April 1723, Sarah Priddon was indicted at the Old Bailey, for making a violent assault on the Hon.

J—F—, and stabbing him with a knife in his left breast, and giving him a wound of which he long languished, with an intent to kill and murder him.

Mrs. Priddon, or rather Salisbury (for that was the name by which she was best known), was a woman of the town, who was well acquainted with the gentleman whom she wounded. It appeared on the trial that Mr. F. having gone to the Three Tuns tavern in Chandos Street, Covent Garden, about midnight, Sally followed him thither soon afterwards. The drawer, after he had waited on Mr. F. went to bed; but at two in the morning he was called up, to draw a pint of Frontiniac for Mrs. Salisbury. This he did, and carried it to her with a French roll and a knife. The prisoner was now in company and conversation with Mr. F. and the drawer heard them disputing about an Opera ticket, which he had presented to her sister; and, while they were talking, she stabbed him; on which he put his hand to his breast, and said, 'Madam, you have wounded me.'

No sooner had she committed the fact than she appeared sincerely to regret what she had done: she sent for a surgeon, who finding it necessary to extend the wound, that the blood might flow outwardly, she seemed terrified, and, calling out 'O Lord! what are you doing?' fainted away.

On her recovery, she asked Mr. F. how he did; to which he answered, 'Very bad, and worse than you imagine.' She endeavoured to console him in the best manner she could, and, after some time, the parties went away in separate chairs; but not till the wounded gentleman had forgiven her, and saluted her as a token of that forgiveness.

The counsel for the prisoner endeavoured to prove that she had no intention of wounding him with malice *prepense*; and that what she did arose from a sudden start of passion, the consequence of his having given an Opera ticket to her sister, with a view to ingratiate her affections, and debauch her.

The counsel for the Crown ridiculed this idea, and insinuated that a woman of Mrs. Salisbury's character could not be supposed to have any very tender regard for her sister's reputation. They allowed that Mr. F. had readily forgiven her at the time; but insisted that this was a proof of the placability of his temper, and no argument in her favour.

They said that, if the gentleman had died of the wound, she would have been deemed guilty of murder, as she had not received the least provocation to commit the crime; and that the event made no difference with respect to the malignity of her intentions.

The jury, having considered the circumstances of the case, found her guilty of assaulting and wounding Mr. F. but acquitted her of doing it with an intent to kill and murder him. In consequence hereof she was sentenced to pay a fine of one hundred pounds, to be imprisoned for a year, and then to find security for her good behaviour for two years; but, when she had suffered about nine months' imprisonment, she died in Newgate, and was buried in the churchyard of St. Andrew, Holborn.

The case of the unhappy woman who has been the subject of this narrative will afford matter for serious reflection. She had been acquainted with the gentleman whom she stabbed, and there is nothing ungenerous in supposing that their acquaintance was of the criminal kind.

It was insinuated by the counsel for the Crown that it could not be supposed that Mrs. Salisbury had any regard for the reputation of her sister. But why so? It is to be presumed that a woman of any sensibility, who had been unhappy enough to forfeit her own character, should become the more anxious to preserve that of one to whom she was bound by the ties of consanguinity. It does not follow that, because a woman has failed in the great article of personal chastity, she must therefore be deficient in every other virtue that can adorn the female mind.

Too frequently, indeed, it happens that women in this predicament become dead to all those finer feelings that do honor to their sex in particular, and to humanity in general. But then what shall be said of those men who reduce them to a situation so calamitous? Will the sudden impulse of passion be pleaded in mitigation of a crime which, in its consequences, almost always detaches a woman from the company of the virtuous of her own sex, and renders her, in a great degree, an outcast of society?

If there be any truth in the common opinion that women in general are weaker than men, it follows, of course, that the wisest ought to be the most virtuous; and that the man who seduces a woman is more criminal in that act than she is in yielding to the seduction: yet so ungenerous is the vulgar opinion, that a woman for ever loses her character in consequence of an offence which is hardly deemed criminal in a man.

ROCHE AND HIS ASSOCIATES THROWING THE MASTER AND MATE OVERBOARD.

PHILIP ROCHE

Executed for piracy and murder.

———

WE have already commented upon the foul crime of piracy. The account now to be given of this atrocious offender will show to what a horrid pitch it has been carried; and happy should we feel ourselves if we could add that this was a singular case. In latter years we find that murder, foul as that committed by Roche, was practised on board of one of our men of war, in which Captain Pigot, her commander, was barbarously killed; and the mutinous crew seized the frigate, and delivered her to the enemy.

This detested monster, Philip Roche, was a native of Ireland, and, being brought up to a seafaring life, served for a considerable time on board some coasting vessels, and then sailed to Barbadoes on board a West-Indiaman. Here he endeavoured to procure the place of a clerk to a factor; but, failing in this, he went again to sea, and was advanced to the station of a first mate.

He now became acquainted with a fisherman named Neale, who hinted to him large sums of money might be acquired by insuring ships, and then causing them to be sunk, to defraud the insurers.

Roche was wicked enough to listen to this horrid idea, and, becoming acquainted with a gentleman who had a ship bound to Cape Breton, he got a station on board, next in command to the captain, who, having a high opinion of him, trusted the ship to his management, directing the seaman to obey his commands.

If Roche had entertained any idea of sinking the ship, he seemed now to have abandoned it; but he had brought on board with him five Irishmen, who were concerned in the shocking tragedy that ensued.

When they had been only a few days at sea, the plan was executed as follows: One night, when the captain and most of the crew were asleep, Roche gave orders to two of the seamen to furl the sails, which being immediately done, the poor fellows no sooner descended on the deck, than Roche and his hellish associates murdered them, and threw them overboard. At this instant a man and a boy at the yard-arm, observing what passed, and dreading a similar fate, hurried towards the topmast-head, when one of the Irishmen, named Cullen, followed them, and, seizing the boy, threw him into the sea. The man, thinking to effect at least a present escape, descended to the main deck, where Roche instantly seized, murdered, and then threw him overboard.

The noise occasioned by these transactions alarming the sailors below, they hurried up with all possible expedition;

but they were severally seized and murdered as fast as they came on deck, and, being first knocked on the head, were thrown into the sea. At length the master and mate came on the quarter-deck, when Roche and his villainous companions seized them and, tying them back to back, committed them to the merciless waves.

These execrable murders being perpetrated, the murderers ransacked the chests of the deceased then sat down to regale themselves with liquor; and, while the profligate crew were carousing, they determined to commence pirates, and that Roche should be the captain as the reward of his superior villainy.

They had intended to have sailed up the Gulf of St. Lawrence; but as they were within a few days' sail of the Bristol Channel when the bloody tragedy was acted, and finding themselves short of provisions, they put into Portsmouth, and, giving the vessel a fictitious name, they painted her afresh, and then sailed for Rotterdam. At this city they disposed of their cargo, and took in a fresh one. Here they were unknown, and an English gentleman, named Annesley, shipped considerable property on board, and took his passage with them for the port of London; but the villains threw this unfortunate gentleman overboard, after they had been only one day at sea.

When the ship arrived in the river Thames, Mr. Annesley's friends made inquiry after him, in consequence of his having sent letters to England, describing the ship in which he proposed to embark; but Roche denied any knowledge of the gentleman, and even disclaimed his own name.

Notwithstanding his confident assertions, it was rightly presumed who he was, and a letter which he sent to his wife being stopped, he was taken into custody. Being carried before the Secretary of State for examination, he averred that he was not Philip Roche; and said that he knew no person of that. Hereupon the intercepted letter was shown him, on which he instantly confessed his crimes, and was immediately committed to take his trial at the next Admiralty sessions.

It was intimated to Roche that he might expect a pardon if he would impeach any three persons who were more culpable than himself, so that they might be prosecuted to conviction; but not being able to do this, he was brought to his trial, and found guilty: judgment of death was awarded against him.

After conviction he professed to be of the Roman Catholic faith, but was certainly no bigot to that religion, since he attended the devotions according to the Protestant form. He was hanged at Execution Dock on the 5th of August, 1723; but was so ill at the time, that he could not make any public declaration of the abhorrence of the crime for which he suffered.

It is impossible to read this shocking narrative without execrating the very memory of the wretches whose crimes gave rise to it. History has not furnished us with any account of what became of the wicked accomplices of Roche; but there can be little doubt of their having dragged on a miserable existence, if they did not end their lives at the gallows.

The mind of the guilty must be perpetually racked with torments; and the murderer who is permitted to live does but live in wretchedness and despair. His days must be filled with anxiety, and his nights with torture.

From the fate of the miserable subject of this narrative, let our sailors be taught that an honest pursuit of the duties of their station is more likely to ensure happiness to them than the possession of any Sum of money unlawfully obtained. Our brave tars are not, from their situation in life, much accustomed to the attendance on religious duties: but it can cost them no trouble to recollect that to 'do justice and love mercy' is equally the character of the brave man and the Christian.

BUTLER, A THIEF, DISCOVERED UNDER A TUB BY JONATHAN WILD.

JONATHAN WILD

Executed for feloniously conniving with thieves.

———

OF all the thieves that ever infested London, this man was the most notorious. That eminent vagabond, Bamfylde Moore Carew, was recognised as 'King of the Beggars';—in like manner may the name and memory of Jonathan Wild be ever held in abhorrence as 'The Prince of Robbers.'

The history of the arts, deceptions, cruelty, and perfidy of this man, have alone filled a volume; and, should he occupy more room in our epitome than may be deemed necessary, we have only to observe, that the whole catalogue of other crimes exposed in this Chronology, centred in one individual, would scarcely produce a parallel with this thief-taker, and most finished thief.

Jonathan Wild was born at Wolverhampton, in Staffordshire, about the year 1682. He was the eldest son of his parents, who, at a proper age, put him to a day-school, which he continued to attend till he had gained a sufficient knowledge in reading, writing, and accounts, to qualify him for business. His father had intended to bring him up to his own trade; but changed that design, and, at about the age of fifteen, apprenticed him for seven years to a buckle-maker in Birmingham. Upon the expiration of this term he returned to Wolverhampton, married a young woman of good character, and gained a tolerable livelihood by working at his business.

About two years after, in the course of which time his wife gave birth to a son, he formed the resolution of visiting London, deserted his wife and child, and set out for the metropolis, where he got into employment, and maintained himself by his trade; being, however, of an extravagant disposition, many months had not elapsed after his arrival before he was arrested for debt, and thrown into Wood Street Compter, where he remained upwards of four years. In a pamphlet which he published, and which we shall more particularly mention hereafter, he says, that during his imprisonment 'it was impossible but he must, in some measure, be let into the secrets of the criminals there under confinement, and particularly Mr. Hitchin's management.'

Whilst in the Compter, Wild assiduously cultivated the acquaintance of his fellow-captives, and attended to their accounts of the exploits in which they had been engaged with singular satisfaction. In this prison was a woman named Mary Milliner, who had long been considered as one of the most abandoned prostitutes and pickpockets on the town. After having escaped the punishment due to the variety of felonies of which she had been guilty, she was put under confinement for debt. An intimacy soon commenced between this woman and Wild, and they had no sooner obtained their freedom than they lived under the denomination of man and wife. By their iniquitous practices they quickly obtained a sum of money, which enabled them to open a little public house in Cock Alley, facing Cripplegate church.

Milliner being personally acquainted with most of the depraved characters by whom London and its environs were infested, and perfectly conversant as to the manner of their proceedings, she was considered by Wild as a most useful companion; and indeed very materially contributed towards rendering him one of the most accomplished proficients in the arts of villainy. He industriously penetrated into the secrets of felons of every description, who resorted in great numbers to his house, in order to dispose of their booties; and they looked upon him with a kind of awe, arising from the consciousness that their lives were at all times in his power.

Wild was at little trouble to dispose of the articles brought to him by thieves at something less than their real value, no law existing at this period for the punishment of the receivers of stolen goods; but the evil increased at length to so enormous a degree, that it was deemed expedient by the legislature to frame a law for its suppression. An act was passed, therefore, consigning such as should be convicted of receiving goods, knowing them to have been stolen, to transportation for the space of fourteen years.

Wild's practices were considerably interrupted by abovementioned law; to elude the operation of which, however, he adopted the following plan:—he called a meeting of all the thieves known to him, and observed that, if they carried their booties to such of the pawnbrokers as were known to be not much affected by scruples of conscience, they would scarcely receive on the property one-fourth of the real value; and that if they were offered to strangers, either for sale, or by way of deposit, it was a chance of ten to one but the parties offering were rendered amenable to the laws. The most industrious thieves, he said, were now scarcely able to obtain a livelihood, and must either submit to be half starved, or live in great and continual danger of Tyburn. He informed them that he had devised a plan for removing the inconveniences under which they laboured, recommended them to follow his advice, and to behave towards him with honour; and concluded by proposing that, when they made prize of any thing, they should deliver it to him, instead of carrying it to the pawnbroker, saying he would *restore the goods to the owners*, by which means greater sums might be raised, while the thieves would remain perfectly secure from detection.

This proposal was received with general approbation, and it was resolved to carry it into immediate execution. All the stolen effects were to be given into the possession of Wild, who soon appointed convenient places wherein they were to be deposited, rightly judging that it would not be prudent to have them left at his own house.

The infamous plan being thus concerted, it became the business of Wild to apply to persons who had been robbed, pretending to be greatly concerned at their misfortunes, saying that some suspected property had been stopped by a very honest man, a broker, with whom he was acquainted, and that, if their goods happened to be in the hands of his friend, restitution should be made. But he failed not to suggest that the broker ought to be rewarded for his trouble and disinterestedness; and to use every argument in his power towards exacting a promise that no disagreeable consequences should ensue to his friend, who had imprudently neglected to apprehend the supposed thieves.

Happy in the prospect of regaining their property, without the trouble and expense necessarily attending prosecutions, people generally approved of the conduct of Wild, and sometimes rewarded him even with one half of the real value of the goods restored. It was not, however, uniformly so; and sundry pertinacious individuals, not satisfied with Wild's superficial statement, questioned him particularly as to the *manner* of their goods being discovered. On these occasions he pretended to feel hurt that his honour should be disputed, alleging that his motive was to afford all the service in his power to the injured party, whose goods he imagined might possibly be those stopped by his friend; but since his honest intentions had been received in so ungracious a manner, and himself interrogated respecting the robbers, he had nothing further to say on the subject, but must take his leave; adding, that his name was Jonathan Wild, and that he was every day to be found at his house in Cock Alley, Cripplegate. This affectation of resentment seldom failed to answer the purposes proposed by it; and a more favorable estimate of his principles and character thus formed, he had an opportunity of advancing his demands.

Wild received in his own name no gratuity from the owners of stolen goods, but deducted his profit from the money which was to be paid *the broker*: thus did he amass considerable sums without danger of prosecution, his offences coming under the operation of no law then in existence. For several years indeed he preserved a tolerably fair character, so consummate was the art employed in the management of his schemes.

Our hero's business greatly increasing, and his name becoming well known, he altered his mode of action. Instead of applying directly to parties who had been plundered, he opened an office, to which great numbers resorted, in hopes of recovering their effects. He made a great parade in his business, and assumed a consequence which enabled him

more effectually to impose upon the public. When persons
came to his office, they were informed that they must each
pay a crown in consideration of receiving his advice. This
ceremony being dispatched, he entered in his book the
name and address of the applicants, with all the particulars they could communicate respecting the robberies, and
the rewards that would be given provided the goods were
recovered: they were then desired to call again in a few
days, when he hoped he should be able to give them some
agreeable intelligence. Upon returning to know the success
of his inquiries, he told them that he had received some
information concerning their goods, but that the agent he
had employed to trace them had apprised him that the robbers pretended they could raise more money by pawning
the property than by restoring it for the promised reward;
saying, however, that, if he could by any means procure an
interview with the villains, he doubted not of being able to
settle matters agreeably to the terms already stipulated;
but, at the same time, artfully insinuating that the safest
and most expeditious method would be to make some addi-
tion to the reward.

Wild, at length, became eminent in his profession,
which proved highly lucrative. When he had discovered
the utmost sum that it was likely would be given for the
recovery of any property, he requested its owner to apply at
a particular time, and, meanwhile, caused the goods to be
ready for delivery.

Considerable advantages were derived from examining the person who had been robbed; as he thence became
acquainted with particulars which the thieves might omit to
communicate, and was enabled to detect them if they concealed any part of their booties. Being in possession of the
secrets of every notorious thief, they were under the necessity of complying with whatever terms he thought proper
to exact, being aware that, by opposing his inclination, they

should involve themselves in the most imminent danger of being sacrificed to the injured laws of their country.

Through the infamous practices of this man, articles which had been before considered as of little use but to the owners now became matters claiming particular attention from the thieves, by whom the metropolis and its environs were haunted. Pocket-books, books of accounts, watches, rings, trinkets, and a variety of articles of but small intrinsic worth, were at once esteemed very profitable plunder. Books of accounts, and other writings, being of great importance to the owners, produced very handsome rewards; and the same may be said of pocket-books, which generally contained curious memorandums, and sometimes bank-notes and other articles on which money could be readily procured.

Wild accumulated cash so fast, that he considered himself a man of consequence; and, to support his imaginary dignity, dressed in laced clothes and wore a sword, which martial instrument he first exercised on the person of his accomplice and reputed wife, Mary Milliner, who having on some occasion provoked him, he instantly struck at her with it, and cut off one of her ears. This event was the cause of a separation; but, in acknowledgment of the great services she had rendered him, by introducing him to so advantageous a *profession*, he allowed her a weekly stipend till her decease.

Before Wild had brought the plan of his office to perfection, he for some time acted as an assistant to Charles Hitchin, once city-marshal, a man as wicked as himself. These celebrated copartners in villainy, under the pretext of controlling the enormities of the dissolute, paraded the streets from Temple-bar to the Minories, searching houses of ill fame, and apprehending disorderly and suspected persons; but those who complimented these *public* reformers with *private* douceurs were allowed to practise every species of wickedness with impunity. Hitchin and Wild, however, grew jealous of each other, and, an open rupture taking place, they parted, each pursuing the business of thief-taking on his own account.

In the year 1715 Wild removed from his house in Cock Alley to a Mrs. Seagoe's, in the Old Bailey, where he pursued his business with the usual success, notwithstanding the efforts of Hitchin, his rival in iniquity, to suppress his proceedings.

The reader's astonishment will increase when we state that these two abandoned miscreants had the daring effrontery to appeal to the public, and attacked each other with all possible scurrility in pamphlets and advertisements. Never, surely, was the press so debased as in disgorging the filth of their pens. Hitchin published what he called 'The Regulator; or a Discovery of Thieves and Thief-takers.' It is an ignorant and impudent insult to the reader, and replete with abuse of Wild, whom he brands, in his capacity of thief-taker, with being worse than the thief. Wild retorts with great bitterness; and his pamphlet containing much curious information, we shall incorporate a part of it, requesting the reader to bear in mind that it refers to a previous part of our hero's career.

Hitchin having greatly debased the respectable post of city marshal, the lord mayor suspended him from that office. In order to repair his loss, he determined, as the most prudent step, to strive to bury his aversion, and confederate with Wild. To effect this, he wrote as follows:

'I am very sensible, that you are let into the knowledge of the secrets of the Compter, particularly with relation to the securing of pocket-books; but your experience is inferior to mine: I can put you in a far better method than you are acquainted with, and which may be done with safety; for, though I am suspended, I still retain the power of acting as constable, and, notwithstanding I cannot be heard before my lord mayor as formerly, I have interest among the aldermen upon any complaint.

'But I must first tell you that you spoil the trade of thief-taking, in advancing greater rewards than are necessary. I give but half-a-crown a book, and, when the thieves and pickpockets see you and I confederate, they will submit to our terms, and likewise continue their thefts, for fear of coming to the gallows by our means. You shall take a turn with me, as my servant or assistant, and we'll commence our rambles this night.'

Wild, it appears, readily accepted the ex-marshal's proposals: towards dark they proceeded to Temple-bar, and called in at several brandy-shops and alehouses between that and Fleet Ditch; some of the masters of these houses complimented the marshal with punch, others with brandy, and some presented him with fine, ale, offering their service to their worthy protector. Hitchin made them little answer; but gave them to understand all the service he expected from them was, to give information of pocket-books, or any goods stolen, as a pay-back: 'For you women of the town,' addressing himself to some females in one of the shops, 'make it a common practice to resign things of this nature to the bullies and rogues of your retinue; but this shall no longer be borne with. I'll give you my word both they and you shall be detected, unless you deliver all the pocket-books you meet with to me. What do you think I bought my place for, but to make the most of it? and you are to understand this is my man (pointing to our buckle-maker) to assist me. And if you at any time, for the future, refuse to yield up the watches or books you take, either to me or my servant, you may be assured of being all sent to Bridewell, and not one of you shall be permitted to walk the streets longer. For, notwithstanding I am under suspension (chiefly for not suppressing the practices of such vermin as you), I have still a power of punishing, and you shall dearly pay for not observing deference to me.' Strutting along a little farther, he on a sudden seized two or three dexterous pickpockets, reprimanding them for not paying their respects, asking to what part of the town they were rambling, and whether they did not see him? They answered that they saw him at a distance, but he caught hold of them so hastily that they had no time to address him. 'We have been strolling,' said they, 'over Moorfields, and from thence to the Blue Boar, in pursuit of you; but not finding you, as usual, were under some fears that you were indisposed.' The marshal replied, he should have given them a meeting there, but had been employed the whole day with his new man. 'You are to be very careful,' said he, 'not to oblige any person but myself, or servant, with pocket-books; if you presume to do otherwise you shall swing for it, and we are out in the city every night to observe your motions.' These instructions given, the pick-pockets left, making their master a low congee, and promising obedience. Such was the progress of the first night with the buckle-maker, whom he told that his staff of authority terrified the ignorant to the extent of his wishes.

Some nights afterwards, walking towards the back part of St. Paul's, the ex-marshal thus addressed Jonathan:—'I will now show you a brandy-shop that entertains no company but whores and thieves. This is a house for our purpose, and I am informed that a woman of the town who frequents it has lately robbed a gentleman of his watch and pocket-book: this advice I received from her companion, with whom I have a good understanding. We will go into this house, and, if we can find this woman, I will assume a sterner countenance (though at best I look like an infernal), by continued threats extort a confession, and by that means get possession of the watch and pocket-book; in order to which, do you slily accost her companion.'—Here he described her.—'Call to her, and say that your master is in a damned ill humour, and swears if she does not instantly make a discovery where the watch and pocket-book may be found, at farthest by to-morrow, he will certainly send her to the Compter, and thence to the work-house.'

The means being thus concerted to obtain the valuable goods, both master and man entered the shop in pursuit of the game, and, according to expectation, found the person wanted, with several others; where-upon the marshal, showing an enraged countenance becoming the design, and Wild being obliged to follow his example, the company said that the master and man looked as sour as two devils. 'Devils!' said the marshal; 'I'll make some of you devils, if you do not immediately discover the watch and pocket-book I am employed to procure.' 'We do not know your meaning, Sir,' answered some.—'Who do you discourse to?' said others; 'we know nothing of it.' The marshal replied in a softer tone, 'You are ungrateful to the last degree to deny me this small request, when I was never let into the secret of any thing to be taken from a gentleman but I communicated it to you, describing the person so exactly that you could not mistake your man; and there is so little got at this rate, that the devil may trade with you for me!'

This speech being made, the marshal gave a nod to his man, who called one of the women to the door, and, telling the story above directed, the female answered, 'Unconscionable devil! when he gets five or ten guineas, not to bestow above as many shillings upon us unfortunate wretches! but, however, rather than go to the Compter, I'll try what is to be done.'

The woman, returning to Hitchin, asked him what he would give for the delivery of the watch, being seven or eight pounds in value, and the pocket-book, having in it various notes and goldsmiths' bills: to whom the marshal answered, a guinea; and told her it was much better to comply than to go to Newgate, which she must certainly expect upon her refusal. The woman replied that the watch was in pawn for forty shillings, and if he did not advance that sum she should be obliged to strip herself for its redemption; though, when her furbelowed scarf was laid aside, she had nothing underneath but furniture for a paper-mill. After abundance of words, he allowed her thirty shillings for the watch and book, which she accepted, and the watch was never returned to the owner!

Some little time after this, a gentleman in liquor going into the. Blue Boar, near Moorfields, with a woman of the town, immediately lost his watch. He applied to the ex-marshal, desiring his assistance; but the buckle-maker, being well acquainted with the walk between Cripplegate and Moorfields, had the fortune to find the woman. The master immediately seized her, on notice given, and by vehement threatenings obliged her to a confession. She declared that she had stolen the watch, and carried it to a woman that kept a brandy-shop near, desiring her to assist in the sale of it. The mistress of the brandy-shop readily answered that she had it from an honest young woman who frequented her house, whose husband was gone to sea; whereupon she pawned the watch for its value, and ordered the sale.

This story seeming reasonable, a watchmaker had purchased the watch, and gave the money agreed for it, which was fifty shillings. Thus the sale of the watch being discovered, the marshal, with his staff and assistant, immediately repaired to the watchmaker's house, and, seizing the watchmaker in the same manner as a. person would do the greatest criminal, carried him to a public house, telling him that if he did not forthwith send for the watch he should be committed to Newgate.

The watchmaker, not being any ways accustomed to unfair dealings, directly answered that he bought the watch, and the person he had it of would produce the woman that stole it, if it were stolen, the woman being then present.

The marshal replied he had no business with the persons that stole the property, but with him in whose possession it was found; and that, if he did not instantly send for the watch, and deliver it without insisting upon any money, but on the contrary return him thanks for his civility, which deserved five or ten pieces, he would without delay send him to Newgate.

Hereupon the innocent artisan, being much surprised, sent for the watch, and surrendered it; and since that it has sufficiently appeared that the owner made a present to Hitchin of three guineas for his trouble, whilst the poor watchmaker underwent a dead loss of his fifty shillings. This story and the following afford a pretty good example of the honesty of this city-marshal:

A biscuit-baker near Wapping having lost a pocket-book, wherein was, among other papers, an ex-chequer-bill for 100*l*. applied himself to the marshal's man, the buckle-maker, for the recovery thereof: the buckle-maker advised him to advertise it, and stop the payment of the bill, which he did accordingly; but, having no account of his property, he came to Wild several times about it; and, at length, told him that he had received a visit from a tall man, with a long peruke and sword, calling himself the city-marshal, who asked him if he had lost his pocket-book. The biscuit-baker answered yes; and desiring to know his reasons for putting such a question, or whether he could give him any intelligence; he replied, no, he could not give him any intelligence of it as yet, but wished to be informed whether he had employed any person to search after it. To which the biscuit-baker answered, he had employed one Wild. Hereupon the marshal told him he was under a mistake; that he should have applied to him, who was the only person in England that could serve him, being well assured it was entirely out of the power of Wild, or any of those fellows, to know where the pocket-book was (this, says the pamphlet,

was very certain, he having it at that time in his custody);
and begged to know the reward that would be given. The
biscuit-baker replied he would give 10*l*. The marshal said
that a greater reward should be offered, for that exchequer-
bills and those things were ready money, and could immediately be sold; and that, if he had employed him in the
beginning, and offered 40*l*. or 50*l*. he would have served
him.

The biscuit-baker having acquainted Wild with this
story, the latter gave it as his opinion that the pocket-book
was in the marshal's possession, and that it would be to no
purpose to continue advertising it, he being well assured
that the marshal would not have taken the pains to find out
the biscuit-baker, unless he knew how to get at it.

Upon the whole, therefore, he advised the owner rather
to advance his bidding, considering what hands the note
was in, especially as the marshal had often told his servant
how easily he could dispose of bank-notes and exchequer-
bills at gaming-houses, which he very much frequented.

Pursuant to this advice, the losing party went a second
time to the marshal, and bid 40*l*. for his pocket-book and
bill. 'Zounds, sir,' said the marshal, 'you are too late!' which
was all the satisfaction he gave him. Thus was the poor biscuit-baker tricked out of his exchequer-bill, which was paid
to another person, though it could never be traced back; but
it happened, a short time after, that some of the voting fry of
pickpockets under the tuition of the marshal fell out in sharing the money given them for this very pocket-book; whereupon one of them came to Wild, and discovered the whole
matter, *viz.* that he had sold the pocket-book, with the 100*l*.
exchequer-note in it, and other bills, to the city-marshal, at
a tavern in Aldersgate Street, for four or five guineas.

A person standing in the pillory, near Charing Cross,
a gentleman in the crowd was deprived of a pocket-book,
which had in it bills and lottery-tickets to the value of

several hundred pounds; and a handsome reward (30*l.*) was at first offered for it in a public advertisement. The marshal, having a suspicion that a famous pickpocket, known by his lame hand, had taken the book, he applied to him; and, to enforce a confession and delivery, told him, with a great deal of assurance, that he must be the person, such a man, with a lame hand, having been described by the gentleman to have been near him, and whom he was certain had stolen his book. 'In short,' says he, 'you had the book, and you must bring it to me, and you shall share the reward; but, if you refuse to comply with such advantageous terms, you must never expect to come within the city gates; for, if you do, Bridewell, at least, if not Newgate, shall be your residence.'

After several meetings, the marshal's old friend could not deny that he had the pocket-book: but he said to the marshal, 'I did not expect this rigorous treatment from you, after the services I have done you, in concealing you several times, and. by that means keeping you out of a gaol. It is not the way to expect any future service, when all my former good offices are forgotten.' Notwithstanding these reasons, Hitchin still insisted upon what he had at first proposed; and at length the pickpocket, considering that he could not repair to the Exchange, or elsewhere, to follow his pilfering employment, without the marshal's consent, and fearing to be made a mark of his revenge, condescended to part with the pocket-book upon terms reasonable between buyer and seller. Whereupon says the marshal, 'I lost all my money last night at gaming, except a gold watch in my pocket, which I believe there will be no inquiry after, it coming to hand by an intrigue with a woman of the town, whom the gentleman will be ashamed to prosecute for fear of exposing himself. I'll exchange goods for goods with you.' So the pickpocket, rather than he would risk the consequence of disobliging his master, concluded the bargain.

One night, not far from St. Paul's, the marshal and his man met with a detachment of pickpocket boys, who instantly, at the sight of their master, took to their heels and ran away. The buckle-maker asked the meaning of their surprise. To which the marshal answered, 'I know their meaning, a pack of rogues! they were to have met me in the fields, this morning, with a book I am informed they have taken from a gentleman, and they are afraid of being secured for their disobedience. There is Jack Jones among them.—We'll catch the whore's bird.' Jack Jones, running behind a coach to make his escape, was taken by the marshal and his man. The master carried him to a tavern, and threatened him severely, telling him he believed they were turned housebreakers, and that they were concerned in a burglary lately committed by four young criminals. This happened to be the fact, and the boy fearing the marshal had been informed of it, he, for his own security, confessed, and the marshal promised to save his life on his becoming evidence: whereupon the marshal committed the boy to the Compter till the next morning, when he carried him before a justice of the peace, who took his information, and issued a warrant for the apprehension of his companions.

Notice being given where the criminals were to be found, *viz.* at a house in Beech Lane, Hitchin and Wild went privately in the night thither, and, listening at the door, they overheard the boys, with several others, in a mixed company. Entering the house, they met ten or twelve persons, who were in a great rage, inquiring what business the marshal had there, and saluting him with a few oaths, which occasioned the marshal to make a prudent retreat, pulling the door after him, and leaving his little man to the mercy of the savage company.

In a short time the marshal returned with eight or ten watchmen and a constable; and, at the door, out of his dastardly disposition, though his pretence was a ceremonious respect, obliged the constable to go in first; but the constable and marshal were both so long with their compliments that the man thought neither of them would enter in: at last the constable appearing, with his long staff extended before him, the marshal manfully followed, crying out, 'Where are the rebel villains? Why don't ye secure them?' Wild answered that they were under the table; upon which the constable pulled out the juvenile offenders, neither of whom were above twelve years of age. The two boys now taken were committed to Newgate; but the fact having been perpetrated in the county of Surrey, they were afterwards removed to the Marshalsea prison. The assizes coming on at Kingston, and Jones giving his evidence against his companions before the grand jury, a true bill was found, and the marshal indorsed his name on the back of it, to have the honour of being an evidence against these monstrous housebreakers. On the trial, the nature of the fact was declared; but the parents of the offenders appeared, and satisfied the Court that the marshal was the occasion of the ruin of these boys, by taking them into the fields, and encouraging them in the stealing of pocket-books; and told him, on his affirming they were thieves, that he had made them such. The judge, observing the marshal's views were more to get the reward than to do justice, summed up the charge to the jury in favour of the boys, who were thereupon acquitted, and the marshal reprimanded. He was so enraged at this, and so angry with himself for not accusing them of other crimes, that he immediately returned to London, leaving his man to discharge the whole reckoning at Kingston.

A gentleman, who had lost his watch when in company with a woman of the town, applied to a person belonging to the Compter, who recommended him to the buckle-maker, to procure the same; and the gentleman applying accordingly to him, and giving him a description of the woman,

the buckle-maker, a few days after, traversing Fleet Street
with his master in an evening, happened to meet with the
female (as he apprehended by the description of the gentleman) who had stolen the watch, and, coming nearer, was
satisfied therein.

He told his master that she was the very person
described: to which the master answered, with an air of
pleasure, 'I am glad to find we have a prospect of something to-night to defray our expenses,' and immediately,
with the assistance of Wild, seized the female and carried
her to a public house, where, upon examination, she confessed it was in her power to serve the marshal in it telling him that if he would please to go with her home, or
send his man, the watch would be returned, with a suitable
reward for his trouble. The man asked his master his opinion, whether he thought he might pursue the woman with
safety? To which the other replied, Yes, for that he knew
her, at the same time giving hints of his following at a reasonable distance, for his security, which he did with a great
deal of precaution, as will appear; for, proceeding with the
female, she informed him that her husband, who had the
watch about him, was at a tavern near Whitefriars, and, if
he would condescend to go thither, he might be furnished
with it without giving himself any farther trouble, together
with the reward he deserved.—To which Wild consenting,
they came to the tavern, where she made inquiry for the
company she had been with but a short space before; and,
being informed they were still in the house, she sent in word
by the drawer that the gentlewoman who had been with
them that evening desired the favour to speak with them.
The drawer going in, and delivering the message, immediately three or four men came from the room to the female:
she gave them to understand that the marshal's man had
accused her of stealing a watch, telling them she supposed
it must be some other woman who had assumed her name,

and desired their protection: upon this the whole company sallied out, and attacked the marshal's man in a very violent manner, to make a rescue of the female, upbraiding him for degrading a gentlewoman of her reputation.

The marshal having followed at a little distance, and observed the ill success of his man, fearing the like discipline, made off, hugging himself that he had escaped the severe treatment he had equally deserved. Jonathan in the struggle showed his resentment chiefly against the female; who, after a long contest, was thrust out at the back door; and immediately the watch being called, he and the rest of the party were seized.

As they were going to the Compter, the marshal overtook them near Bow church, and, coming up to Wild in great haste, asked him the occasion of his long absence: the man said, that he had been at a tavern with the woman, where he thought he saw him: the master answered, that indeed he was there; but seeing the confusion so great, he went off to call the watch and constables. The marshal used his interest to get his servant off, but to no purpose, he being carried to the Compter with the rest of the company, in order to make an agreement there.

The next morning the woman sent to her companions in the Compter, letting them know that, if they could be released, the watch should be returned without any consideration, which was accordingly done, and a small present made to the marshal's man for smart-money. They were now all discharged, paying their fees.

The watch being thus ready to be produced to the owner, the marshal insisted upon the greatest part of the reward, as being the highest person in authority: the man declared this unreasonable, he himself having received the largest share of the bastinado. 'But, however,' says the marshal, 'I have now an opportunity of playing my old game; I'll oblige the gentleman to give me ten guineas to save his reputation, which is so nearly concerned with a common prostitute.' But the gentleman knew too much of his character to be thus imposed upon, and would give him no more than what he promised, which was three guineas. Hitchin at first refused; but his man (who had the most right to make a new contract) advising him to act cautiously, he at last agreed to accept the reward first offered, giving Jonathan only one guinea for his services and the cure of his wounds. The above is a farther instance of the marshal's cowardice and inhumanity.

The marshal, going one night up Ludgate Hill, observed a well-dressed woman walking before, whom he told Wild was a lewd woman, for that he saw her talking with a man. This was no sooner spoke but he seized her, and asked who she was. She made answer that she was a bailiff's wife. 'You are more likely to be a whore,' said the marshal, 'and as such you shall go to the Computer.'

Taking the woman through St. Paul's Church-yard, she desired liberty to send for some friends; but he would not comply with her request. He forced her into the Nag's Head tavern in Cheapside, where he presently ordered a hot supper and plenty of wine to be brought in; commanding the female to keep at a distance from him, and telling her that he did not permit such vermin to sit in his company, though he intended to make her pay the reckoning.

When the supper was brought to the table, he fell to it lustily, and would not allow the woman to eat any part of the supper with him, or to come near the fire, though it was extreme cold weather. When he had supped, he stared round, and, applying himself to her, told her that if he had been an informer, or such a fellow, she would have called for eatables and wine herself, and not have given him the trouble of direction, or else would have slipped a piece into his hand; adding, 'You may do what you please: but I can assure you it is in my power, if I see a woman in the hands of informers, to discharge her, and commit them. You are not so ignorant but you must guess my meaning.' She replied, that she had money enough to pay for the supper, and about three half-crowns more. This desirable answer being given, he ordered his attendant to withdraw, while he compounded the matter with her.

When Wild returned, the gentlewoman was civilly asked to sit by the fire, and eat the remainder of the supper, and in all respects treated very kindly, only with a pretended reprimand to give him better language whenever he should speak to her for the future; and, after another bottle drank at her expense, she was discharged. This is an excellent method to get a good supper gratis, and to fill an empty pocket.

The marshal, previous to his suspension, had daily meetings with the pickpocket boys in Moorfields, and treated them there plentifully with cakes and ale; offering them sufficient encouragement to continue their thefts: and at a certain time it happened that one of the boys, more cunning than his companions, having stolen an alderman's pocketbook, and finding, on opening it, several bank bills, he gave the marshal to understand that it was worth a great deal beyond the usual price; and, the notes being of considerable value, insisted upon five pieces. The marshal told the boy that five pieces were enough to break him at once; that if he gave him two guineas he would be sufficiently paid; but assured him that, if he had the good luck to obtain a handsome reward, he would then make it up five pieces. Upon this present encouragement and future expectation the boy delivered up the pocket-book, and a few days afterwards, being informed that a very large reward had been given for the notes, he applied to the marshal for the remaining three guineas, according to promise; but all the satisfaction he got was, that he should be sent to the house of correction if he continued to demand it; the marshal telling him that such rascals as he were ignorant how to dispose of their money.

This conniving at the intrigues of the pickpockets, taking the stolen pocket-book and sending threatening letters to the persons that lost them, under pretence that they had been in company with lewd women; extorting money also from persons in various other ways; were the causes of the marshal's being suspended; and this most detestable villain having subsequently been fined twenty pounds, and pilloried, for a crime too loathsome to be named in these pages, left Wild at length alone to execute his plans of depredation on the public.

We shall now, quitting Mr. Wild's recriminating pamphlet, proceed in our regular account of the hero of this narrative.—When the vagabonds with whom he was in league faithfully related to him the particulars of the robberies they had committed, and intrusted to him the disposal of their booties, he assured them that they might safely rely on him for protection against the vengeance of the law; and indeed it must be acknowledged that in cases of this nature he would persevere in his utmost endeavours to surmount very great difficulties rather than wilfully falsify his word.

Wild's artful behaviour, and the punctuality with which he discharged his engagements, obtained him a great share of confidence among thieves of every denomination; insomuch, that if he caused it to be intimated to them that he was desirous of seeing them, and that they should not be molested, they would attend him with the utmost willingness, without entertaining the most distant apprehension of danger, although conscious that he had informations against them, and that their lives were absolutely in his power; but if they presumed to reject his proposals, or proved otherwise refractory, he would address them to the following effect: 'I have given you my word that you should come and go in safety, and so you shall; but take care of yourself, for, if ever you see me again, you see an enemy.'

The great influence that Wild obtained over the thieves will not be thought a very extraordinary matter, if it is considered that, when he promised to use his endeavours for rescuing them from impending fate, he was always desirous, and generally able, to succeed. Such as complied with his measures he would never interrupt; but, on the contrary, afford them every encouragement for prosecuting their iniquitous practices; and, if apprehended by any other person, he seldom failed of procuring their discharge. His most usual method (in desperate cases, and when matters could not be managed with more ease and expedition) was to procure them to be admitted evidences, under pretext that it was in their power to make discoveries of high importance to the public. When they were in prison he frequently attended them, and communicated to them from his own memorandums such particulars as he judged it would be prudent for them to relate to the Court. When his accomplices were apprehended, and he was not able to prevent their being brought to trial, he contrived stratagems (in which his invention was amazingly fertile) for keeping the principal witnesses out of Court; so that the delinquents were generally dismissed in defect of evidence.

Jonathan was ever a most implacable enemy to those who were hardy enough to reject his terms, and dispose of their stolen effects for their own separate advantage. He was industrious to an extreme in his efforts to surrender them into the hands of justice; and, being acquainted with all their usual places of resort, it was scarcely possible for them to escape his vigilance.

By his subjecting such as incurred his displeasure to the punishment of the law, he obtained the rewards offered for pursuing them to conviction; greatly extended his ascendancy over the other thieves, who considered him with a kind of awe; and, at the same time, established his character as being a man of great public utility.

It was the practice of Wild to give instructions to the thieves whom he employed as to the manner in which they should conduct themselves; and, if they followed his directions, it was seldom that they failed of success. But if they neglected a strict observance of his rules, or were, through inadvertency or ignorance, guilty of any kind of mismanagement or error in the prosecution of the schemes he had suggested, it was to be understood almost as an absolute certainty that he would procure them to be convicted at the next sessions, deeming them to be unqualified for the profession of roguery.

He was frequently asked how it was possible that he could carry on the business of restoring stolen effects, and yet not be in league with the robbers; and his replies were always to this purpose:—'My acquaintance among thieves is very extensive, and, when I receive information of a robbery, I make inquiry after the suspected parties, and leave word at proper places that, if the goods are left where I appoint, the reward shall be paid, and no questions asked. Surely no imputation of guilt can fall upon me; for I hold no interviews with the robbers, nor are the goods given into my possession.'

We will now give a relation of the most remarkable exploits of the hero of these pages; and our detail must necessarily include many particulars relating to other notorious characters of the same period.

A lady of fortune being on a visit in Piccadilly, her servants, leaving her sedan at the door, went to refresh themselves at a neighbouring public house. Upon their return the vehicle was not to be found; in consequence of which the men immediately went to Wild, and having informed him of their loss, and complimented him with the usual fee, they were desired to call upon him again in a few days. Upon their second application, Wild extorted from them a considerable reward, and then directed them to attend the chapel in Lincoln's Inn Fields on the following morning, during the time of prayers. The men went according to the appointment, and under the piazzas of the chapel perceived the chair, which upon examination they found to contain the velvet seat, curtains, and other furniture, and that it had received no kind of damage.

A young gentleman, named Knap, accompanied his mother to Sadler's Wells, on Saturday, March 31, 1716. On their return they were attacked, about ten at night, near the wall of Gray's Inn Gardens, by five villains. The young gentleman was knocked down, and his mother, being exceedingly alarmed, called for assistance; upon which a pistol was discharged at her, and she instantly fell down dead. A considerable reward was offered by proclamation in the Gazette for the discovery of the perpetrator of this horrid crime; and Wild was remarkably assiduous in his endeavours to apprehend the offenders. From a description given of some of the villains, Wild immediately judged the gang to be composed of William White, Thomas Thurland, John Chapman, alias Edward Darvel, Timothy Dun, and Isaac Rag.

On the evening of Sunday, April 8, Wild received intelligence that some of the above-named men were drinking with their prostitutes at a house kept by John Weatherly, in Newtoner's Lane. He went to Weatherly's, accompanied by his man Abraham, and seized White, whom he brought away about midnight, in a hackney-coach, and lodged him in the round-house.

White being secured, information was given to Wild that a man named James Aires was then at the Bell Inn, Smithfield, in company with a woman of the town. Having an information against Aires, Wild, accompanied by his assistants, repaired to the inn, under the gateway of which they met Thurland, whose person had been mistaken for that of Aires. Thurland was provided with two brace of pistols; but, being suddenly seized, he was deprived of all opportunity of making use of those weapons, and taken into custody.

They went on the following night to a house in White Horse Alley, Drury Lane, where they apprehended Chapman, alias Darvel. Soon after the murder of Mrs. Knap, Chapman and others stopped the coach of Thomas Middlethwaite, Esq. but that gentleman escaped being robbed by discharging a blunderbuss, and wounding Chapman in the arm, on which the villains retired.

In a short time after, Wild apprehended Isaac Rag at a house which he frequented in St. Giles's, in consequence of an information charging him with a burglary. Being taken before a magistrate, in the course of his examination Rag impeached twenty-two accomplices, charging them with being housebreakers, footpads, and receivers of stolen effects; and, in consequence thereof, was admitted an evidence for the crown. This man had been convicted of a misdemeanour in January, 1714-15, and sentenced to stand three times in the pillory. He had concealed himself in the dust-hole belonging to the house of Thomas Powell, where being discovered, he was searched, and a pistol, some matches, and a number of pick-lock keys, were found in his possession. His Intention was evidently to commit a burglary; but, as he did not enter the house, he was indicted for a misdemeanour in entering the yard with intent to steal. He was indicted in October, 1715, for a burglary, in the house of Elizabeth Stanwell, on the 24th of August; but he was acquitted of this charge.

White, Thurland, and Chapman were arraigned on the 18th of May, 1716, at the sessions-house in the Old Bailey, on an indictment for assaulting John Knap, putting him in fear, and taking from him a hat and wig, on the 31st of March, 1716. They were also indicted for the murder of Mary Knap, widow: White by discharging a pistol loaded with powder and bullets, and thereby giving her a wound, of which she immediately died, March 31, 1716. They were a second time indicted for assaulting and robbing John Gough. White was a fourth time indicted with James Russel for a burglary in the house of George Barklay. And Chapman was a fourth time indicted for a burglary in the house of Henry Cross. These three offenders were executed at Tyburn on the 8th of June, 1716.

Wild was indefatigable in his endeavours to apprehend Timothy Dun, who had hitherto escaped the hands of justice by removing to a new lodging, where he concealed himself in the most cautious manner. Wild, however, did not despair of discovering this offender, whom he supposed must either perish through want of the necessaries of life, or obtain the means of subsistence by returning to his felonious practices; and so confident was he of success, that he made a wager of ten guineas that he would have him in custody before the expiration of an appointed time.

Dun's confinement, at length, became exceedingly irksome to him; and he sent his wife to make inquiries respecting him of Wild, in order to discover whether he was still in danger of being apprehended. Upon her return Wild ordered one of his people to follow her home. She took water at Blackfriars, and landed at the Falcon; but suspecting the man was employed to trace her, she again took water, and crossed to Whitefriars: observing that she was still followed, she ordered the waterman to proceed to Lambeth, and having landed there, it being nearly dark, imagined she had escaped the observation of Wild's man, and therefore walked immediately home. The man traced her to Maid Line, near the Bank-side, Southwark, and perceiving her enter a house, he marked the wall with chalk, and then returned to his employer, with an account of the discovery he had made.

Wild, accompanied by a fellow named Abraham, a Jew, who acted the part himself had formerly done to the worthless marshal, one Riddlesden, and another man, went on the following morning to the house where the woman had been seen to enter. Dun, hearing a noise, and thence suspecting that he was discovered, got through a back-window on the second floor upon the roof of the pantry, the bottom of which was about eight feet from the ground. Abraham discharged a pistol, and wounded Dun in the arm; in consequence of which he fell from the pantry into the yard; after his fall Riddlesden fired also, and wounded him in the face with small-shot. Dun was secured and carried to Newgate, and being tried at the ensuing sessions, was soon after executed at Tyburn.

Riddlesden was bred to the law, but he entirely neglected that business, and abandoned himself to every species of wickedness. His irregular course of life having greatly embarrassed his circumstances, he broke into the chapel of Whitehall, and stole the communion-plate. He was convicted of this offence, and received sentence of death; but, through the exertion of powerful interests, a pardon was obtained, on condition of transporting himself for the term of seven years. He went to America, but soon returned in England, and had the address to himself into the favour of a young lady, daughter to a merchant at Newcastle-Upon-Tyne. Before he could get his wife's fortune, which was considerable, into his hands, he was discovered and committed to Newgate. She followed him, and was brought to bed in the prison. Her friends, however, being apprized of her unhappy situation, caused her to return home. He contracted an intimacy with the widow of Richard Revel, one of the turnkeys of Newgate; and, being permitted to transport himself again, that woman went with him to Philadelphia, under the character of his wife. In consequence, however, of a disagreement between them, Mrs. Revel returned, and took a public house in Golden Lane; but what became of Riddlesden does not appear.

One night, during the connexion of Wild with Hitchin the city marshal, being abroad in their walks, not far from the Temple, they discovered a clergyman standing against the wall in an alley, to which he had retired, as persons frequently do, on account of modesty and decency. Immediately a woman of the town, lying in wait for prey, brushing by, the clergyman exclaimed aloud, 'What does the woman want?' The marshal instantly rushed in upon them, and seized the clergyman, bidding his man secure the woman. The clergyman resisted, protesting his innocence which his language to the woman confirmed; but, finding it to no purpose, he at last desired that he might be permitted to go into an ironmonger's house near this, the marshal refused, and dragged the clergyman to the end of Salisbury Court, in Fleet Street, where he raised a mob about him; and two or three gentlemen, who knew the parson, happening to come by, asked the mob what they were doing with him, telling them he was chaplain to a noble lord. The rough gentry answered, 'Damn him, we believe he's chaplain to the devil, for we caught him with a whore.'

Hereupon the gentlemen desired the marshal to go to a tavern, that they might talk with him without noise and tumult, which he consented to. When they came into the tavern, the clergyman asked the marshal by what authority he thus abused him. The marshal replied he was a city officer (pulling out his staff), and would have him to the Compter, unless he gave very good security for his appearance next morning, when he would swear that he caught him with a whore.

The clergyman seeing him so bent upon perjury, which would very much expose him, sent for other persons to vindicate his reputation, who, putting a purse of gold into the marshal's hand (which they found was the only way to deal with such a monster in iniquity), the clergyman was permitted to depart.

A thief of most infamous character, named Arnold
Powel, being confined in Newgate, on a charge of having
robbed a house in the neighbourhood of Golden Square of
property to a great amount, was visited by Jonathan, who
informed him that, in consideration of a sum of money,
he would save his life; adding that, if the proposal was
rejected, he should inevitably die at Tyburn for the offence
on account of which he was then imprisoned. The prisoner, however, not believing that it was in Wild's power to
do him any injury, bade him defiance. Powel was brought
to trial; but, through a defect of evidence, he was acquitted. Having gained intelligence that Powel had committed
a burglary in the house of Mr. Eastlick, near Fleet Ditch,
Wild caused that gentleman to prosecute the robber. Upon
receiving information that a bill was found for the burglary, Powel sent for Wild, and, a compromise was effected
according to the terms which Wild himself had proposed,
in consequence of which Powel was assured that his life
should be preserved. Upon the approach of the sessions,
Wild informed the prosecutor that the first and second
days would be employed in other trials, and, as he was willing Mr. Eastlick should avoid attending with his witnesses
longer than was necessary, he would give timely notice
when Powel would be arraigned. But he contrived to have
the prisoner put to the bar; and, no persons appearing
to prosecute, he was ordered to be taken away; but after
some time he was again set to the bar, then ordered away,
and afterwards put up a third time, proclamation being
made each time for the prosecutor to appear. At length the
jury were charged with the prisoner, and, as no accusation
was adduced against him, he was necessarily dismissed;
and the Court ordered Mr. Eastlick's recognisances to be
estreated.

Powel was ordered to remain in custody till the next
sessions, there being another indictment against him; and

Mr. Eastlick represented the behaviour of Wild to the Court, who justly reprimanded him with great severity.

Powel put himself into a salivation, in order to avoid being brought to trial the next sessions; but, notwithstanding this stratagem, he was arraigned and convicted, and executed on the 20th of March, 1716-7.

At this time Wild had quitted his apartments at Mrs. Seagoe's, and hired a house adjoining to the Coopers' Arms, on the opposite side of the Old Bailey. The unexampled villainies of this man were now become an object of so much consequence, as to excite the particular attention of the legislature. In the year 1718 an act was passed, deeming every person guilty of a capital offence who should accept a reward in consequence of restoring stolen effects without prosecuting the thief. It was the general opinion that this law would effectually suppress the iniquitous practices of Wild; but, after some interruption to his proceedings, he devised means for evading it, which were for several years attended with success.

He now declined the custom of receiving money from the persons who applied to him; but, upon the second or third time of calling, informed them that all he had been able to learn respecting their business was, that, if a sum of money was left at an appointed place, their property would be restored the same day.

Sometimes, as the person robbed was returning from Wild's house, he was accosted in the street by a man who delivered the stolen effects, at the same time producing a note, expressing the sum that was to be paid for them.

In cases wherein he supposed danger was to be apprehended, he advised people to advertise that whoever would bring the stolen goods to Jonathan Wild should be rewarded, and no questions asked.

In the two first instances it could not be proved that he either saw the thief, received the goods, or accepted of a reward; and in the latter case he acted agreeably to the directions of the injured party, and there appeared no reason to criminate him as being in confederacy with the felons.

When he was asked what would satisfy him for his trouble, he told the persons who had recovered their property that what he had done was without any interested view, and merely from a principle of doing good; that therefore he made no claim; but, if he accepted a present, he should not consider it as being his due, but as an instance of generosity, which he should acknowledge accordingly.

Our adventurer's business increased exceedingly, and he opened an office in Newtoner's Lane, to the management of which he appointed his man Abraham. This Israelite proved a remarkably industrious and faithful servant to Jonathan, who intrusted him with matters of the greatest importance.

By too strict an application to business Wild much impaired his health, so that he judged it prudent to retire into the country for a short time. He hired a lodging at Dulwich, leaving both offices under the direction of Abraham.

A lady had her pocket picked of bank-notes to the amount of seven thousand pounds. She related the particulars of her robbery to Abraham, who in a few days apprehended three pickpockets, and conducted them to Jonathan's lodgings at Dulwich. Upon their delivering up all the notes, Wild dismissed them. When the lady applied to Abraham, he restored her property, and she generously made him a present of four hundred pounds, which he delivered to his employer. These three pickpockets were afterwards apprehended for some other offences, and transported. One of them carefully concealed a bank-note for a thousand pounds in the lining of his coat. On his arrival at Maryland, he procured cash for the note, and, having purchased his freedom, went to New York, where he assumed the character of a gentleman.

Wild's business would not permit him to remain long at Dulwich; and being under great inconvenience from the want of Abraham's immediate assistance, he did not keep open his office in Newtoner's Lane for more than three months.

About a week after the return of Jonathan from Dulwich, a mercer in Lombard Street ordered a porter to carry to a particular inn a box, containing goods to the amount of two hundred pounds. In his way the porter was observed by three thieves, one of whom, being more genteelly dressed than his companions, accosted the man in the following manner: 'If you are willing to earn sixpence, my friend, step to the tavern at the end of the street, and ask for the roquelaure I left at the bar; but, lest the waiter should scruple giving it to you, take my gold watch as a token. Pitch your burden upon this bulk, and I will take care of it till you return; but be sure you make haste.' The man went to the tavern, and, having delivered his message, was informed that the thing he inquired for had not been left there; upon which the porter said, 'Since you scruple to trust me, look at this gold watch, which the gentleman gave me to produce as a token.' What was called a gold watch, being examined, proved to be only pewter lacquered. In consequence of this discovery, the porter hastened back to where he had left the box; but neither that nor the sharpers were to be found.

The porter was, with reason, apprehensive that he should incur his master's displeasure if he related what had happened; and, in order to excuse his folly, he determined upon the following stratagem:—he rolled himself in the mud, and then went home, saying he had been knocked down, and robbed of the goods.

The proprietor of the goods applied to Wild, and related to him the story he had been told by his servant. Wild told him he had been deceived as to the manner in which the trunk was lost, and that he should be convinced of it if he would send for the porter. A messenger was accordingly dispatched for him, and, upon his arrival, Abraham conducted him into a room separated from the office only by a slight partition. 'Your master,' said Abraham, 'has just been here concerning the box you lost; and he desired that you might be sent for, in order to communicate the particulars of the robbery.—What kind of people were the thieves, and in what manner did they take the box away?' In reply the man said, 'Why, two or three fellows knocked me down, and then carried off the box.' Hereupon Abraham told him, that, 'if they knocked him down, there was but little chance of the property being recovered, since that offence rendered them liable to be hanged. But,' continued he, 'let me prevail upon you to speak the truth; for, if you persist in a refusal, be assured we shall discover it by some other means. Pray, do you recollect nothing about a token? Were you not to fetch a roquelaure from a tavern? and did you not produce a gold watch as a token to induce the waiter to deliver it?'—Astonished at Abraham's words, the porter declarcd 'he believed he was a witch,' and immediately acknowledged in what manner he had lost the box.

One of the villains concerned in the above transaction lived in the house formerly inhabited by Wild, in Cock Alley, near Cripplegate. To this place Jonathan and Abraham repaired, and, when they were at the door, they overheard a dispute between the man and his wife, during which the former declared that he would set out for Holland the next day. Upon this they forced open the door; and Wild, saying he was under the necessity of preventing his intended voyage, took him into custody, and conducted him to the Compter. On the following day, the goods being returned to the owner, Wild received a handsome reward; and he contrived to procure the discharge of the thief.

On the 23d or 24th of January, 1718-19, Margaret Dodwell and Alice Wright went to Wild's house, and desired

to have a private interview with him. Observing one of
these women to be with child, he imagined she might want
a father to her expected issue; for it was a part of his business to procure persons to stand in the place of the real
fathers of children born in consequence of illicit commerce.
Being shown into another room, Dodwell spoke in the following manner:—'I do not come, Mr. Wild, to inform you
that I have met with any loss, but that I wish to find something. If you will follow my advice, you may acquire a thousand pounds, or perhaps many thousands.' Jonathan here
expressed the utmost willingness to engage in an enterprise
so highly lucrative, and the woman proceeded thus: 'My
plan is this: you must procure two or three stout resolute
fellows who will undertake to rob a house in Wormwood
Street, near Bishopsgate. This house is kept by a cane chair
maker, named John Cooke, who has a lodger, an ancient
maiden lady, immensely rich; and she keeps her money in
a box in her apartment; she is now gone into the country
to fetch more. One of the men must find an opportunity of
getting into the shop in the evening, and conceal himself
in a saw-pit there: he may let his companions in when the
family are retired to rest. But it will be particularly necessary to secure two stout apprentices, and a boy, who lie in
the garret. I wish, however, that no murder may be committed.' Upon this Wright said, 'Phoo! phoo! when people
engage in matters of this sort, they must manage as well as
they can, and so as to provide for their own safety.' Dodwell
now resumed her discourse to Jonathan. 'The boys having
been secured, no kind of difficulty will attend getting possession of the old lady's money, she being from home, and
her room under that where the boys sleep. In the room facing that of the old lady, Cooke and his wife lie: he is a man
of remarkable courage; great caution, therefore, must be
observed respecting him; and indeed I think it would be as
well to knock him on the head; for then his drawers may be

rifled, and he is never without money. A woman and a child lie under the room belonging to the old lady, but I hope no violence will be offered to them.'

Having heard the above proposal, Wild took the women into custody, and lodged them in Newgate. It is not to be supposed that his conduct in this affair proceeded from a principle of virtue or justice, but that he declined engaging in the iniquitous scheme from an apprehension that their design was to draw him into a snare.

Dodwell had lived five months in Mr. Cooke's house, and, though she paid no rent, he was too generous to turn her out, or in any manner to oppress her. Wild prosecuted Dodwell and Wright for a misdemeanor, and, being found guilty, they were sentenced each to six months' imprisonment.

Wild had inserted in his book a gold watch, a quantity of fine lace, and other property of considerable value, which one John Butler had stolen from a house at Newington Green; but Butler, instead of coming to account as usual, had declined his felonious practices, and lived on the produce of his booty. Wild, highly enraged at being excluded his share, determined to pursue every possible means for subjecting him to the power of justice.

Being informed that he lodged at a public house in Bishopsgate Street, Wild went to the house early one morning, when Butler, hearing him ascending the stairs, jumped out of the window of his room, and, climbing over the wall of the yard, got into the street. Wild broke open the door of the room; but was exceedingly disappointed and mortified to find that the man of whom he was in pursuit had escaped. In the mean time Butler ran into a house, the door of which stood open, and, descending to the kitchen, where some women were washing, told them he was pursued by a bailiff, and they advised him to conceal himself in the coalhole.

Jonathan, coming out of the ale-house, and seeing a shop on the opposite side of the way open, he inquired of the master, who was a dyer, whether a man had not taken refuge in his house. The dyer answered in the negative, saying he had not left his shop more than a minute since it had been opened. Wild requested to search the house, and the dyer readily complied. Wild asked the women if they knew whether a man had taken shelter in the house, which they denied; but, informing them that the man he sought was a thief, they said he would find him in the coalhole.

Having procured a candle, Wild and his attendants searched the place without effect, and they examined every part of the house with no better success. He observed that the villain must have escaped into the street; on which the dyer said that could not be the case; that if he had entered, he must still be in the house, for he had not quitted the shop, and it was impossible that a man could pass to the street without his knowledge; advising Wild to search the cellar again. They now all went into the cellar, and, after some time spent in searching, the dyer turned up a large vessel, used in his business, and Butler appeared. Wild asked him in what manner he had disposed of the goods he stole from Newington Green, upbraided him as being guilty of ingratitude, and declared that he should certainly be hanged.

Butler, however, knowing the means by which an accommodation might be effected, directed our hero to go to his lodging, and look behind the head of the bed, where he would find what would recompense him for his time and trouble. Wild went to the place, and found what perfectly satisfied him; but, as Butler had been apprehended in a public manner, the other was under the necessity of taking him before a magistrate, who committed him for trial. He was tried the ensuing sessions at the Old Bailey; but, by the artful management of Wild, instead of being condemned to die, he was only sentenced to transportation.

Being at an inn in Smithfield, Wild observed a large trunk in the yard, and, imagining that it contained property of

value, he hastened home, and instructed one of the thieves
he employed to carry it off. The man he used in this matter was named Jeremiah Rann, and he was reckoned one
of the most dexterous thieves in London. Having dressed
himself so as exactly to resemble a porter, he carried away
the trunk without being observed.

Mr. Jarvis, a whipmaker by trade, and the proprietor
of the trunk, had no sooner discovered his loss than he
applied to Wild, who returned him the goods, in consideration of receiving ten guineas. Some time after, a disagreement taking place between Jonathan and Rann, the former
apprehended the latter, who was tried and condemned to
die. The day preceding that on which Rann was executed
he sent for Mr. Jarvis, and related to him all the particulars
of the trunk. Wild was threatened with a prosecution by
Mr. Jarvis; but all apprehensions arising hence were soon
dissipated by the decease of that gentleman.

Wild, being much embarrassed in endeavoring to find
out some method by which he might safely dispose of the
property that was not claimed by the respective proprietors,
revolved in his mind a variety of schemes; but at length
he adopted that which follows: he purchased a sloop, in
order to transport the goods to Holland and Flanders, and
gave the command of the vessel to a notorious thief, named
Roger Johnson.

Ostend was the port where this vessel principally traded;
but, when the goods were not disposed of there, Johnson
navigated her to Bruges, Ghent, Brussels, and other places.
He brought home lace, wine, brandy, &c. and these com-
modities were landed in the night, without making any
increase to the business of the revenue officers. This trade
was continued about two years, when, five pieces of lace
being lost, Johnson deducted the value of them from the
mate's pay. Violently irritated by this conduct, the mate

lodged an information against Johnson for running a great quantity of various kinds of goods.

In consequence of this the vessel was exchequered, Johnson cast in damages to the amount of 700*l.* and the commercial proceedings were entirely ruined.

A disagreement had for some time subsisted between Johnson and Thomas Edwards, who kept a house of resort for thieves in Long Lane, concerning the division of some booty. Meeting one day in the Strand, they charged each other with felony, and were both taken into custody. Wild bailed Johnson, and Edwards was not prosecuted. The latter had no sooner recovered his liberty than he gave information against Wild, whose private warehouses being searched, a great quantity of stolen goods were there found. Wild now arrested Edwards in the name of Johnson, to whom he pretended the goods belonged, and he was taken to the Marshalsea, but the next day procured bail. Edwards determined to wreak his revenge upon Johnson, and for some time industriously sought him in vain; but, meeting him accidentally in Whitechapel Road, he gave him into the custody of a peace-officer, who conducted him to an adjacent alehouse. Johnson sent for Wild, who immediately attended, accompanied by his man, Quilt Arnold. Wild promoted a riot, during which Johnson availed himself of an opportunity of effecting an escape.

Information being made against Wild for the rescue of Johnson, he judged it prudent to abscond, and he remained concealed for three weeks; at the end of which time, supposing all danger to be over, he returned to his house. Being apprized of this, Mr. Jones, high-constable of Holborn division, went to Jonathan's house in the Old Bailey, on the 15th of February, 1725, apprehended him and Quilt Arnold, and took them before Sir John Fryer, who committed them to Newgate on a charge of having assisted in the escape of Johnson.

On Wednesday, the 24th of the same month, Wild moved to be either admitted to bail or discharged, or brought to trial that sessions. On the following Friday a warrant of detainer was produced against him in Court, and to it was affixed the following articles of information:

I. That for many years past he had been a confederate with great numbers of highwaymen, pick-pockets, house-breakers, shop-lifters, and other thieves.

II. That he had formed a kind of corporation of thieves, of which he was the head or director; and that notwith-standing his pretended services, in detecting and pros-ecuting offenders, he procured such only to be hanged as concealed their booty, or refused to share it with him.

III. That he had divided the town and country into so many districts, and appointed distinct gangs for each, who regularly accounted with him for their robberies. That he had also a particular set to steal at churches in time of divine service: and likewise other moving detachments to attend at Court on birth-days, balls, &c. and at both houses of parliament, circuits, and country fairs.

IV. That the persons employed by him were for the most part felon convicts, who had returned from transporta-tion before the time for which they were transported was expired; and that he made choice of them to be his agents, because they could not be legal evidences against him, and because he had it in his power to take from them what part of the stolen goods he thought fit, and otherwise use them ill, or hang them, as he pleased.

V. That he had from time to time supplied such convicted felons with money and clothes, and lodged them in his own house, the better to conceal them: particularly some against whom there are now informations for counterfeiting and diminishing broad pieces and guineas.

VI. That he had not only been a receiver of stolen goods, as well as of writings of all kinds, for near fifteen years past, but had frequently been a confederate, and robbed along with the above-mentioned convicted felons.

VII. That in order to carry on these vile practices, and to gain some credit with the ignorant multitude, he usually carried a short silver staff, as a badge of authority from the government, which he used to produce when he himself was concerned in robbing.

VIII. That he had, under his care and direction, several ware houses for receiving and concealing stolen goods; and also a ship for carrying off jewels, watches, and other valuable goods, to Holland, where he had a superannuated thief for his factor.

IX. That he kept in pay several artists to make alterations, and transform watches, seals, snuffboxes, rings, and other valuable things, that they might not be known, several of which he used to present to such persons as he thought might be of service to him.

X. That he seldom or never helped the owners to the notes and papers they had lost unless he found them able exactly to specify and describe them, and then often insisted on more than half the value.

XI. And, lastly, it appears that he has often sold human blood, by procuring false evidence to swear persons into facts they were not guilty of; sometimes to prevent them from bring evidences against himself, and at other times for the sake of the great reward given by the government.

The information of Mr. Jones was also read in Court, setting forth that two persons would be produced to accuse the prisoner of capital offences. The men alluded to in the above affidavit were John Follard and Thomas Butler, who had been convicted; but, it being deemed expedient to grant them a pardon on condition of their appearing in support of a prosecution against Wild, they pleaded to the same, and were remanded to Newgate till the next sessions.

Saturday, the 12th of April, Wild, by counsel, moved that his trial might be postponed till the ensuing sessions; and an affidavit made by the prisoner was read in Court, purporting that till the preceding evening he was entirely ignorant of a bill having been found against him; that he knew not what offence he was charged with, and was unable to procure two material witnesses, one of them living near Brentford, and the other in Somersetshire. This was opposed by the counsel for the crown, who urged that it would be improper to defer the trial on so frivolous a pretext as that made by the prisoner; that the affidavit expressed an ignorance of what offence he was charged with, and yet declared that two nameless persons were material witnesses.

The prisoner informed the Court that his witnesses were—Hays, at the Pack Horse, on Turnham Green, and—Wilson, a clothier, at Frome; adding that he had heard it slightly intimated that he was indicted for a felony upon a person named Stretham. Wild's counsel moved that the names of Hays and Wilson might be inserted in the affidavit, and that it should be again sworn to by the prisoner. The counsel for the prosecution observed that justice would not be denied the prisoner, though it could not be reasonably expected that he would be allowed any extraordinary favours or indulgences. Follard and Butler were, at length, bound each in the penalty of 500*l.* to appear at the ensuing sessions, when it was agreed that Wild's fate should be determined.

Saturday, May 15, 1725, Jonathan Wild was indicted for privately stealing in the house of Catherine Stretham, in the parish of St. Andrew, Holborn, fifty yards of lace, the property of the said Catherine, on the 22d of January, 1724-5. He was a second time indicted for feloniously receiving from the said Catherine, on the 10th of March, ten guineas, on account, and under pretence, of restoring the said lace, without apprehending and prosecuting the felon who stole the property.

Previous to his trial Wild distributed among the jury-men, and other persons who were walking on the leads before the Court, a great number of printed papers, under the title of 'A List of Persons discovered, apprehended, and convicted of several Robberies on the Highway; and also for Burglary and Housebreaking; and also for returning from Transportation: by Jonathan Wild.' This list contained the names of thirty-five for robbing on the highway, twenty-two for housebreaking, and ten for returning from transporta-tion. To the list was annexed the following *Nota Bene:*—

'Several others have been also convicted for the like crimes, but, remembering not the persons' names who had been robbed, I omit the criminals' names.

'Please to observe that several others have been also convicted for shop-lifting, picking of pockets, &c. by the female sex, which are capital crimes, and which are too tedious to be inserted here, and the prosecutors not willing of being exposed.

'In regard, therefore, of the numbers above convicted, some, that have yet escaped justice, are endeavouring to take away the life of the said.'

'JONATHAN WILD.'

The prisoner, being put to the bar, requested that the witnesses might be examined apart, which was complied with. Henry Kelly deposed that by the prisoner's direction he went, in company with Margaret Murphy, to the pros-ecutor's shop, under pretence of buying some lace; that he stole a tin box, and gave it to Murphy in order to deliver to Wild, who waited in the street for the purpose of receiv-ing their booty, and rescuing them if they should be taken into custody; that they returned together to Wild's house, where the box, being opened, was found to contain eleven pieces of lace; that Wild said he could afford to give no more than five guineas, as he should not be able to get more than went to America, but soon returned to England, and had the address to ingratiate himself into the favour of a young lady, daughter to an opulent merchant at Newcastle-upon-Tyne. Before he could get his wife's fortune, which was considerable, into his hands, he was discovered and committed to Newgate. She followed him, and was brought to bed in the prison. Her friends, however, being apprized of her unhappy situation, caused her to return home. He contracted an intimacy with the widow of Richard Revel, one of the turnkeys of Newgate; and, being permitted to transport himself again, that woman went with him to Philadelphia, under the character of his wife. In consequence, however, of a disagreement between them, Mrs. Revel returned, and took a public house in Golden Lane; but what became of Riddlesden does not appear.

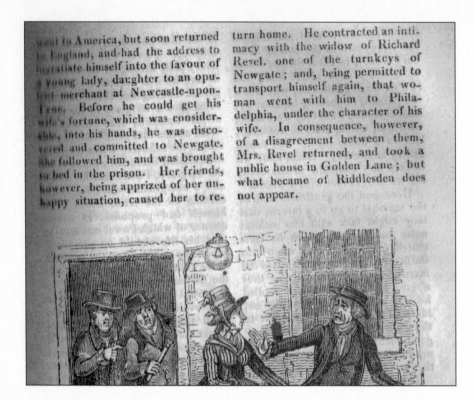

ten guineas for returning the goods to the owner; that he received, as his share, three guineas and a crown, and that Murphy had what remained of the five guineas.

Margaret Murphy was next sworn, and her evidence corresponded in every particular with that of the former witness.[1]

Catherine Stretham, the elder, deposed that, between three and four in the afternoon of the 22d of January, a man and woman came to her house, pretending that they wanted to purchase some lace; that she showed them two or three parcels, to the quality and price of which they objected; and that in about three minutes after they had left the shop she missed a tin box, containing a quantity of lace, the value of which she estimated at 50*l*.

---

[1] Margaret Murphy was executed March 27, 1728, for stealing plate.

The prisoner's counsel observed that it was their opinion he could not be legally convicted, because the indictment positively expressed that *he stole* the lace *in* the house, whereas it had been proved in evidence that he was at a considerable distance when the fact was committed. They allowed that he might be liable to conviction as an accessory before the fact, or guilty of receiving the property, knowing it to be stolen; but conceived that he could not be deemed guilty of a capital felony unless the indictment declared (as the act directs) that he did *assist, command*, or *hire*.

Lord Raymond presided when Wild was tried, and, in summing up the evidence, his lordship observed that the guilt of the prisoner was a point beyond all dispute; but that, as a similar case was not to be found in the law-books, it became his duty to act with great caution: he was not perfectly satisfied that the construction urged by the counsel for the crown could be put upon the indictment; and, as the life of a fellow-creature was at stake, recommended the prisoner to the mercy of the jury, who brought in their verdict Not Guilty.

Wild was indicted a second time for an offence committed during his confinement in Newgate. The indictment being opened by the counsel for the crown, the following clause in an act passed in the 4th year of Geo. I. was ordered to be read:

'And whereas there are divers persons who have secret acquaintance with felons, and who make it their business to help persons to their stolen goods, and by that means gain money from them, which is divided between them and the felons, whereby they greatly encourage such offenders:— Be it enacted, by the authority aforesaid, that whenever any person take the money or reward, directly or indirectly, under pretence, or upon account, of helping any person or persons to any stolen goods or chattels, every such person so taking money or reward as aforesaid (unless such person do apprehend, or cause to be apprehended, such felon who stole the same, and give evidence against him) shall be guilty of felony, according to the nature of the felony committed in stealing such goods, and in such and the same manner as if such offender had stolen such goods and chattels in the manner, and with such circumstances, as the same were stolen.'

Catherine Stretham deposed to the following effect: 'A box of lace being stolen out of my shop on the 22d of January, I went in the evening of the same day to the prisoner's house, in order to employ him in recovering my goods; but, not finding him at home, I advertised them, offering a reward of fifteen guineas, and saying no questions should be asked. The advertisement proved ineffectual: I therefore went again to the prisoner's house, and by his desire gave the best description that I was able of the persons I suspected to be the robbers; and, promising to make inquiry after my property, he desired me to call again in two or three days. I attended him a second time, when he informed me that he had learnt something concerning my goods, and expected more particular information in a short time. During this conversation we were joined by a man who said he had reason to suspect that one Kelly, who had been tried for circulating plated shillings, was concerned in stealing the lace. I went to the prisoner again on the day he was apprehended, and informed him that, though I had advertised a reward of no more than fifteen, I would give twenty or twenty-five guineas, rather than not recover my property; upon which he desired me not to be in too great a hurry, and said the people who had the lace were gone out of town, but that he would contrive to foment a disagreement between them, by which means he should be enabled to recover the goods on more easy terms. He sent me word, on the 10th of March, that if I would attend him in Newgate, and bring ten guineas with me, the goods should be returned. I went to the prisoner, who desired a person to call a porter, and then gave me a letter, saying it was the direction he had received where to apply for the lace. I told him I could not read, and gave the letter to the man he had sent for, who appeared to be a ticket-porter. The prisoner then told me I must give the porter ten guineas, that he might pay the people who had my goods, otherwise they would not return them. I gave the money, and the man went out of the prison; but in a short time he returned with a box sealed up, though it was not the box I lost. I opened it, and found all my lace, excepting one piece. I asked the prisoner what satisfaction he expected; and he answered, 'Not a farthing; I have no interested views in matters of this kind, but act from a principle of serving people under misfortune. I hope I shall soon be able to recover the other piece of lace, and to return you the ten guineas, and perhaps cause the thief to be apprehended. For the service I can render you I shall only expect your prayers. I have many enemies, and know not what will be the consequence of this imprisonment.'

The prisoner's counsel argued that as Murphy had deposed that Wild, Kelly, and herself, were concerned in the felony, the former could by no means be considered as coming within the description of the act on which the indictment was founded, for the act in question was not meant to operate against the actual perpetrators of felony, but to subject such persons to punishment as held a correspondence with felons.

The counsel for the crown observed that, from the evidence adduced, no doubt could remain of the prisoner's coming under the meaning of the act, since it had been proved that he had engaged in combinations with felons, and had not discovered them.

The judge recapitulated the arguments enforced on each side, and was of opinion that the case of the prisoner was clearly within the meaning of the act; for it was plain that he had maintained a secret correspondence with felons, and received money for restoring stolen goods to the owners, which money was divided between him and the felons, whom he did not prosecute. The jury pronounced him guilty, and he was executed at Tyburn on Monday, the 24th of May, 1725, along with Robert Harpham.

Wild, when he was under sentence of death, frequently declared that he thought the service he had rendered the public in returning the stolen goods to the owners, and apprehending felons, was so great as justly to entitle him to the royal mercy. He said that, had he considered his case as being desperate, he should have taken timely measures for inducing some powerful friends at Wolverhampton to intercede in his favour; and that he thought it not unreasonable to entertain hopes of obtaining a pardon through the interest of some of the dukes, earls, and other persons of high distinction, who had recovered their property through his means. It was observed to him that he had trained up a great number of thieves, and must be conscious that he had not enforced the execution of the law from any principle of virtue, but had sacrificed the lives of a great number of his accomplices, in order to provide for his own safety, and to gratify his desire of revenge against such as had incurred his displeasure.

He was observed to be in an unsettled state of mind, and, being asked whether he knew the cause thereof, he said he attributed his disorder to the many wounds he had received in apprehending felons, and particularly mentioned two fractures of his skull, and his throat being cut by Blueskin.

He declined attending divine service in the chapel, excusing himself on account of his infirmities, and saying that there were many people highly exasperated against him, and therefore he could not expect but that his devotions would be interrupted by their insulting behaviour. He said he had fasted four days, which had greatly increased his weakness. He asked the Ordinary the meaning of the words 'Cursed is every one that hangeth on a tree'; and what was the state of the soul immediately after its departure from the body. He was advised to direct his attention to matters of more importance, and sincerely to repent of the crimes he had committed.

By his desire the Ordinary administered the sacrament to him, and during the ceremony he appeared to be somewhat attentive and devout. The evening preceding the day on which he suffered he inquired of the Ordinary whether self-murder could be deemed a crime, since many of the Greeks and Romans, who had put a period to their own lives, were so honorably mentioned by historians. He was informed that the most wise and learned heathens accounted those guilty of the greatest cowardice who had not fortitude sufficient to maintain themselves in the station to which they had been appointed by the providence of Heaven; and that the Christian doctrines condemned the practice of suicide in the most express terms.

He pretended to be convinced that self-murder was a most impious crime; but about two in the morning he endeavoured to put an end to his life by drinking laudanum: however, on account of the largeness of the dose, and his having fasted for a considerable time, no other effect was produced than drowsiness, or a kind of stupefaction. The situation of Wild being observed by two of his fellow-prisoners, they advised him to rouse his spirits, that he might be able to attend to the devotional exercises, and, taking him by the arms, they obliged him to walk, which he could not have done alone, being much afflicted with the gout. The exercise revived him a little, but he presently became exceedingly pale, then grew very faint; a profuse sweating ensued, and soon afterwards his stomach discharged the greatest part of the laudanum. Though he was somewhat recovered, he was nearly in a state of insensibility; and in this situation he was put into the cart and conveyed to Tyburn.

In his way to the place of execution the populace treated this offender with remarkable severity, incessantly pelting him with stones, dirt, &c. and execrating him as the most consummate villain that had ever disgraced human nature.

Upon his arrival at Tyburn he appeared to be much recovered from the effects of the laudanum; and the executioner informed him that a reasonable time would be allowed him for preparing himself for the important change that he must soon experience. He continued sitting some time in the cart; but the populace were at length so enraged at the indulgence shown him, that they outrageously called to the executioner to perform the duties of his office, violently threatening him with instant death if he presumed any longer to delay. He judged it prudent to comply with their demands, and when he began to prepare for the execution the popular clamour ceased.

About two o'clock on the following morning the remains of Wild were interred in St. Pancras Church-yard; but a few nights afterwards the body was taken up (for the use of the surgeons, as it was supposed). At midnight a hearse and six was waiting at the end of Fig Lane, where the coffin was found the next day.

Wild had by the woman he married at Wolverhampton a son about nineteen years old, who came to London a short time before the execution of his father. He was a youth of so violent and ungovernable a disposition, that it was judged prudent to confine him while his father was conveyed to Tyburn, lest he should create a tumult, and prove the cause of mischief among the populace. Soon after the death of his father he accepted a sum of money to become a servant in one of our plantations.

Besides the woman to whom he was married at Wolverhampton, five others lived with him under the pretended sanction of matrimony: the first was Mary Milliner; the second Judith Nun, by whom he had a daughter; the third Sarah Grigson, alias Perrin; the fourth Elizabeth Man, who cohabited with him above five years; the fifth, whose real name is uncertain, married some time after the death of Wild.

History can scarcely furnish an instance of such complicated villainy as was shown in the character of Jonathan Wild, who possessed abilities which, had they been properly cultivated, and directed into a right course, would have rendered him a respectable and useful member of society; but it is to be lamented that the profligate turn of mind which distinguished him in the early part of his life disposed him to adopt the maxims of the abandoned people with whom he became acquainted.

During his apprenticeship Wild was observed to be fond of reading; but, as his finances would not admit of his buying books, his studies were confined to such as casually fell in his way; and they unfortunately happened to contain those abominable doctrines to which thousands have owed the ruin of both their bodies and souls. In short, at an early period of life he imbibed the principles of deism and atheism; and the sentiments he thus early contracted he strictly adhered to nearly till the period of his dissolution.

Voluminous writings were formerly beyond the purchase of persons in the inferior classes of life; but the great encouragement that has of late years been given to the publication of weekly numbers has so liberally diffused the streams of knowledge, that but few even of the lower ranks of society can be sensible of any impediment to the-gratification of the desire of literary acquirements.

Wild trained up and instructed his dependents in the practice of roguery; and, when they became the objects of his displeasure, he labored with unremitting assiduity to procure their deaths. Thus his temporal and private interest sought gratification at the expense of every religious and moral obligation. We must conceive it to be impossible for a man acknowledging the existence of an Almighty Being to expect his favor, while devising the means of corrupting his fellow-creatures, and cutting them off 'even in the blossom of their sins': but the atheist, having nothing after this world either to hope or fear, is only careful to secure himself from detection; and the success of one iniquitous scheme naturally induces him to engage in others, and the latter actions are generally attended with circumstances of more aggravated guilt than the former.

There is a principle, implanted in our nature, which will exert itself when we are approaching to a state of dissolution, and impress our minds with a full confidence in the existence of an eternal God, who will reward or punish us according to our deserts or demerits. Thus it happened to the miserable subject of these pages, who, when he had relinquished the hope of surviving the sentence of the law, anxiously inquired into the meaning of several texts of scripture, and concerning the intermediate state of the soul. The horrors of his guilt rushed upon his conscience with such force that reflection became intolerable; and, instead of repenting of his enormous crimes, he employed the last of his moments that were enlightened by reason (the distinguished characteristic of humanity) in meditating the means of self-destruction.

CATHERINE HAYES AND HER ACCOMPLICES CUTTING OFF HER HUSBAND'S HEAD.

CATHERINE HAYES

Burnt alive for the murder of her husband.

———

We give the history of the enormous sins and dreadful sufferings of this abominable woman just as they came to our hands—altogether too shocking for a single comment.

Catherine Hayes was the daughter of a poor man of the name of Hall, who lived near Birmingham. She remained with her parents till she was about fifteen years old, and then, having a dispute with her mother, left her home, and set out with a view of going to London. Her person being rather engaging, some officers in the army, who met with

her on the road, prevailed on her to accompany them to
their quarters at Great Ombersley, in Worcestershire, where
she remained with them a considerable time.—On being
dismissed by these officers, she strolled about the country,
till, arriving at the house of Mr. Hayes, a farmer in War-
wickshire, the farmer's wife hired her as a servant. When
she had continued a short time in this service, Mr. Hayes's
son fell violently in love with her, and a private marriage
took place, which was managed in the following manner:
Catherine left the house early in the morning, and the
younger Hayes, being a carpenter, prevailed on his mother
to let him have some money to buy tools; but as soon as he
had got it he set out, and, meeting his sweetheart at a place
they had agreed on, they went to Worcester, where the nuptial rites were celebrated. At this time it happened that the
officers by whom she had been seduced were at Worcester;
and, hearing of her marriage, they caused young Hayes to
be taken out of bed from his wife, under pretence that he
had enlisted in the army. Thus situated, he was compelled
to send an account of the whole transaction to his father,
who, though offended with his son for the rash step he had
taken, went to a magistrate, who attended him to Worcester, and demanded by what authority the young man was
detained. The officers endeavoured to excuse their conduct;
but the magistrate threatening to commit them to prison
if they did not release him, the young fellow immediately
obtained his liberty. The father, irritated at the imprudent
conduct of his son, severely censured his proceedings; but,
considering that what was passed could not be recalled, had
good sense enough not to persevere in his opposition to an
unavoidable event.—Mr. Hayes now furnished his son with
money to begin business for himself; and the young couple
were in a thriving way, and appeared to live in harmony; but
Mrs. Hayes, being naturally of a restless disposition, prevailed on her husband to enlist for a soldier. The regiment

in which he served being ordered to the Isle of Wight, Catherine followed him thither. He had not been long there before his father procured his discharge, which, as it happened in the time of war, was attended with an expense of 60*l*. On the return of young Hayes and his wife, the father gave them an estate of 10*l*. per annum, to which he afterwards added another of 16*l*. which, with the profit of their trade, would have been amply sufficient for their support. The husband bore the character of an honest well-disposed man; he treated his wife very indulgently, yet she constantly complained of the covetousness of his disposition; but *he* had much more reason to complain of *her* disposition, for she was turbulent, quarrelsome, and perpetually exciting disputes among her neighbours. The elder Mr. H. observing with concern how unfortunately his son was matched, advised him to leave her, and settle in some place where she might not find him. Such, however, was his attachment to her, that he could not comply with this advice; and she had the power of persuading him to come to London, after they had been married about six years. On their arrival in the metropolis, Mr. Hayes took a house, part of which he let in lodgings, and opened a shop in the chandlery and coal trade, in which he was as successful as he could have wished. Exclusive of his profit by shop-keeping, he acquired a great deal of money by lending small sums on pledges, for at this time the trade of pawnbroking was followed by any one at pleasure, it having been then subjected to no regulation. Mrs. Hayes's conduct in London was still more reprehensible than it had been in the country. The chief pleasure of her life, consisted in creating and encouraging quarrels among her neighbours; and, indeed, her unhappy temper discovered itself on every occasion. Sometimes she would speak of her husband, to his acquaintance, in terms of great tenderness and respect; and at other times she would represent him to her female associates as a compound of every thing that was contemptible in human nature. On a particular occasion, she told a woman of her acquaintance that she should think it no more sin to murder him than to kill a dog. At length her husband, finding she made perpetual disturbances in the neighbourhood, thought it prudent to remove to Tottenham Court Road, where he carried on his former business; but not being as successful here as he could have wished, he took another house in Tyburn Road, since called Oxford Road. Here he continued his practice of lending small sums of money on pledges, till, having acquired a decent competency, he left off housekeeping, and hired lodgings near the same spot.—Thomas Billings, a journeyman tailor, and a supposed son of Mrs. Hayes by her former connexions, lodged in the house with Mrs. Hayes; and the husband having gone into the country on business, his wife and this man indulged themselves in every species of extravagance. On Hayes's return some of his neighbours told him how his wife had been wasting his substance, on which he severely censured her conduct, and, a quarrel arising between them, they proceeded from words to blows. It was commonly thought that she formed the resolution of murdering him at this time, as the quarrel happened only six weeks before his fatal exit. She now began to sound the disposition of Billings, to whom she said it was impossible for her to live longer with her husband; and she urged all possible arguments to prevail on him to aid her in the commission of the murder, which Billings resisted for some time, but at length complied.

At this period Thomas Wood, an acquaintance of Mr. Hayes, arrived from the country; and, as he was apprehensive of being impressed, Hayes kindly took him into his house, and promised to use his interest in procuring him some employment. After a few days' residence Mrs. Hayes proposed to him the murder of her husband: but the man was shocked at the thought of destroying his friend and benefactor, and told her he would have no concern in so atrocious a deed. However, she artfully urged that 'he was an atheist, and it could be no crime to destroy a person who had no religion or goodness—that he was himself a murderer, having killed a man in the country, and likewise two of his own children; one of whom he buried under a pear-tree, and the other under an apple-tree.' She likewise said that her husband's death would put her in possession of 1500*l*., of the whole of which Wood should have the disposal, if he would assist her and Billings in the perpetration of the murder. Wood went out of town a few days after this, and on his return found Mr. and Mrs. Hayes and Billings in company together, having drank till they had put themselves into the utmost apparent good humour. Wood sitting down at Hayes's request, the latter said they had drank a guinea's worth of liquor, but, notwithstanding this, he was not drunk. A proposal was now made by Billings, that, if Hayes could drink six bottles of mountain without being drunk, he would pay for it; but that Hayes should be the paymaster, if the liquor made him drunk, or if he failed of drinking the quantity. This proposal being agreed to, Wood, Billings, and Mrs. Hayes, went to a wine-vault to buy the wine, and, on their way, this wicked woman reminded the men that the present would be a good opportunity of committing the murder, as her husband would be perfectly intoxicated. The mind of Wood was not yet wrought up to a proper pitch for the commission of a crime so atrocious as the murder of a man who had sheltered and protected him, and this too at a time when his mind must necessarily be unprepared for his being launched into eternity. Mrs. H. had therefore recourse to her former arguments, urging that it would be no sin to kill him; and Billings seconded all she said, and, declaring he was ready to take a part in the horrid deed, Wood was at length prevailed on to become one of the execrable butchers. Thus agreed, they went to a wine-vault, where Mrs. Hayes paid half a guinea for six bottles of wine, which, being sent home by a porter, Mr. Hayes began to drink it, while his intentional murderers regaled themselves with beer. When he had taken a considerable quantity of the wine, he danced about the room like a man distracted, and at length finished the whole quantity: but, not being yet in a state of absolute stupefaction, his wife sent for another bottle, which he likewise drank, and then fell senseless on the floor. Having lain some time in this condition, he got, with much difficulty, into another room, and threw himself on a bed. When he was asleep, his wife told her associates that this was the time to execute their plan, as there was no fear of any resistance on his part. Accordingly Billings went into the room with a hatchet, with which he struck Hayes so violently that he fractured his skull. At this time Hayes's feet hung off the bed, and the torture arising from the blow made him stamp repeatedly on the floor, which being heard by Wood, he also went into the room, and, taking the hatchet out of Billings's hand, gave the poor man two more blows, which effectually dispatched him. A woman, named Springate, who lodged in the room over that where the murder was committed, hearing the noise occasioned by Hayes's stamping, imagined that the parties might have quarrelled in consequence of their intoxication; and going down stairs, she told Mrs. Hayes that the noise had awakened her husband, her child, and herself. Catherine had a ready answer to this: she said some company had visited them, and were grown merry but they were on the point of taking their leave; with which answer Mrs. Springate returned to her room well satisfied. The murderers now consulted on the best manner of disposing of the body, so as most effectually to prevent detection. Mrs. Hayes proposed to cut off the head, because, if the body was found whole, it would be more likely to be known. The villains agreeing to this proposition, she fetched a pail, lighted a candle, and all of them going into the room, the men drew the body partly off the bed, when Billings supported the head, while Wood, with his pocket-knife, cut it off, and the infamous woman held the pail to receive it, being as careful as possible that the floor might not be stained with the blood. This being done, they emptied the blood out of the pail into a sink by the window, and poured several pails of water after it; but, notwithstanding all this care, Mrs. Springate observed some congealed blood the next morning; though at that time she did not in the least suspect what had passed. It was likewise observed that the marks of the blood were visible on the floor for some weeks afterwards, though Mrs. Hayes had washed and scraped it with a knife. When the head was cut off, this she-devil recommended boiling it till the flesh should part from the bones; but the other parties thought this operation would take up too much time, and therefore advised the throwing it into the Thames, in expectation that it would be carried off by the tide, and sink. This agreed to, the head was put into the pail, and Billings took it under his great coat, being accompanied by Wood; but, making a noise in going down stairs, Mrs. Springate called, and asked what was the matter; to which Mrs. Hayes answered that her husband was going on a journey, and, with incredible dissimulation, affected to take leave of him; and, as it was now past eleven, pretended great concern that he was under a necessity of going at so late an hour. By this artifice Wood and Billings passed out of the house unnoticed, and went to Whitehall, where they intended to have thrown in the head; but the gates being shut, they went to a wharf near the Horse Ferry, Westminster. Billings putting down the pail, Wood threw the head into the dock, expecting it would have been carried away by the stream; but at this time the tide was ebbing, and a ligherterman, who was then in his vessel, heard something fall into the dock, but it was too dark for him to distinguish objects. The murderers, having thus disposed of the head, went home, and were let in by Mrs. Hayes, without the knowledge of the lodgers. On the following morning, soon after day-break, as a watchman, named Robinson, was going off his stand, he saw the pail, and, looking into the dock, observed the head of a man. Having procured some witnesses to this spectacle, they took out the head; and, observing the pail to be bloody, concluded that it was brought therein from some distant part. The lighterman now said that he had heard something thrown into the dock; and the magistrates and parish officers, having assembled, gave strict orders that the most diligent search should be made after the body, which, however, was not found till some time afterwards; for, when the murderers had conversed together on the disposal of the body, Mrs. Hayes had proposed that it should be put into a box and buried; and the others agreeing to this, she purchased a box, which, on being sent home, was found too little to contain it: she therefore recommended the chopping off the legs and arms, which was done; but the box being still too small, the thighs were likewise cut off, all the parts packed up together, and the box put by till night, when Wood and Billings took out the pieces of the mangled body, and, putting them into two blankets, carried them into a pond near Marylebone; which being done, they returned to their lodgings, and Mrs. Springate, who had still no suspicion of what had passed, opened the door for them. In the interim the magistrates directed that the head should be washed clean, and the hair combed, after which it was put on a pole in the churchyard of St. Margaret, Westminster, that an opportunity might be afforded for its being viewed by the public.[2]

---

[2] It was formerly customary to oblige persons suspected of murder to touch the murdered body, for the discovery of their guilt or innocence.

This way of finding murderers was practised in Denmark by King Christianus H. and permitted all over his kingdom; the occasion whereof is this:—Certain gentlemen being on an evening together in a stove, or tavern, fell out among themselves, and from words came to blows, (the caudles being out), insomuch that one of them was stabbed with a poniard. Now the murderer was unknown, by reason of the number, although the person stabbed accused a pursuivant of the king's, who was one of the company.

The king, to find out the homicide, caused them all to come together in the stove, and, standing round the corpse, he commanded that they should, one after another, lay their right hand on the stain gentleman's naked breast, swearing that they had not killed him. The gentlemen did so, and no sign appeared against them; the pursuivant only remained, who, condemned before in his own conscience, went, first of all, and kissed the dead man's feet; but, as soon as he had laid his hand upon his breast, the blood gushed forth in abundance, both out of his wound and his nostrils; so that, urged by this evident accusation, he confessed the murder, and was, by the king's own sentence, immediately beheaded. Such was the origin of this practice, which was so common in many of the countries in Europe, for finding out unknown murderers.

Orders were likewise given that the parish officers should attend this exhibition of the head, to take into custody any suspicious person who might discover signs of guilt on the sight of it.

The high constable of Westminster, on a presumption that the body might, on the following night, be thrown where the head had been, gave private orders to the inferior constables to attend during the night, and stop all coaches, or other carriages, or persons with burdens, coming near the spot, and examine if they could find the body, or any of the limbs. The head being exposed on the pole so excited the curiosity of the public, that immense crowds of people, of all ranks, went to view it; and among the rest was a Mr. Bennet, apprentice to the king's organ-builder, who, having looked at it with great attention, said he thought it was the head of Hayes, with whom he had been some time acquainted; and hereupon he went to Mrs. Hayes, and, telling her his suspicions, desired she would go and take a view of the head. In answer hereto she told him that her husband was in good health, and desired him to be cautious of what he said, as such a declaration might occasion Hayes a great deal of trouble; on which, for the present, Bennet took no farther notice of the affair. A journeyman tailor, named Patrick, who worked in Monmouth Street, having likewise taken a view of the head, told his master on his return that he was confident it was the head of Hayes; on which some other journeymen in the same shop, who had likewise known the deceased, went and saw it, and returned perfectly assured that it was so. Now Billings worked at this very shop in Monmouth Street: one of these journeymen observed, therefore, to him, that he must know the head, as he lodged in Hayes's house; but Billings said he had left him well in bed when he came to work in the morning, and therefore it could not belong to him. On this same day Mrs. Hayes gave Wood a suit of clothes which had belonged to her husband, and sent him to Harrow-on-the-Hill. As Wood was going down stairs with the bundle of clothes, Mrs. Springate asked him what he had got; to which Mrs. Hayes readily replied, A suit of clothes he had borrowed of an acquaintance. On the second day after the commission of the murder, Mrs. Hayes being visited by a Mr. Longmore, the former asked what was the news of the town; when the latter said that the public conversation was wholly engrossed by the head which was fixed in St. Margaret's church-yard. Hereupon Catherine exclaimed against the wickedness of the times, and said she had been told that the body of a murdered woman had been found in the fields that day. Wood coming from Harrow-on-the-Hill on the following day, Catherine told him that the head was found; and giving him some other clothes that had belonged to her husband, and five shillings, said she would continue to supply him with money. After the head had been exhibited four days, and no discovery made, a surgeon named Westbrook was desired to put it in a glass of spirits, to prevent its putrefying, and keep it for the farther inspection of all who chose to take a view of it, which was accordingly done. Soon after this Mrs. Hayes quitted her lodgings, and removed to the house of Mr. Jones, a distiller, paying Mrs. Springate's rent also at the former lodgings, and taking her with her. Wood and Billings like-wise removed with her, whom she continued to supply with money, and employed herself principally in collecting cash that had been owing to her late husband. A sister of Mr. Hayes's, who lived in the country, having married a Mr. Davies, Hayes had lent Davies some money, for which he had taken his bond. Catherine finding this bond among Mr. Hayes's papers, she employed a person to write a letter in the name of the deceased, demanding ten pounds in part of payment, and threatening a prosecution in case of refusal. Mr. Hayes's mother being still living, and Davies unable to pay the money, he applied to the old gentlewoman for assistance, who agreed to pay the sum on condition that the bond was sent into the country; and wrote to London, intimating her consent so to do, having no suspicion of the horrid transaction which had taken place. Amongst the incredible numbers of people who resorted to see the head was a poor woman from Kingsland, whose husband had been absent from the very time that the murder was perpetrated. After a minute survey of the head, she believed it to be that of her husband, though she could not be absolutely positive. However, her suspicions were so strong, that strict search was made after the body, on a presumption that the clothes might help her to ascertain it. Meanwhile, Mr. Hayes not being visible for a considerable time, his friends could not help making inquiry after him. A Mr. Ashby, in particular, who had been on the most friendly terms with him, called on Mrs. Hayes, and demanded what had become of her husband. Catherine pretended to account for his absence by communicating the following intelligence, as a matter that must be kept profoundly secret: 'Some time ago (said she) he happened to have a dispute with a man, and from words they came to blows, so that Mr. Hayes killed him. The wife of the deceased made up the affair, on Mr. Hayes's promising to pay her a certain annual allowance; but he not being able to make it good, she threatened to inform against him, on which he has absconded.' This method of accounting for the absence of his friend was by no means satisfactory to Mr. Ashby, who asked her if the head that had been exposed on the pole was that of the man who had been killed by her husband. She readily answered in the negative, adding, that the party had been buried entire; and that the widow had her husband's bond for the payment of fifteen pounds a year. Ashby inquired to what part of the world Mr. Hayes was gone: she said to Portugal, in company with some gentlemen; but she had yet received no letter from him. The whole of this story seeming highly improbable to Mr. Ashby, he went to Mr. Longmore, a gentleman nearly related to Hayes, and it was agreed between them that Mr. Longmore should call on Catherine, and have some conversation, but not let her know that Ashby had been with him, as they supposed that, by comparing the two accounts together, they might form a very probable judgment of the matter of fact. Accordingly Longmore went to Catherine, and inquired after her husband. In answer to his questions, she said she presumed Mr. Ashby had related the circumstance of his misfortune; but Longmore replied that he had not seen

Ashby for a considerable time, and expressed his hope that her husband was not imprisoned for debt. 'No,' she replied, 'it is much worse than that.' 'Why,' said Longmore, 'has he murdered any one?' To this she answered in the affirmative; and, desiring him to walk into another room, told him almost the same story as she had done to Mr. Ashby, but instead of naming Portugal, said he was retired into Hertfordshire, and, in fear of being attacked, had taken four pistols to defend himself. It was now remarked by Mr. Longmore that it was imprudent for him to travel thus armed, as he was liable to be taken up-on suspicion of being a highwayman, and if such a circumstance should happen, he would find it no easy matter to procure a discharge. She allowed the justice of this remark, but said that Mr. Hayes commonly travelled in that manner. She likewise said that he *was* once taken into custody on suspicion of being a highwayman, and conducted to a magistrate; but a gentleman who was casually present, happening to know him, gave bail for his appearance. To this Longmore observed that the justice of peace must have exceeded his authority, for that the law required that two parties should bail a person charged on suspicion of having robbed on the highway. In the course of conversation Mr. Longmore asked her what sum of money her husband had in his possession. To which she replied that he had seventeen shillings in his pocket, and about twenty-six guineas sewed within the lining of his coat. She added that Mrs. Springate knew the truth of all these circumstances, which had induced her to pay that woman's rent at the former lodgings, and bring her away. Mrs. Springate, having been interrogated by Longmore, averred the truth of all that Catherine had said; and added, that Mr. Hayes was a very cruel husband, having behaved with remarkable severity to his wife; but Mr. Longmore said this must be false, for to his knowledge he was remarkably tender and indulgent to her. Longmore went immediately to Mr. Ashby, and said that, from the difference of the stories Catherine had told them, he had little doubt but that poor Hayes had been murdered. Hereupon they determined to go to Mr. Eaton, who was one of the life-guards, and nearly related to the deceased, and to communicate their suspicions to him; but Eaton happening to be absent from home, they agreed to go again to Westminster, and survey the head with more care and attention than they had hitherto done. On their arrival the surgeon told them that a poor woman from Kingsland had, in part, owned the head as that of her husband, but she was not so absolutely certain as to swear that it was so, and that they were very welcome to take another view of it. This they did, and coincided in opinion that it was actually the head of Hayes. On their return, therefore, they called at Eaton's house, and took him with them to dine at Mr. Longmore's, where the subject of conversation ran naturally on the supposed discovery they had made. A brother of Mr. Longmore, coming in at this juncture, listened to their conversation; and, remarking that they proposed Mr. Eaton should go to Mrs. Hayes at the expiration of two or three days, and make inquiries after her husband similar to those which had been made by the others, this gentleman urged his objections; observing that, as they had reason to think their suspicions so well founded, it would be very ill policy to lose any time, since the murderers would certainly effect an escape, if they should hear they were suspected; and as Wood and Billings were drinking with Mr. Hayes the last time he was seen, he advised that they should be immediately taken into custody. This advice appeared so reasonable, that all the parties agreed to follow it; and, going soon afterwards to Justice Lambert, they told him their suspicions, and the reasons on which they were founded. The magistrate immediately granted his warrant for the apprehension of Catherine Hayes, Thomas Wood, Thomas

Billings, and Mary Springate, on suspicion of their having been guilty of the murder of John Hayes; and Mr. Lambert, anxious that there should be no failure in the execution of the warrant, determined to attend in person. Hereupon, having procured the assistance of two officers of the life-guards, and taking with him the several gentlemen who had given the information, they went to Mr. Jones, the distiller's (Mrs. Hayes's lodgings), about nine o'clock at night. As they were going up stairs without any ceremony, the distiller desired to know by what authority they made so free in his house; but Mr. Lambert informing him who he was, no farther opposition was made to their proceedings. The magistrate, going to the door of Mrs. Hayes's room, rapped with his cane; on which she said 'Who is there?' and he commanded her to open the door immediately, or it should be broken open. To this she replied, that she would open it as soon as she had put on her clothes, and she did so in little more than a minute, when the justice ordered the parties present to take her into custody. At this time Billings was sitting on the side of the bed, bare-legged; on which Mr. Lambert asked if they had been sleeping together; to which Catherine replied 'No'; and said that Billings had been mending his stockings; on which the justice observed that 'his sight must be extremely good, as there was neither fire nor candle in the room when they came to the door.' Some of the parties remaining below, to secure the prisoners, Mr. Longmore went up stairs with the justice, and took Mrs. Springate into custody; and they were all conducted together to the house of Mr. Lambert. This magistrate having examined the prisoners separately for a considerable time, and all of them positively persisting in their ignorance of any thing respecting the murder, they were severally committed for re-examination on the following day, before Mr. Lambert and other magistrates. Mrs. Springate was sent to the Gate-house, Billings to New Prison,

and Mrs. Hayes to Tothill-fields Bridewell. When the peace
officers, attended by Longmore, went the next day to fetch
up Catherine to her examination, she earnestly desired to
see the head; and it being thought prudent to grant her
request, she was carried to the surgeon's, and no sooner
was the head shown to her than she exclaimed 'Oh, it is my
dear husband's head!' It is my dear husband's head!' She
now took the glass in her arms, and shed many tears while
she embraced it. Mr. Westbrook told her that he would take
the head out or the glass, that she might have a more perfect view of it, and be certain that it was the same. The
surgeon doing as he had said, she seemed to be greatly
affected, and, having kissed it several times, she begged to
be indulged with a lock of the hair; and, on Mr. Westbrook
expressing his apprehension that she had too much of his
blood already, she fell into a fit, and on her recovery was
conducted to Mr. Lambert's, to take her examination with
the other parties. On the morning of this day, as a gentleman and his servant were crossing the fields Marylebone,
they observed something lying in a ditch, and, taking a
nearer view of it, found that it consisted of some of the
parts of a human body. Shocked at the sight, the gentleman
dispatched his servant to get assistance to investigate the
affair farther; and some labouring men being procured,
they dragged the pond, and found the other parts of the
body wrapped in a blanket, but no head was to be found. A
constable brought intelligence of this fact while Mrs. Hayes
was under examination before the justices, a circumstance
that contributed to strengthen the idea conceived of her
guilt. Notwithstanding this, she still persisted in her innocence: but the magistrates, paying no regard to her declarations, committed her to Newgate for trial. Wood being at
this time out of town, it was thought prudent to defer the
farther examination of Billings and Springate till he should
be taken into custody. On the morning of the succeeding

Sunday he came on horseback to the house where Mrs. Hayes had lodged when the murder was committed; when he was told that she had removed to Mr. Jones's. Accordingly he rode thither, and inquired for her; when the people, knowing that he was one of the parties charged with the murder, were disposed to take him into custody: however, their fear of his having pistols prevented their doing so; but, unwilling that such an atrocious offender should escape, they told him that Mrs. Hayes was gone to the Green Dragon, in King Street, on a visit (which house was kept by Mr. Longmore), and they sent a person with him, to direct him to the place. The brother of Longmore being at the door on his arrival, and knowing him well, pulled him from his horse, and accused him of being an accomplice in the murder. He was immediately delivered to the custody of some constables, who conducted him to the house of Justice Lambert, before whom he underwent an examination; but, refusing to make any confession, he was sent to Tothill-fields Bridewell for farther examination. On his arrival at the prison he was informed that the body had been found: and, not doubting but that the whole affair would come to light, he begged that he might be carried back to the justice's house. This being made known to Mr. Lambert, he sent for the assistance of two other magistrates, and the prisoner being brought up, he acknowledged the particulars of the murder, and signed his confession. It is thought that he entertained some hope of being admitted an evidence; but as his surrender was not voluntary, and his accomplices were in custody, the magistrates told him he must abide the verdict of a jury. This wretched man owned that, since the perpetration of the crime, he had been terrified at the sight of every one he met, that he had not experienced a moment's peace, and that his mind had been distracted with the most violent agitations. His commitment was made out for Newgate; but so exceedingly were the passions of the populace agitated on the occasion, that it was feared he would be torn to pieces by the mob; wherefore it was thought prudent to procure a guard of a sergeant and eight soldiers, who conducted him to prison with their bayonets fixed. A gentleman, named Mercer, having visited Mrs. Hayes in Newgate the day before Wood was taken into custody, she desired he would go to Billings, and urge him to confess the whole truth, as the proofs of their guilt were such, that in advantage could be expected him a farther denial of the fact. Accordingly the gentleman went to Billings, who, being carried before Justice Lambert, made a confession agreeing in all its circumstances with that of Wood; and thereupon Mrs. Springate was set at liberty, as her Innocence was evident from their concurrent testimony. Numbers of people now went to see Mrs. Hayes in Newgate; and on her being asked what could induce her in commit so atrocious a crime, she gave very different answers at different times; but frequently alleged that Mr. Hayes had been an unkind husband to her, a circumstances which was contradicted by the report of every person who knew the deceased. In the history of this woman there is a strange mystery. She called Billings her son, and sometimes averred that he was really so; but he knew nothing of her being his mother, nor did her relations know anything of the birth of such a child. To some people she would affirm he was the son of Mr. Hayes, born after marriage; but that, his father having an aversion to him while an infant, he was put to nurse in the country, and all farther care of him totally neglected on their coming to London. But this story is altogether incredible, because Hayes was not a man likely to have deserted his child to the frowns of fortune; and his parents had never heard of the birth of such a son. Billings was equally incapable of giving a satisfactory account of his own origin. All he knew was, that he had lived with a country shoemaker, who passed for his father, and had sent him to school, and then put him apprentice to a tailor. It is probable she discovered him to be her son when she afterwards became acquainted with him in London; and as some persons, who came from the same part of the kingdom, said that Billings was found in a basket near a farmhouse, and supported at the expense of the parish, it may be presumed that he was dropped in that manner by his unnatural mother.

Thomas Wood was born near Ludlow, in Shropshire, and brought up to the business of husbandry. He was so remarkable for his harmless and sober conduct, when a boy, as to be very much esteemed by his neighbours. On the death of his father, his mother took a public house for the support of her children, of whom this Thomas was the eldest; and he behaved so dutifully that the loss of her husband was scarcely felt. He was equally diligent abroad and at home; for, when the business of the house was insufficient to employ him, he worked for the farmers, by which he greatly contributed to the support of the family. On attaining years of maturity he engaged himself as a waiter at an inn in the country, from thence removed to other inns, and in all his places preserved a fair character. At length he came to London; but, being afraid of being impressed, as already mentioned, obtained the protection of Mr. Hayes, who behaved in a very friendly manner to him, till the arts of a vile woman prevailed on him to imbrue his hands in the blood of his benefactor.

Billings and Wood having already made confessions, and being penetrated with the thought of the heinous nature of their offence, determined to plead guilty to the indictment against them: but Mrs. Hayes, having made no confession, flattered herself there was a chance of her being acquitted, and therefore resolved to put herself on her trial, in which she was encouraged by some people that she met with in Newgate.

The malignancy of the crime with which this woman was charged induced the king to direct his own counsel to carry on the prosecution; and these gentlemen did all in their power to convince the Court and jury that the most striking example should be made of one who had so daringly defied the laws of God and man. The indictment being opened, and the witnesses heard, the jury, fully convinced of the commission of the fact, found her guilty. The prisoners being brought to the bar to receive sentence, Mrs. Hayes entreated that she might not be burnt, according to the then law of petty treason, alleging that she was not guilty, as she did not strike the fatal blow; but she was informed by the Court that the sentence awarded by the law could not be dispensed with. Billings and Wood urged that, having made so full and free a confession, they hoped they should not be hung in chains; but to this they received no answer.

After conviction the behaviour of Wood was uncommonly penitent and devout; but while in the condemned hold he was seized with a violent fever, and, being attended by a clergyman to assist him in his devotions, he confessed he was ready to suffer death, under every mark of ignominy, as some atonement for the atrocious crime he had committed: however, he died in prison, and thus defeated the final execution of the law. At particular times Billings behaved with sincerity; but at others prevaricated much in his answers to the questions put to him. On the whole, however, he fully confessed his guilt, acknowledged the justice of his sentence, and said no punishment could be adequate to the excess of the crime of which he had been guilty. The behaviour of Mrs. Hayes was somewhat similar to her former conduct. Having an intention to destroy herself, she procured a phial of strong poison, which being casually tasted by a woman who was confined with her, it burnt her lips; on which she broke the phial, and thereby frustrated the design. On the day of her death Hayes received the sacrament, and was drawn on a sledge to the place of execution. Billings was executed in the usual manner, and hung in chains, not far from the pond in which Mr. Hayes's body was found, in Marylebone Fields. When the wretched woman had finished her devotions, an iron chain was put round her body, with which she was fixed to a stake near the gallows. On these occasions, when women were burnt for petty treason, it was customary to strangle them, by means of a rope passed round the neck, and pulled by the executioner, so that they were dead before the flames reached the body. But this woman was literally burnt alive; for the executioner letting go the rope sooner than usual, in consequence of the flames reaching his hands, the fire burnt fiercely round her, and the spectators beheld her pushing away the faggots, while she rent the air with her cries and lamentations. Other faggots were instantly thrown on her; but she survived amidst the flames for a considerable time, and her body was not perfectly reduced to ashes in less than three hours.[3] They suffered at Tyburn, May 9, 1726.

---

[3] Until the thirtieth year of the reign of King George III this punishment was inflicted on women convicted of murdering their husbands, which crime is denominated petit-treason. It has frequently, from some accident happening in strangling the malefactor, produced the horrid effects above related. In the reign of Mary (the cruel) this death was commonly practised upon the objects of her vengeance; and many bishops, rather than deny their religious opinions, were burnt even without previous strangulation. It was high time this part of the sentence, the type of barbarism, should be dispensed with. The punishment now inflicted for this most unnatural and abhorred crime is hanging; but once convicted, a woman need never look for mercy.

EVERETT AND BIRD STOPPING A STAGE-COACH ON HOUNSLOW HEATH.

JOHN EVERETT

Executed for highway robbery.

———

WAS a native of Hitchin, in Hertfordshire, and had been well educated, his father possessing 300*l*. per annum. He was apprenticed to a salesman; but, running away from his master, he entered into the army, and served in Flanders, where he behaved so well that he was promoted to the rank of sergeant. On the return of his regiment to England he purchased his discharge, and, repairing to London, bought the place of an officer in White-chapel Court, in which he continued about seven years; but, having given liberty to some persons whom he had arrested, one Charlesworth, a solicitor of that Court, caused him to be discharged, and then sued him for the amount of the debts of the parties whom his inconsiderate good nature had liberated. To evade imprisonment, Everett enlisted in Lord Albemarle's company of footguards; and, soon after his again engaging in the army, he fell into company with Richard Bird, with whom he had been formerly acquainted.

This Bird hinted that great advantages might be acquired in a particular way, if Everett could be trusted; and the latter, anxious to know what the plan was, learnt that it was to go on the road; on which an agreement was immediately concluded. Hereupon they set out on their expedition, and robbed several stages in the counties adjacent to London, from which they obtained considerable booty in jewels, money, and valuable effects. Thus successful in their first exploits, they went to Hounslow Heath, where they stopped two military officers, who were attended by servants armed with blunderbusses; but they obliged them to submit, and robbed them of their money and watches: the watches were afterwards left, according to agreement, at a coffee-house near Charing Cross, and the thieves received twenty guineas for restoring them. Soon after they stopped a gentleman in an open chaise, near Epsom. The gentleman drew his sword, and made several passes at them; yet they robbed him of his watch, two guineas, his sword, and some writings; but they returned the writings at the earnest request of the injured party. They also made a practice of robbing the butchers and hagglers on Epping Forest, on their way to London. One of these robberies was singular:—Meeting with an old woman, a higgler, they searched the lining of a high-crowned hat, which she said had been her mother's, in which they found about three pounds; but returned her hat. Soon after this they stopped a coach on Hounslow Heath, in which were

two Quakers; who, calling them *sons of violence,* jumped
out of the coach to oppose them; but their fellow-travellers
making no resistance, and begging them to submit, all the
parties were robbed of their money. Everett, observing that
one of the Quakers wore a remarkably good wig, snatched
it from his head, and gave him in return an old black tie,
which he had purchased for half a crown of a Chelsea pen-
sioner. This sudden metamorphosis caused great mirth
among the company in the coach. About ten days after this
he and his companion walked to Hillingdon Common,
where, seeing two gentlemen on horseback, Everett stopped
the foremost, and Bird the other, and robbed them of
upwards of three guineas and their gold watches; they then
cut the girths of the saddles, and secured the bridles, to
prevent a pursuit. They now hastened to Brentford, where,
understanding that they were followed, they got into the
ferry to cross the Thames; and when they were three parts
over, so that the river was fordable, they gave the ferrymen
ten shillings, and obliged them to throw their oars into
the river. They then jumped overboard, and got on shore,
while the spectators thought it was only a drunken frolic,
and the robbers got safe to London. Some time after this
Everett was convicted of an attempt to commit a robbery
on the highway, for which he was sentenced to three years'
imprisonment in New Prison, Clerkenwell. After some time
he was employed to act here as turnkey; and his conduct
meeting with approbation, he remained in that station
after the term of his imprisonment was expired; but the
keeper dying, he took a public house in Turnmill Street. He
had not been long in this station when the new keeper who
had been appointed frequently called on him, and made
him advantageous offers, on the condition of his resuming
the office of turnkey. This he did; but, when Everett had
perfectly instructed him in the management of the prison,
he dismissed him, without assigning any reason for such

ungenerous conduct.—Everett being now greatly in debt, was consequently obliged to remove within the rules of the Fleet prison, took a public house in the Old Bailey; after which he took the Cock alehouse, in the same street, which he kept three years with reputation, when the Warden of the Fleet persuaded him to keep the tap-house of the said prison. While in this station he was charged with being concerned with the keeper in some mal-practices, for which the House of Commons ordered him to be confined in Newgate; but he obtained his liberty at the end of the session, as no bill had been found against him. During his confinement his brewer seized his stock of beer, to the amount of 300*l.* which reduced him to circumstances of great distress; but he even now resolved on a life of industry, if he could have got employment; yet his character was such that no person would engage him. Thus perplexed, he once more equipped himself for the highway, with a view, as he solemnly declared after sentence of death, to raise only fifty pounds, as his brewer would have given him credit if he could have possessed himself of that sum. Having stopped a coach on the Hampstead road, in which were a lady, her daughter, and a child about five years old, the child was so terrified at his presenting a pistol, that he withdrew it at the request of the lady, who gave him a guinea and some silver; and though he observed she had a watch and some gold rings, &c. he did not demand them. Some company riding up, he was followed to the end of Leather Lane, where he evaded the pursuit by turning into Hatton Garden, and going into the Globe tavern. Here he called for wine, and, while he was drinking, he saw his pursuers pass; on which he paid his reckoning, and slipped into a public house in Holborn, where he again saw them pass. Thinking himself safe, he remained here a considerable time. When he thought the pursuit was over, he called a coach at the end of Brook Street, and, driving to Honey Lane Market, purchased a duck for his supper, and a turkey for his Christmas dinner: he then went to his lodging in Newgate Market. On the following day one Whitaker (called 'the boxing drover') circulated a report that Everett had committed a highway robbery; on which the latter loaded a brace of pistols, and vowed he would be revenged. He went to Islington in search of Whitaker, and visited several public houses which he used to frequent; but, not meeting with him, the crime of murder was happily prevented. A woman in the neighbourhood of Newgate Market having buried her husband, who had left her enough to support herself and children with decency, Everett repeatedly visited the widow, was received with too great marks of esteem, and assisted her in the dissipation of that money which should have provided for her family. The widow's son, jealous of this connexion, remonstrated with his mother on the impropriety of her conduct, and told her it would end in her ruin. This made Everett and her more cautious in their meetings; but the son watched them with the utmost degree of vigilance and circumspection. Having one evening observed them go into a tavern, he provided himself with a large and sharp knife, and, entering the room where they were sitting, swore he would stab Everett to the heart; but the latter, by superiority of strength, disarmed him. The young fellow was at length persuaded to sit down, when Everett assured him that he entertained the utmost respect both for himself and his mother; but the youth answered he was a liar, and the mutual destruction both of mother and children must follow their unlawful connexion. As the lad grew warm, Everett affected great coolness and good humour, and considered how he might most readily get rid of so unwelcome a guest, as he was unwilling so soon to part with the widow. At length he determined to make the young fellow drunk, and plied him with such a quantity of liquor that he fell fast asleep, in which condition he was left, while the other parties adjourned to a distant tavern, where they remained till morning, when Everett borrowed seven guineas of the widow, under pretence of paying her in a week. Not long after this Everett was married to this very widow at Stepney church, by which he came into possession of money and plate to a considerable amount, and might have lived happily with her if he would have taken her advice; but the extravagance of his disposition led to his ruin. When he was in very low circumstances he casually met his old accomplice, Bird, and joined with him in the commission of a robbery in Essex. They were both taken, and lodged in Chelmsford gaol; but Everett having turned evidence, the other was convicted and executed. As soon as he obtained his liberty he committed several robberies in the neighbourhood of London, the last of which was on a lady named Ellis, whom he stopped near Islington; but, being taken into custody on the following day, he was tried, and capitally convicted. He had been married to three wives, who all visited him after sentence of death. He was likewise visited by the son of the widow; but, recollecting what had formerly passed between them, Everett would have stabbed him with a penknife, but was prevented by one of his wives; for which in her position he afterwards expressed the greatest happiness. What gave him most uneasiness was the crime of perjury, of which he had been guilty, with a view to take away the life of an innocent man. One Pickett, a cooper, having affronted him, he swore a robbery against him; but, the jury not being satisfied with the evidence, the man was fortunately acquitted. Mr. Nicholson, the then minister of St. Sepulchre's church, attended the prisoner while under sentence of death, and kindly exerted himself to convince him of the atrocious nature of his offences; but the number of people who visited him from motives of curiosity took off his attention from his more important duties. However, he was at times serious, and would then advise his brethren in affliction to prepare for that death which now appeared unavoidable.

The gaol distemper having seized him while in Newgate, a report was propagated that he had taken poison; but this was totally false. He wrote letters to some of his acquaintance, begging they would take warning by his unhappy fate, and avoid those steps which led him to his ruin.

At the place of execution, at Tyburn, February 20, 1729, he behaved in such a manner as induced the spectators to think that his penitence for his past crimes was unaffected.

MISS HONEYMAN ESCAPING FROM THE PIRATES, WITH THE FAMILY PAPERS.

JOHN GOW, and OTHERS

Executed for piracy.

———

JOHN GOW was a native of one of the Orkney Islands, in the north of Scotland, and was instructed in maritime affairs, in which he became so expert, that he was appointed second mate of a ship, in which he sailed on a voyage to Santa Cruz.

When the vessel was ready to weigh anchor from the place above mentioned, the merchants who had shipped goods on board her came to pay a parting visit to the captain and to give him their final instructions.

On this occasion, the captain, agreeably to custom, entertained his company under an awning on the quarter-deck; and, while they were regaling, some of the sailors preferred a complaint of ill treatment they pretended to have received, particularly with regard to short allowance.

The captain was irritated at so undeserved a charge, which seemed calculated to prejudice him in the opinion of his employers: but, conscious of the uprightness of his intentions, he did not reply in anger, only saying that there was a steward on board, who had the care of the provisions, and that all reasonable complaints should be redressed: on which the seamen retired with apparent satisfaction.

The wind being fair, the captain directed his men to weigh anchor as soon as the merchants had quitted the vessel. It was observed that Paterson, one of the complainants, was very dilatory in executing his orders; on which the captain demanded why he did not exert himself to unfurl the sails; to which he made no direct answer, but was heard to mutter, 'As we eat, so shall we work.' The captain heard this, but took no notice of it, as he was unwilling to proceed to extremities.

The ship had no sooner sailed than the captain considered his situation as dangerous; on reflecting that his conduct had been complained of, and his orders disobeyed. Hereupon he consulted the mate, and they agreed to deposit a number of small-arms in the cabin, in order to defend themselves in case of an attack. This precaution might have been extremely salutary, but that they spoke so loud as to be overheard by two of the conspirators, who were on the quarterdeck.

The captain likewise directed the mate to order Gow, who was second mate and gunner, to clean the arms; a circumstance that must plainly insinuate to the latter that the conspiracy was at least suspected.

Those who had overheard the conversation between the captain and mate communicated the substance of it to

Gow and the other conspirators, who thereupon resolved to carry their plan into immediate execution. Gow, who had previously intended to turn pirate, thought the present an admirable opportunity, as there were several chests of money on board the ship: wherefore he proposed to his companions that they should immediately embark in the enterprise; and they determined to murder the captain, and seize the ship.

Half of the ship's company were regularly called to prayers in the great cabin at eight o'clock in the evening, while the other half were doing duty on deck; and, after service, those who had been in the cabin went to rest in their hammocks. The contrivance was, to execute the plot at this juncture. Two of the conspirators only remained on duty, the rest being among those who retired to their hammocks.

Between nine and ten at night a kind of watchword was given, which was, 'Who fires first?' On this some of the conspirators left their hammocks, and, going to the cabins of the surgeon, chief mate, and supercargo, they cut their throats while they were asleep.

The surgeon, finding himself violently wounded, quitted his bed, and soon afterwards dropped on the floor, and expired. The mate and supercargo held their hands on their throats, and, going on the quarter-deck, solicited a momentary respite, to recommend their souls to Heaven: but even this favour was denied; for the villains, who found their knives had failed to destroy them, dispatched them with pistols.

The captain, hearing a noise, demanded the occasion of it. The boatswain replied that he did not know; but was apprehensive that some of the men had either fallen, or been thrown, overboard. The captain hereupon went to look over the ship's side, on which two of the murderers followed, and tried to throw him into the sea; but he disengaged himself, and turned about to take a view of them;

when one of them cut his throat, but not so as to kill him. He now solicited mercy; but, instead of granting it, the other stabbed him in the back with a dagger, and would have repeated his blow, but he had struck with such force that he could not draw back the weapon.

At this instant Gow, who had been assisting in the murders between the decks, came on the quarter-deck, and fired a brace of balls into the captain's body, which put a period to his life.

The execrable villains concerned in this tragical affair having thrown all the dead bodies overboard, Gow was unanimously appointed to the command of the ship.

Those of the sailors who had not been engaged in the conspiracy secreted themselves, some in the shrouds, some under the stores, in dreadful apprehension of sharing the fate of the captain and their murdered companions.

Gow now assembled his associates on the quarter-deck; and, appointing them their different stations on board, it was agreed to commence pirates. The new captain now directed that the men who had concealed themselves should be informed that no danger would happen to them if they did not interfere to oppose the new government of the ship, but kept such stations as were assigned them.

The men, whose fears had taught them to expect immediate death, were glad to comply with these terms; but the pirates, to enforce obedience to their orders, appointed two conspirators to attend with drawn cutlasses, to awe them, if necessary, into submission.

Gow and his companions now divided the most valuable effects in the cabin; and then, ordering liquor to be brought on the quarter-deck, they consumed the night in drinking, while those unconnected in the conspiracy had the care of working the ship.

The ship's crew originally consisted of twenty-four men, of whom four had been murdered, and eight were conspirators; and, before morning, four of the other twelve having approved of the proceedings of the pirates, there were only eight remaining in any kind of opposition to the usurped authority.

On the following day the new captain summoned these eight to attend him, and, telling them he was determined to go on a cruising voyage, said that they should be well treated if they were disposed to act in concert with the rest of the crew. He observed that every man should fare in the same manner, and that good order and discipline was all that would be required. He said further that the late captain's inhumanity had produced the consequences which had happened: that those who had not been concerned in the conspiracy had no reason to fear any ill resulting from it: that they had only to discharge their duty as seamen, and every man should be rewarded according to his merit.

To this address these unfortunate honest men made no kind of reply; and Gow interpreted their silence into an assent to measures which it was not in their power to oppose. After this declaration of the will of the new captain they were permitted to range the ship at pleasure; but, as some of them appeared to act very reluctantly, a strict eye was kept on their conduct; for, guilt being ever suspicious, the pirates were greatly apprehensive of being brought to justice by means of some of these men.

An individual named Williams now acted as lieutenant of the vessel; and, being distinguished by the ferocity of his nature, he had an opportunity of exerting it by beating these unhappy fellows; a privilege he did not fail to exercise with a degree of severity that must render his memory detestable.

The ship thus seized had been called the George Galley, but the pirates gave her the name of the Revenge; and, having mounted several guns, they steered towards Spain and Portugal, in expectation of making a capture of wine, of which article they were greatly deficient.

They soon made prize of an English vessel laden with fish, bound from Newfoundland to Cadiz; but, having no use for the cargo, they took out the captain and four men, who navigated the ship, which they sunk.

One of the seamen whom they took out of the captured vessel was named James Belvin; a man admirably calculated for their purpose, as he was by nature cruel, and by practice hardened in that cruelty. He said to Gow that he was willing to enter into all his schemes, for he had been accustomed to the commission of acts of barbarity. This man was thought a valuable acquisition to the crew, as several of the others appeared to act from motives of fear rather than of inclination.

The next vessel taken by the pirates was a Scotch ship bound to Italy with pickled herrings; but this cargo, like the former, being of no use to them, they sunk the vessel, having first taken out the men, arms, ammunition, and stores.

After cruising eight or ten days, they saw a vessel about the size of their own, to which they gave chase. She hoisted French colours, and crowded all her sail in order to get clear of them; and, after a chase of three days and nights, they lost her in a fog.

Being distressed for water, they now steered towards the Madeira Islands, of which they came in sight in two days; but, not thinking it prudent to enter the harbour, they steered off and on for several days, in the hope of making prize of some Portuguese or Spanish vessel; but these expectations were frustrated.

Their distress increasing, they stood in for the harbour, and brought the ship to an anchor, but at a considerable distance from the shore. This being done, they sent seven men, well armed, in a boat, with instructions to board a ship, cut her cables, and bring her off; but, if they failed in this, they were to attempt to make prize of wine and water, conveying them in the boat to the ship. Both these schemes were, however, frustrated, since it was easily known, from the distance they lay at, that they were pirates.

When they had cruised off for some days they found themselves in such distress that it became absolutely necessary to seek immediate relief; on which they sailed to Port Santa, a Portuguese settlement, at the distance of about ten leagues.

On their arrival off this place they sent their boat on shore, with a present of salmon and herrings for the governor, and the name of a port to which they pretended to be bound. The persons sent on shore were civilly treated by the governor, who accompanied some of his friends on board the ship. Gow and his associates received the governor very politely, and entertained him and his company in the most hospitable manner; but the boat belonging to the pirates not coming on board with some provisions they had expected, and the governor and his attendants preparing to depart, Gow and his people threatened to take away their lives unless they instantly furnished them with what they required.

The surprise of the Portuguese governor and his friends on this occasion is not to be expressed. They dreaded instant death, and, with every sign of extreme fear, solicited that their lives might be spared. Gow being peremptory in his demands, the governor sent a boat repeatedly ashore, till the pirates were furnished with such articles as they wanted.

This business being ended, the Portuguese were permitted to depart, and the pirates determined to steer towards the coast of Spain, where they soon arrived. After cruising a few days off Cape St. Vincent, they fell in with an English vessel bound from the coast of Guinea to America with slaves, but which had been obliged to put into the port of Lisbon. Now although it was of no use for them to make capture of such a vessel, yet they did take it, and, again putting on board the captain and men, but taking out all the provisions and some of the sails, they left the ship to proceed on her voyage.

Falling in with a French ship, laden with wine, oil, and fruit, they took out the lading, and gave the vessel to the Scotch captain, in return for the ship which they had sunk. The Scotchman was likewise presented with some valuable articles, and permitted to take his men to sail with him; all of whom did so, except one, who continued with the pirates through choice.

About the same time they observed another French ship bearing down towards them, on which Gow ordered his people to lay to; but, observing that the vessel mounted two-and-thirty guns, and seemed proportionably full of men, he assembled his people, and observed to them that it would be madness to think of engaging so superior a force.

The crew in general were of Gow's opinion; but Williams, the lieutenant, said Gow was a coward, and unworthy to command the vessel. The fact is, that Gow possessed somewhat of calm courage, while Williams's impetuosity was of the most brutal kind. The latter, after behaving in a very abusive manner, demanded that the former should give orders for fighting the vessel; but Gow refusing to comply, the other presented his pistol to shoot him; but it only flashed in the pan.

This being observed by two of the pirates, named Winter and Paterson, they both fired at Williams, when one of them wounded him in the arm, and the other in the belly. He dropped as soon as the pieces were discharged, and the other seamen, thinking he was dead, were about to throw him overboard, when he suddenly sprang on his feet, jumped into the hold, and swore he would set fire to the powder-room; and, as his pistol was yet loaded, there was every reason to think he would actually have done so, if he had not been instantly seized, and his hands chained behind him, in which condition he was put among the

French prisoners, who were terrified at the sight of him; for the savage ferocity and barbarity of this man's nature are not to be described, it being a common practice with him to beat the prisoners in the severest manner, for his diversion, (as he called it), and then threaten to murder them.

No engagement happened with the French ship, which held on her way; and two days afterwards the pirates took a ship belonging to Bristol, which was laden with salt fish, and bound from Newfoundland to Oporto. Having taken out the provisions, and many of the stores, they compelled two of the crew to sail with them, and then put the French prisoners on board the newly-captured vessel, which was just on the point of sailing, when they began to reflect in what manner that execrable villain, Williams, should be disposed of.

At length it was determined to put him on board the Bristol ship, the commander of which was desired to turn him over to the first English man of war he should meet with, that he might experience the justice due to his crimes; and in the mean time to keep him in the strictest confinement.

The cruelty of Williams's disposition has been already mentioned, and the following is a most striking instance of it:—Among the arguments used by Gow against engaging the French ship, one was, that they had already more prisoners than they had proper accomodation for, on which Williams proposed that those in their possession might be brought up singly, their throats cut, and their bodies thrown overboard; but Gow said there had been too much blood spilled already—this being too horrid a proposal even for pirates to consent to.

The fact is that Williams would have been hanged at the yard-arm if an opportunity had not offered of putting him on board the Bristol ship. When he learnt their intention respecting him, he earnestly besought a reconciliation; but this being refused him, and he brought on deck in irons, he begged to be thrown overboard, as he was certain of an ignominious death on his arrival in England; but even this poor favour was denied him, and his companions only wished him 'a good voyage to the gallows.'

When the captain of the Bristol ship reached the port of Lisbon he delivered his prisoner on board an English man of war, which conveyed him to England, where he had afterwards the fate of being hanged with his companions, as we shall see in the sequel.

As soon as the Bristol ship had left them, Gow and his crew began to reflect on their situation. They were apprehensive that, as soon as intelligence of their proceedings reached Portugal, some ships would be sent in pursuit of them. Hereupon they called a kind of council, in which every one gave his opinion, as dictated either by his hopes of profit or by his fears.

Some of them advised going to the coast of Guinea, others to North America, and others again to the West Indies; but Gow proposed to sail to the Isles of Orkney, on the north of Scotland, where, he said, they might dispose of their effects, and retire and live on the produce. To induce his people to comply with this proposal, Gow represented that they were much in want of water, and provisions of every kind; that their danger would be great if they continued longer on the high seas; and, above all, that it was highly necessary for them to repair their ship, which they could not do with any degree of safety in a southern port.

He likewise said that, if any ships should be dispatched in quest of them, they would not think of searching for them in a northern latitude, so that their voyage that way would be safe; and, if they would follow his directions, much booty might be obtained by plundering the houses of the gentlemen sailing near the sea-coast. The danger of alarming the country was objected to these proposals; but Gow said that they should be able to dispatch all their business, and sail again, before such an event could happen.

Apparently convinced by this reasoning, they steered northward, and, entering a bay of one of the Orkney Islands, Gow assembled his crew, and instructed them what tale they should tell to the country people, to prevent suspicion: and it is probable that they might, at least for the present, have escaped detection, if his instructions had been literally obeyed.

These instructions were, to say they were bound from Cadiz to Stockholm; but contrary winds driving them past the Sound, till it was filled with ice, they were under the necessity of putting in to clean their ship; and that they would pay ready money for such articles as they stood in need of.

It happened that a smuggling vessel lay at this time in the bay. It belonged to the Isle of Man; and, being laden with brandy and wine from France, had come north-about, to steer clear of the Custom-house cutters. In their present situation Gow thought it prudent to exchange goods with the commander of the vessel, though in any other he would hardly have been so ceremonious. A Swedish vessel entering the bay two days afterwards, Gow likewise exchanged some goods with the captain.

Now it was that the fate of the pirates seemed to be approaching; for such of the men as had been forced into the service began to think how they should effect their escape, and secure themselves, by becoming evidence against their dissolute companions.

When the boat went ashore one evening, a young fellow, who had been compelled to take part with the pirates, got away from the rest of the boat's crew, and, after lying concealed some time at a farmhouse, hired a person to show him the road to Kirkwall, the principal place on the islands, about twelve miles distant from the bay where their ship lay at anchor. Here he applied to a magistrate, said he had been forced into their service, and begged that he might be entitled to the protection of the law, as the fear of death alone had induced him to be connected with the pirates.

Having given information of what he knew of their irregular proceedings, the sheriff issued his precepts to the constables and other peace-officers to call in the aid of the people, to assist in bringing such villains to justice.

About this juncture ten other of Gow's sailors, who had taken an involuntary part with the pirates, seized the long boat, and, having made the main land of Scotland, coasted the country till they arrived at Edinburgh, where they were imprisoned on suspicion of being pirates.

Notwithstanding these alarming circumstances, Gow was so careless of his own safety that he did not put immediately to sea, but resolved to plunder the houses of the gentlemen on the coast, to furnish himself with fresh provisions.

In pursuance of this resolution, he sent his boatswain and ten armed men to the house of Mr. Honeyman, high-sheriff of the county; and, the master being absent, the servants opened the door without suspicion. Nine of the gang went into the house to search for treasure, while the tenth was left to guard the door. The sight of men thus armed occasioned much terror to Mrs. Honeyman and her daughter, who shrieked with dreadful apprehensions for their personal safety; but the pirates, employed in the search of plunder, had no idea of molesting the ladies.

Mrs. Honeyman, running to the door, saw the man who stood guard there, whom she asked what could be the meaning of the outrage: to which he calmly replied that they were pirates, and had come thither only to ransack the house. Recollecting that she had a considerable quantity of gold in a bag, she returned and put it in her lap, and ran by the man at the door, who had no idea but that the wish to preserve her life occasioned her haste.

The boatswain, missing this part of the expected treasure, declared that he would destroy the family writings: but this being overheard by Miss Honeyman, she threw the writings out of the window, and jumping out after them, escaped unhurt, and carried them off. In the interim the pirates seized the linen, plate, and other valuable articles, and then walked in triumph to their boat, compelling one of the servants to play before them on the bagpipes.

On the following day they set sail, but in the evening came again to anchor near another island. Here the boat-swain and some men were sent on shore in search of plunder, but did not obtain any. However, they met with two women, whom they conveyed to the ship, where they detained them three days, and treated them in so shocking a manner, that one of them expired soon after they had put them on shore.

This atrocious offence was no sooner committed than they sailed to Calf-Sound, with an intention of robbing the house of Mr. Fea, who had been an old school-fellow with Gow. This house was the rather pitched upon, as Gow sup-posed that Mr. Fea could not have yet heard of the trans-actions at Mr. Honeyman's; but in this he was mistaken, though Fea could not oppose the pirates on that occasion, on account of the indisposition of his wife.

Mr. Fea's house was situated near the sea-shore: he had only six servants at home when the pirates appeared off the coast; and these were by no means equal to sustain a con-test. It may not be improper to remark that the tide runs so high among these islands, and beats with such force against the rocks, that the navigation is frequently attended with great danger.

Gow, who had not boats to assist him in an emergency, and was unskilled in the navigation of those seas, made a blunder in turning into the bay of Calf-Sound; for, standing too near the point of a small island called the Calf, the ves-sel was in the utmost danger of being run on shore. This little island was merely a pasture for sheep belonging to Mr. Fea, who had at that time six hundred feeding on it.

Gow having cast his anchor too near the shore, so that the wind could not bring him off, sent a boat with a letter to Mr. Fea, requesting that he would lend him another boat, to assist him in heaving off the ship, by carrying out an anchor; and assuring him that he would not do the least injury to any individual.

As Gow's messenger did not see Mr. Fea's boat, the latter gave him an evasive answer, and, on the approach of night, ordered his servants to sink his own boat, and hide the sails and rigging.

While they were obeying this order five of Gow's men came on shore in the boat, and proceeded, doubly armed, towards Fea's house. Hereupon the latter advanced towards them with an assurance of friendship, and begged they would not enter the house, for that his wife was exceedingly ill; that the idea of their approach had greatly alarmed her, and the sight of them might probably deprive her of life. The boatswain replied that they had no design to terrify Mrs. Fea, or any other person; but that the most rigorous treatment must be expected if the use of the boat was denied them.

Mr. Fea represented how dangerous it would be for him to assist them, on account of the reports circulated to their discredit: but he offered to entertain them at an adjacent alehouse; and they accepted the invitation, as they observed that he had no company. While they were drinking, Mr. Fea ordered his servants to destroy their boat, and, when they had done so, to call him hastily out of the company, and inform him of it.

These orders were exactly complied with; and, when he had left the pirates, he directed six men, well armed, to station themselves behind a hedge, and, if they observed him to come alone with the boatswain, instantly to seize him; but, if he came with all the five desperadoes, he would walk forward, so as to give them an opportunity of firing without wounding himself.

After giving these orders Fea returned to the company, whom he invited to his house, on the promise of their behaving peaceably, and said he would make them heartily welcome. They all expressed a readiness to attend him, in the hope of getting the boat: but he told them he would rather have the boatswain's company only, and would afterwards send for his companions.

This being agreed to, the boatswain set forward with two brace of pistols, and, walking with Mr. Fea till they came to the hedge where the men were concealed, that gentleman then seized him by the collar, while the others took him into custody before he had time to make any defence. The boatswain called aloud for his men; but Mr. Fea, forcing a handkerchief into his mouth, bound him hand and foot, and then left one of his own people to guard him, while himself and the rest went back to the public house.

There being two doors to the house, they went some to the one, and some to the other; and, rushing in at once, made prisoners of the other four men before they had time to have recourse to their arms for defence.

The five pirates, being thus in custody, were sent to an adjacent village, and separately confined, and in the interim Mr. Fea sent messengers round the island to acquaint the inhabitants with what had been done; to desire them to haul their boats on the beach, that the pirates should not swim to and steal them; and to request that no person would venture to row within reach of the pirates' guns.

On the following day the wind shifted to the north-west, and blew hard, on which the pirates conceived hopes of getting out to sea; but the person employed to cut the cable missing some of his strokes, the ship's way was checked, she turned round, and, the cable parting, the vessel was driven on Calf Island.

Reduced to this dilemma, without even a boat to assist in getting off the ship, Gow hung out a white flag, as an intimation that he was willing to treat on friendly terms; but Mr.Fea, having now little doubt of securing the whole of the gang, wrote to Gow, and told him he had been compelled to make prisoners of his men on account of their insolent behaviour. He likewise told him that the whole country was alarmed, and that the most probable chance of securing his own life would be by surrendering, and becoming an evidence against his accomplices.

Four armed men in an open boat carried this letter to Gow, who sent for answer that he would give goods to the value of a thousand pounds to be assisted in his escape; but, if this should be refused, he would set fire to the ship rather than become a prisoner. He even said that he would trust to the mercy of the waves, if Mr. Fea would indulge him with a boat.

On reading this letter, Fea determined to persuade him to submit, and therefore took four men well armed in a boat, and rowed towards the ship: but he previously placed a man with a flag in his hand at the top of his house, to make such signals as might be proper to prevent his falling a sacrifice to any artifice of the pirates.

The instructions given to the servant were, that he should wave the flag once if he saw one of the pirates swim towards the shore; but, if he beheld four or more of them, he should wave it constantly till his master got out of danger. Mr. Fea, rowing forwards, spoke through a trumpet, asking Gow to come on shore and talk with him, which the latter said he would. Hereupon Fea lay-to, in waiting for him; but at this juncture he saw a man swimming from the ship with a white flag in his hand, on which the man on the house waved his flag; but soon afterwards he was observed to wave it continually, on which Mr. Fea's boat retired, and those in her presently saw five more of the pirates swimming towards them; but they returned to the ship as soon as they saw the others were aware of the artifice.

The first pirate, who carried the white flag, now retired to the corner of the island, and, calling to Mr. Fea, told him that 'the captain had sent him a bottle of brandy.' Fea replied that he hoped to see Gow hanged, and that he was inclined to shoot the messenger for his insolence; on which the fellow decamped with great precipitation.

Soon after this Gow wrote a most humble letter to Mrs. Fea, imploring her interference in his behalf; and, though she had determined not to interest herself in his favour, yet he resolved to go on shore; and, taking a white flag in his hand, he made signals for a parley; on which Mr. Fea sent some armed men to seize him living or dead.

On their meeting, Gow insisted that one of their men should be left as a hostage; and this circumstance being seen by Mr. Fea, from the windows of his house, he sailed over to the island, where he reprimanded his people for delivering the hostage, and likewise told Gow that he was his prisoner. Gow replied, that could not be, since a hostage had been delivered for him.

To this Mr. Fea replied that he had issued no orders for delivering the hostage, and that the man who had foolishly engaged himself as such must submit to the consequence; but he advised Gow, for his own sake, to make signals that the man might obtain his liberty. This Gow refused to do; but Fea made signals which deceived the pirates, two of whom came on shore with the man, and were instantly taken into custody. Gow was now disarmed of his sword, and made prisoner, after begging to be shot with his sword in his possession.

The leader of the gang being thus secured, Mr. Fea had recourse to stratagem to get all the rest into his power. He now compelled Gow to make signals for some of them to come on shore, which they readily did, mid were apprehended by men concealed to take them as they arrived.

Fea now insinuated to Gow that he would let him have a boat to escape if he would send for his carpenter to repair it, and to bring with him two or three hands to assist him. Gow complied; the men came off, and were severally seized: but as there were other people still mid board, Mr. Fea had recourse to the following contrivance to get them into his possession. He directed his own servants to provide hammers, nails, &c. and make a pretence of repairing the boat; and, while this was doing, told Gow to send for his men, since he must have possession of the ship before he would deliver up the boat.

The pirates, on receiving their late captain's orders to come on shore, were very doubtful how to act; but, after a short debate, and having no officers to command them, they shared what money they possessed, and, coming on shore, were all taken into custody.

Thus, by an equal exertion of courage, conduct, and artifice, did Mr. Fea secure these dangerous men, twenty-eight in number, without a single man being killed or wounded, and with the aid only of a few countrymen; a force apparently very insufficient to the accomplishment of such a business.

When all the prisoners were properly secured, Mr. Fea sent an express to Edinburgh, requesting that proper persons might be sent to conduct them to that city. In the interim Mr. Fea took an inventory of all the effects in the ship, to be appropriated as the government might direct.

Six articles, of which the following is a copy, were found on board the ship, in Gow's hand-writing. It is conjectured that while they were entangled among the rocks of the Orkney Islands these articles were hastily drawn up, and arose from their distressed situation:

I. That every man shall obey his commander in all respects as if the ship was his own, and as if he received monthly wages.

II. That no man shall give or dispose of the ship's provisions; but every one shall have an equal share.

III. That no man shall open or declare to any person or persons who they are, or what designs they are upon; and any persons so offending shall be punished with immediate death.

IV. That no man shall go on shore till the ship is off the ground, and in readiness to put to sea.

V. That every man shall keep his watch night and day; and at the hour of eight in the evening every one shall retire from gaming and drinking, in order to attend his respective station.

VI. Every person who shall offend against any of these articles shall be punished with death, or in such other manner as the ship's company shall think proper.

The express from Mr. Fea being arrived at Edinburgh, another was forwarded to London, to learn the royal pleasure respecting the disposal of the pirates: and the answer brought was, that the lord justice Clerk should immediately send them to London, in order to their being tried by Court of Admiralty, to be held for that purpose.

When these orders reached Edinburgh, a guard of soldiers marched to fetch them to that city; and, on their arrival, they were put on board the Greyhound frigate, which immediately sailed for the Thames.

On their arrival in the river, a detachment of the guards from the Tower attended their landing, and conducted them to the Marshalsea Prison, where they once more saw Lieutenant Williams, who had been conveyed to England by the man of war which received him from the Bristol captain at Lisbon, as before mentioned. This Williams, though certain of coming to an ignominious end, took a malignant pleasure in seeing his companions in like circumstances of calamity.

A commission was now made out for their trial; and, soon after commitment, they underwent separate examinations before the judge of the Admiralty Court in Doctors'

Commons, when five of them, who appeared to be less guilty than the rest, were admitted evidences against their accomplices.

Being removed from the Marshalsea to Newgate, their trials came on at the Old Bailey, when Gow, Williams, and six others, were convicted, and received sentence of death; but the rest were acquitted, as it seemed evident that they had been compelled to take part with the pirates.

The behaviour of Gow, from his first commitment, was reserved and morose. He considered himself as an assured victim to the justice of the laws, nor entertained any hope of being admitted an evidence, as Mr. Fea had hinted to him that he might be.

When brought to trial he refused to plead, in consequence of which he was sentenced to be pressed to death in the usual manner. His reason for this refusal was, that he had an estate which he wished might descend to a relation, and which would have been the case had he died under the pressure.

But, when the proper officers were about to inflict this punishment, he begged to be taken again to the bar to plead, of which the judge being informed, he humanely granted his request; and the consequence was that he was convicted, as above mentioned, on the same evidence as his accomplices.

While under sentence of death he was visited by some Presbyterian ministers, who laboured to convince him of the atrocity of his crime; but he seemed deaf to all their admonitions and exhortations.

Williams's depravity of mind exceeds all description. He seemed equally insensible to the hope of happiness, or the fear of torment, in a future state. He boasted to those who visited him of his constantly advising Gow 'to tie the prisoners back to back, and throw them into the sea,' to prevent their giving evidence against them.

Gow, Williams, and six of their accomplices, were hanged together, at Execution Dock, on the 11th of August, 1729.

A remarkable circumstance happened to Gow at the place of execution. His friends, anxious to put him out of his pain, pulled his legs so forcibly that the rope broke, and he dropped down; on which he was again taken up to the gibbet, and, when he was dead, was hung in chains on the banks of the Thames.

It may be observed, to the credit of recent times, that the crime of piracy is becoming more and more uncommon—our seamen, in general, being as honest as they are brave.

WALLER PELTED TO DEATH BY THE MOB.

JOHN WALLER, alias TREVOR

Pilloried for perjury.

———

THE pillory is an engine made of wood, to punish offenders, by exposing them to public view, and rendering them infamous. There is a statute of the pillory 51 Henry III.; and by statute it is appointed for bakers, forestallers, and those who use false weights, perjury, forgery, &c. Lords of Leets are to have a pillory and tumbrel, or it will be the cause of forfeiture of the leet; and a village may be bound by prescription to provide a pillory, &c.

The name is derived from two Greek words, signifying 'to look through a door'; because one standing on the pillory puts his head, as it were, through a door.

This profligate wretch, Waller, to robbery added the still greater sin of accusing the innocent, in order to receive the reward in certain cases attending conviction. The abominable dealer in human blood was tried at the Old Bailey for robbing, on the highway, one John Edglin, and afterwards, under the name of John Trevor, giving a false evidence against the said John Edglin, whereby his life might have become forfeited to the abused laws of the country. On the latter charge he was found guilty.

It appeared, on this memorable trial, that Waller made it a practice to go the circuits as regularly as the judges and counsel, and to swear robberies against such as he deemed fit objects for his purpose, from no other motive than to obtain the reward given by each county for the apprehension and conviction of criminals for highway robberies and other offences therein committed.

The sentence of the Court was, that he should pay a fine of twenty marks, and be imprisoned for the term of two years, and at the expiration thereof to find good and sufficient security for his good behaviour during the remainder of his life; that he do stand twice in and upon the pillory, bareheaded, with his crime written in large characters; and that he do also stand twice before the pillory, likewise bareheaded, one hour each time.

On Tuesday, the 13th of June, 1732, this wicked man was put in the pillory, pursuant to his sentence, at the Seven Dials, in London; where, so great was the indignation of the populace, that they pelted him to death; and the day after the coroner's inquest gave a verdict, 'Wilful murder by persons unknown.'

THE SEXTON ALARMED ON FINDING POWIS SECRETED IN THE CHURCH.

JOSEPH POWIS

Executed for housebreaking.

———

JOSEPH POWIS was a native of St. Martin's in the Fields; and his father dying while he was an infant, his mother married a smith in St. Martin's Lane, who was remarkable for his ingenuity.

The father-in-law going to Harfleur, in Normandy, with many other skilful artists, to be concerned in an iron manufactory, took Powis with him when he was only eight years of age.

They had not been long here before the father-in-law received a letter, advising him of the death of his wife; on which he left the boy to the care of an Englishman, and came to London in order to settle his affairs, but soon returned to Normandy.

The scheme in which they had embarked failing, they came back to England, and the man, marrying a second wife, took a shop in Chancery Lane, London, and sent young Powis to school, where he made such progress, that a little time gave hope of his becoming a good Latin scholar.

But he had not been long at school before his stepfather took him home, to instruct him in his own business; and hence his misfortunes appear to have arisen; for such was his attachment to literature, that, when he was sent of an errand, he constantly loitered away his time reading at the stall of some bookseller.

When he had been about four years with his father, two lads of his acquaintance persuaded him to take a stroll into the country, and they wandered through the villages adjacent to London for about a week, in a condition almost starving, sometimes begging food to relieve the extremities of hunger, and finally compelled by distress to return to town.

The father-in-law of Powis received him kindly, forgave his fault, and he continued about a year longer with him; but, having read a number of plays, he had imbibed such romantic notions as disqualified him for business.

Inspired with an idea of going on the stage, he offered his services to Mr. Rich, then manager of Covent Garden Theatre; but, having repeated some parts of the tragedy of *Julius Caesar*, Rich told him he was disqualified for the stage, and advised him to attend to his trade.

Soon after this Powis a second time quitted his father-in-law, and rambled through the country some days; but returning on a Sunday, in the absence of the family, he broke open a chest, and, taking out his best clothes, again decamped.

Nothing being missed except the boy's clothes, it was easily judged who must be the thief; wherefore the father-in-law went with a constable in search of the youth, whom he took before a magistrate, in the hope of making him sensible of his folly.

The justice threatening to commit him unless he made a proper submission, he promised to go home and do so; but, dropping his father-in-law in the street, he went to an acquaintance, to whom he communicated his situation, and asked his advice how to act. His friend advised him to go home, and discharge his duty; but this not suiting his inclination, and it being now the time of Bartholomew Fair, he engaged with one Miller to act a part in a farce exhibited at Smithfield.

His next adventure was then going to Dorking, in Surrey, with one Dutton, a strolling player, by whom he was taught to expect great things; but Dutton, having previously affronted the inhabitants, met with no encouragement; on which they proceeded to Horsham, in Sussex, where they were equally unsuccessful.

Powis now slept in a hay-loft, near the kitchen of an inn, and, being almost starved, he used to get in at the window and steal the victuals while the family were in bed. He likewise stole a new pair of shoes belonging to the landlord; but the latter, soon discovering the thief, took the shoes from him, and gave him an old pair instead.

About this time Dutton took Powis's clothes from him, and gave him others that were little better than rags.

Having left this town, they put up at an inn, where the landlord obliged the company to sleep in the hay-loft, admitting none but the manager to come within the house. At night Powis crept into the kitchen, devoured the remains of a cold pie, and stole, a pair of boots and a pair of stockings, with which he retreated into the hay-loft. He continued to steal provisions several nights, till the landlord and Dutton watched, with loaded guns, in expectation of the thief, who, however, came not that night.

Powis, having obtained a few halfpence by one of his petty thefts, stole out from the hay-loft to drink at a public house; but the other landlord, being there, knew the boots to be his; on which our unfortunate adventurer hastily retreated to his loft, where he expected to lie secure; but the landlord, Dutton, and others, following him, seized him, and took him into the kitchen for examination. He readily confessed that he had stolen the victuals; on which he was delivered into the custody of two countrymen to guard him till the next day, when it was proposed to take him before a magistrate.

The family having retired to bed, Powis pretended to fall fast asleep; on which one of his guards said, 'How the poor fellow rests, notwithstanding his misfortunes'; to which the other said, 'Let me sleep an hour, and then I will watch while you sleep.'

In a few minutes both the men were asleep; on which Powis, thinking to escape, attempted to put on the boots; but, making some noise, the landlord heard him, and, coming down stairs, Powis affected to slumber as before. The landlord awakened the guardians, and bade them take more care of their prisoner; which having promised to do, they soon fell asleep again.

Our adventurer now took the boots in his hand, and, getting out of the inn-yard, ran with the utmost expedition till he got out of the town, and then drawing on the boots, he proceeded on his journey to London. However, he missed his way, and, getting on a common, knew not how to proceed; but going into a cow-house, in which was a quantity of flax, he lay down to rest. In the morning the owner of the flax found him, and inquiring what business he had there, Powis said that, being intoxicated, he had lost his way: on which the other directed him into the right road, and our hero hastened forward, in the apprehension of being pursued.

Towards evening he arrived near Dorking, but did not enter the town till it was nearly dark. As he was going through the street he heard a door open; and, turning round, a woman, who had a candle in her hand, called him; and, on his demanding what she wanted, she said to another woman, 'Sure enough it is he.'

This woman, who had washed the players' linen, said that two men had been in pursuit of him; and that his best way would be to avoid the high road, and get to London some other way with all possible expedition.

Powis immediately took this advice, and, quitting the turnpike-road, got to a farm-house, where he stole some books and other trifles, ate some provisions, and then proceeded towards London, stopping at Stock well, at a house kept by the mother of his father-in-law's wife. All this happened in the night; but, knowing the place, he went into the back yard, and lay down to sleep on some straw.

Observing several threshers come to work in the morning, he concealed himself under the straw till night, when he crept out, went to a public house, drank some beer, and returned to his former lodging.

Inspired by the liquor he had drank, he began to sing, which drawing some people round him, they conducted him into the house.

His mother-in-law, happening to be there on a visit, spoke with great kindness to him, and advised him to remain there till she had communicated the affair to her husband.

In a few days the father-in-law came to him, and expressed his readiness to take him home, if he would but attend his business, and decline his present vagrant course of life. This he readily agreed to do, and continued steady during the winter; but on the approach of summer he again left his friends, and rambled about near a month, subsisting on the casual bounty of his acquaintance.

Falling into company with Joseph Paterson, whom he had known among the strolling players, Paterson engaged him to perform a part in the tragedy of 'The Earl of Essex,' at Windmill Hill, near Moorfields, which was then the place of resort for the lower class of spouters in and near London.

The part of *Lord Burleigh* being assigned to Powis, and it being intimated in the printed bills that this part was to be performed by 'A young gentleman, being his first appearance on the stage,' the curiosity of the public was somewhat excited, so that there was a full house. Unfortunately, *Lord Burleigh* was dressed in the shabbiest manner; and, being little better than a compound of rags and dirt, it was with some difficulty the minister of state, went through his part, amidst the laughter and ridicule of the spectators.

Returning home through Ludgate Street, after the play, he saw a gentleman who said he had dropped three guineas, but had picked up one of them. Powis, happening to find the other two, kept one for himself, and gave the other to the owner, who, not knowing that he had retained one, insisted on his drinking a glass of wine, and thanked him for his civility.

Being stopped one night in Chancery Lane by a violent shower of rain, he climbed over a gate, and got under the shelter of a penthouse belonging to the Six Clerks' Office, where he remained till morning, when the clerks came to their business, and he was then afraid to appear, lest he should be taken for a thief from the shabbiness of his dress.

Leaning against a plastered wall, part of it broke; but, as the place he stood in was very dark, no one observed it; on which he resolved to profit by the accident: in consequence of this, he, at night, made the breach wider, and got into the office, whence he stole six guineas, and about fifty shillings in silver.

Having spent this money, he determined to join his old companions on Windmill Hill; and, in his way thither, he observed a fellow pick a countryman's pocket of a bag of money in Smithfield; and a cry of 'Stop thief!' being immediately circulated, the pickpocket dropped the bag, which

Powis took up unobserved, and, retiring to a public house, examined its contents, which he found to amount to above fifty pounds.

Having put the money in his pocket, he threw away the bag, and retired to his lodgings. This money, a greater sum than he had ever before possessed, was soon spent in extravagance, and he was again reduced to great extremities.

Thus distressed, he got into the area of a coffee-house in Chancery Lane, and attempted to force the kitchen-window; but, not succeeding, he secreted himself in the coal-cellar till the following evening, when he got into the house, and hid himself in a hole behind the chimney.

When the family was gone to rest, he stole some silver spoons, and about three shillings' worth of halfpence from the bar, and, having now fasted thirty hours, he ate and drank heartily; but, hearing a person come down stairs, he pulled off his shoes, and, retiring hastily, got into a hole where broken glass was kept, by which his feet were cut in a shocking manner.

It happened to be only the maidservant who came down stairs; and, going into the kitchen, Powis put on his shoes, and ran through the coffee-room into the street.

Being again reduced, he broke into the Chancery Office, where he stole about four pounds ten shillings, which being spent, he looked out for a fresh supply. Going to St. Dunstan's Church, at the time of morning prayers, he hid himself in the gallery till night, and then stole some of the prayer-books, which he proposed to have carried off the next morning, when the sexton appeared, who, being more terrified than the thief, ran to procure the assistance of another man; but in the mean time Powis had so secreted himself that they could not find him after a search of two hours; they therefore at length gave it up, concluding that he had got out through one of the windows. However, he remained in the church all that day, and at the hour of prayer next morning went off with as many books as produced him a guinea.

On the following night he visited an acquaintance in Ram Alley, Fleet Street, where he observed a woman deposit some goods in a room, the door of which she fastened with a padlock. On this he concealed himself in the cellar till towards morning, when he opened the padlock with a crooked nail, and stole two gold rings and a guinea, being baulked in his expectation of a much more valuable prize.

One of the prayer-books which he had stolen from St. Dunstan's Church he sold to a bookseller in the Strand; and, while the lady who had lost it was inquiring at the bookseller's if such a book had fallen into his hands, Powis happened to stop to speak with a gentleman at the door; on which the bookseller said, 'There is the man who sold it to me'; and the lady replied, 'He is a thief, and has stolen it.'

The bookseller, calling Powis into his shop, asked if he had sold him that book, which he acknowledged; and, being desired to recollect how he had obtained it, he said he could not; on which the bookseller threatened to have him committed to prison; but the lady, now earnestly looking at him, asked if his name was Powis. He said it was; on which she burst into tears, and said, 'I am sorry for you, and for your poor father; you are the cause of all his unhappiness.' The bookseller, happening likewise to know Powis's father, delivered the book to the lady, and permitted the young thief to depart, on promise to pay for it on the following day: but the day of payment never came.

A few nights after this he climbed up the sign-post belonging to a pastry-cook in Fleet Street, and got in at a chamber-window, whence he descended into the shop; but, not finding any money in the till, stole only two or three old books, and filled his pockets with tarts, with which he decamped.

Calling some days afterwards at the same shop to buy a
tart, he found the people of the house entertaining themselves with the idea of the disappointment the thief had
met with: and a lady who lodged in the house produced her
gold watch, saying she supposed that had been the object
of his search.

This circumstance encouraged him to make another
attempt; wherefore, on the following night, he again
ascended the sign-post, and got in at the window; but, hearing a person coming down stairs without shoes, he got back
to the sign-post, descended, and ran off. He was instantly
pursued, but escaped through the darkness of the night.

Chagrined at this disappointment, he sauntered into
the fields, and lay down under a hay-rick. He slumbered
awhile; but, being distressed in mind, he imagined he heard
a voice crying, 'Run, run, fly for your life; for you are pursued, and if you are taken you will be hanged.' He started
with wild affright, and large drops of sweat ran down his
face, occasioned by the agitation of his mind.

Finding that he had only been disturbed by a dream, he
again lay down; but the stings of his conscience continuing
to goad him, he dreamt that a person came to him, saying,
'Young man, you must go away from hence; for, were I to
suffer you to remain here, I should expect a judgment to
fall on me: so go away, or I will fetch a constable, who shall
oblige you to go.' Being again terrified, he walked round
the hay-rick, calling out 'Who is there?' but receiving no
answer, he lay down once more, and dreamt that his father-
in-law stood by him, and spoke as follows:—'O son! will you
never take warning till justice overtakes you? The time will
come when you will wish, but too late, that you had been
warned by me.'

Unable now to sleep, through the agonies of his mind,
he wandered about till morning, and had formed a resolution of returning to his father-in-law; but as he was going

to him he met an old acquaintance, who paid him a debt of a few shillings; and, going to drink with him, Powis soon forgot the virtuous resolutions he had formed.

On parting from this acquaintance he went to the house of another, where he slept five hours; and then, being extremely hungry, went to a public house, where he supped, and spent all his money, except eight-pence.

Thus reduced, he resolved to make a fresh attempt on the Chancery-office, for which purpose he broke through the wall, but found no booty.

In the mean time his father-in-law exerted his utmost endeavours to find him, to consult his safety; and, having met with him, told him it would be imprudent for him to stay longer in London, as people began to be suspicious of him: wherefore he advised him to go to Cambridge, and work as a journeyman with a smith of his acquaintance.

Young Powis consenting, the father bought him new clothes, furnished him with some good books, and gave him money to proceed on his journey. He now left the old gentleman; but soon afterwards meeting with six strolling players, one of whom he had formerly known, they sat down to drinking; at which they continued till all Powis's money was spent, and then he sold his new clothes.

Our young adventurer now became so hardened in guilt that there appeared no prospect of his reformation. One Sunday morning early he attempted to break open the house of a baker in Chancery Lane; but the family being alarmed, he was obliged to decamp without his booty, though not without being known. This affair coming to the knowledge of the father, he commissioned some friends to tell the boy, if they should meet him, that he was still ready to receive him with kindness, if he would mend his conduct.

Powis, being now very much distressed, applied to his still generous relation, who advised him to go to the West Indies, as the most effectual method of being out of danger;

and he promised to furnish him with necessaries for the voyage.

Accepting the offer, Powis was properly fitted out, and sent on board a ship in the river, where he was confined in the hold, to prevent his escaping. In a day or two afterwards he was allowed the liberty of the ship; but most of the seamen now going on shore to take leave of their friends, he resolved to seize the opportunity of making his escape, and of taking something of value with him.

Waiting till it was night, he broke open a chest belonging to a passenger, and, having stolen a handsome suit of clothes, he took the opportunity of the people on watch going to call others to relieve them; and, dropping down the side of the ship, got into a boat; but, having only a single oar, he was unable to steer her; and, after striving a considerable time, was obliged to let her drive; the consequence of which was, that she ran on shore below Woolwich.

Quitting the boat, he set off towards London; but near Deptford he met with two men, who asked him to sell his wig; on which he went to a public house with them, where they told him that a friend of theirs had been robbed of such a wig, and they suspected him to be the robber. Powis saw through the artifice, and, calling the landlord, desired that a constable might be sent for to take the villains into custody; but the men immediately threw down their reckoning, and ran off in the utmost haste.

Our adventurer, proceeding to London, changed his clothes, and took to his former practice of housebreaking; in which, however, he was remarkably unsuccessful. Strolling one night to the house where he had formerly been at Stockwell, he got in at the window, and stole a bottle of brandy, a great coat, and some other articles; but the family being alarmed, he was pursued and taken.

As he was known to the people of the house, they threatened to convey him to the ship; but he expressed so much dread at the consequence, that they conducted, him to his father-in-law, whose humanity once more induced him to receive the returning prodigal with kindness.

Powis now lived regularly at home about nine weeks, when, having received about a guinea as Christmas-box money, he got into company, and spent the whole; after which he renewed his former practices.

Having concealed himself under some hay in a stable in Chancery Lane, he broke into a boarding-school adjoining to it, whence he stole some books and a quantity of linen: and, soon after this, he broke into the house of an attorney, and, getting into a garret, struck a light; but some of the family being alarmed, there was an outcry of 'Thieves!' A man ascending a ladder being observed by Powis, he attempted to break through the tiling; but, failing in this, the other cried 'There is the thief!' Terrified by these words, he got into a gutter, whence he dropped down to a carpenter's yard adjoining, but could get no farther.

While he was in this situation, the carpenter, going into the yard with a candle, took him into custody, and lodged him in the roundhouse; but on the following day his father-in-law exerted himself so effectually, that the offence was forgiven, and he was once more taken home to the house of this ever-indulgent friend.

After he had been three months at home, the father-in-law was employed to do some business for Mr. Williams, a Welsh gentleman of fortune, who having brought his lady to London to lie in, she died in child-bed; and it was determined that she should be buried in Wales. Hereupon Powis's father-in-law was sent for to examine all the locks, &c. that the effects might be safe in the absence of Mr. Williams.

Our youth, being employed as a journeyman in this business, found a box of linen that was too full, on which he took out some articles. In removing the linen he found a small box, remarkably heavy, which, on examination, appeared to contain diamonds, jewels, rings, a gold watch, and other articles, to the amount of more than 200*l.* all which he stole and put the box in its place. This being done, he called the maid to see that all was safe, and delivered her the key of the larger box.

Being possessed of this booty, Powis consulted an acquaintance as to the method of disposing of it, who advised him to melt the gold, and throw the jewels into the Thames. This being agreed upon, the acquaintance kept the jewels; and the gold being sold for eleven guineas, Powis had seven of them, which he soon squandered away.

About a fortnight after the effects were stolen Powis was apprehended on suspicion of the robbery, and committed to Newgate; and, being tried at the next sessions, was sentenced to be transported for seven years; the jury having given a verdict that he was guilty of stealing to the value of thirty-nine shillings.

He lay in Newgate a considerable time; till at length his father-in-law, after repeated entreaties, and a promise of a total reformation of manners, made such interest, that he was burnt in the hand, and set at large.

Yet again was this ungrateful boy taken under his parent's roof, where he continued about seven months; when, meeting with one of his dissolute companions, he spent all his money, and was then afraid to return home.

He now refrained some time from acts of theft; and, taking lodgings in an alley in Fleet Street, subsisted by borrowing money of his acquaintance. Soon afterwards, however, he broke open a trunk at his lodgings, and stole some linen, which he pawned for five shillings and sixpence.

On the next day the landlord charged him with the robbery; but, not intending to prosecute him, was content with recovering his linen from the pawnbrokers, and took powis's word for making good the different money.

In less than a week after the adjustment of this affair our young, but hardened, villain broke open the coffee-house in Chancery Lane which we have already mentioned, and stole a few articles, which produced him about thirty shillings: soon afterwards he broke into the chancery-office, where he stole two books, which he sold for half a crown.

On the following evening he went again to the office, and hid himself under the staircase; but, being heard to cough by a man who had been left to watch, he was taken into custody, and conveyed to a tavern in the neighbourhood, where his father-in-law attended, and pleaded so forcibly in his behalf, that he was permitted to go home with him for the night.

On the following day some gentlemen came to examine him, when he denied the commission of a variety of crimes with which he had been charged; but the gentlemen, having consented to his escape for this time, advised him not to appear again in that neighbourhood, as the Masters in Chancery had given strict orders for prosecuting him.

After receiving some good advice from his father-in-law, he was recommended to work with a smith in Milford Lane, in the Strand: but Powis had a brother who called upon him a few days afterwards, and told him that a warrant was issued to apprehend him for robbing the Chancery, which obliged him to abscond.

Strolling one evening in the Spa Fields, near Islington, some constables apprehended him as a vagrant, and lodged him, with several others, in New Prison; and on the following day most of the prisoners were discharged by a magistrate, and Powis was ordered to be set at liberty; but, not having money to pay his fees, he was taken back to the prison, where he remained a few days longer, and was then set at liberty by the charity of a gentleman, who bade him 'thank God, and take care never to get into trouble again.'

In a short time after his discharge he broke into the Earl of Peterborough's house at Chelsea, and stole some trifling articles from the kitchen, which he sold for four shillings; and on the following night he robbed another house in the same neighborhood of some effects, which he sold for ten shillings.

This trifling sum being soon spent, he broke open a house in Lincoln's Inn Fields, where he got a considerable quantity of money; and, to prevent persons who knew him from suspecting that he was the thief, he forged a letter, as coming from his grandfather in Yorkshire, purporting that he had sent him such a sum.

In a short time afterwards, at a kind of ball given by one of his companions to celebrate his birthday, Powis fell in love with a girl who made one of the company.

The girl paying no attention to his addresses, Powis waited on her mother, and, after some conversation with her, was permitted to pay his personal respects to the daughter, to whom he pretended that his grandfather in Yorkshire would leave him a large sum of money; and, in proof of what he said, he showed her some counterfeit letters, appearing to have the post-mark on them.

The girl made no objection to him as a husband; but said it would be prudent in him to visit his grandfather, and ask his consent to the match, which would contribute to her peace of mind. On this he left her, and broke open a house that evening, whence he stole a few things, which he sold for fifteen shillings, and, calling on her the next day, took his leave, as if preparing for his journey.

His plan was to commit some robbery by which he might obtain a considerable sum, and then, concealing himself for some time, return to his mistress, and pretend that his grandfather had given him the money.

Going to see 'The Beggars' Opera,' he was greatly shocked at the appearance of *Macheath* on the stage in fetters, and could not forbear reflecting what might be his own future fate; yet about a week afterwards he broke open a cook's shop, and stole some articles, the sale of which produced him a guinea.

On the following day he called at Newgate, treated the prisoners to the amount of seven shillings, and, on his quitting the prison, met two girls whom he knew; and with them he went to Hampstead, where he treated them to the amount of twelve shillings and sixpence; so that only eighteen pence remained of his last ill-gotten guinea.

On the following day Powis went to the Black Raven, in Fetter Lane, where he observed the landlord put some gold into a drawer, of which he determined, if possible, to possess himself. About midnight he went away, having first stolen the pin that fastened the cellar-window.

Returning at two in the morning, he got into the cellar, and attempted to open the door of the tap-room; but, failing in this, he was about to return by the way he had entered, when a watchman coming by, and seeing the window open, alarmed the family. Powis now escaped into a carpenter's yard, and hid himself: but the landlord coming down, and several persons attending, he was apprehended; not, however, till one person had run a sword through his leg, and another struck him a blow on the head that almost deprived him of his senses; circumstances of severity which could not be justified, as he made no resistance.

The offender was lodged in the Compter for the present, and, being removed to Newgate, was brought to his trial at the Old Bailey, convicted of the burglary, and received sentence of death. The jury, considering the cruelty with which he had been treated, recommended him to mercy: however, the royal favour was not extended to him, as he had before been sentenced to transportation.

When brought up to receive sentence, he begged to be represented as an object worthy of the royal lenity; but was told not to expect such indulgence. He likewise wrote to his sweetheart to exert her influence, which she promised, but could do nothing to serve him.

He was hanged at Tyburn on the 9th of October, 1732, along with William Shelton, at the age of twenty-two years, after admonishing the spectators to take warning by his fatal end, and expressing the utmost detestation of the irregularities of his life.

The case of this malefactor will afford a very striking lesson to youth. In the former part of his life we see the miserable situation of a strolling player; and surely the distresses he encountered will be deemed enough to terrify thoughtless young men, who are fond of what is called spouting, from engaging in this vagrant course of life.

The terrors of Powis's conscience when he lay down to sleep under the hay-rick show that there is no peace to the wicked. One self-approving hour, the consequence of having discharged our duty, must afford more solid satisfaction than whole months spent in that riot and debauchery which may be purchased with ill-gotten wealth.

Nothing, surely, can be equal to the goodness with which Powis was treated by his father-in-law. His kindness appears to have been almost without example, and what could scarcely have been expected even from a real parent.

This offender, then, sinned against all advice, all warning, all indulgence: but we trust his fate will have a forcible effect on young people who may read this narrative. We hope it will, in a particular manner, teach them the necessity of duty to their parents; and that the only way to be happy in advanced life is to be virtuous and religious while they are young.

CAPTAIN PORTEOUS PUT TO DEATH BY THE EDINBURGH MOB.

CAPTAIN JOHN PORTEOUS

Convicted of murder, and murdered by the mob.

———

JOHN PORTEOUS was born of indigent parents, near the city of Edinburgh, who bound him apprentice to a tailor, with whom, after the expiration of his apprenticeship, he worked as journeyman.

Porteous was soon noticed by several reputable gentlemen as a young man of good address and fine accomplishments, and one whom they entertained a desire to serve.

It happened at this time that a gentleman who had been lord provost of Edinburgh, growing tired of his mistress, wished to disengage himself from her in a genteel manner; and, knowing Porteous to be very poor, he proposed his taking her off his hands by making her his wife.

When the proposition was first made to the lady she rejected it with much disdain, thinking it a great degradation to match with a journeyman tailor; but, on the gentleman's promising her a fortune of five hundred pounds, she consented, and they were married accordingly.

Porteous now commenced master, and met with good success for some time; but, being much addicted to company, he neglected his business, by which means he lost many of his customers. His wife, in consequence, was obliged to apply to her old friend the provost, to make some other provision for them.

In Edinburgh there are three companies of men, in number twenty-five each, who are employed to keep the peace, and take up all offenders, whom they keep in custody till examined by a magistrate. An officer is appointed to each of these companies, whom they style Captain, with a salary of eighty pounds a year, and a suit of scarlet uniform, which in that part of the world is reckoned very honorable.

A vacancy happening by the death of one of these captains, the provost immediately appointed his friend Porteous to fill up the place; and the latter, being now advanced to honour, forgot all his former politeness, for which he was so much esteemed when a tradesman, assuming the consequence of a man in authority.

If a riot happened in the city, Porteous was generally made choice of by the magistrates to suppress it, he being a man of resolute spirit, and unacquainted with fear. On these occasions he would generally exceed the bounds of his commission, and would treat the delinquents with the utmost cruelty, by knocking them down with his musket, and frequently breaking legs and arms.

If sent to quell a disturbance in a house of ill fame, notwithstanding he was a most abandoned debauched himself, he would take pleasure in exposing the characters of all he found there, thus destroying the peace of many families: he would treat the unhappy prostitutes with the greatest inhumanity, and even drag them to a prison, though many of them had been seduced by himself.

Amongst other instances of cruelty he committed we shall mention the following, because it procured him the universal hatred of the people in that city:—

A vacancy happening in the lectureship of a neighbouring church, two young gentlemen were candidates; and, having each an equal number of votes, the dispute was referred to the presbytery, who declared in favour of Mr. Dawson. The other candidate, Mr. Wotherspoon, appealed to the synod, who reversed the order of the presbytery. As the parishioners were much exasperated, and a tumult being apprehended at the church on the day Mr. Wotherspoon was to preach his first sermon, Porteous was ordered there to keep the peace; but finding, on his arrival, Mr. Dawson had got possession of the pulpit, he went up the steps without the least ceremony, seized him by the collar, and dragged him down like a thief. In consequence of the wounds he received at this time, Mr. Dawson died a few weeks after.

Mr. Wotherspoon coming in at the time of the affray, Mr. Dawson's friends were so enraged, that they immediately fell on him, whom they beat in such a terrible manner, that he also died about the same time as Mr. Dawson.

Thus the lives of two amiable men were sacrificed to the brutality of this inhuman monster. Many men, women, and children, were also much wounded in the affray; yet the wretch himself escaped unpunished, no regular notice being taken of the affair.

Nothing gave more pleasure to this fellow than his being employed to quell riots, on which occasions he never wanted an opportunity of exercising his savage disposition.

The condemnation and death of Porteous happened in the following most extraordinary manner:—

Smuggling was so much practised in Scotland at that time that no laws could restrain it. The smugglers assembled in large bodies, so that the revenue-officers could not attack them without endangering their lives.

The most active person in striving to suppress these unlawful practices was Mr. Stark, collector for the county of Fife, who, being informed that one Andrew Wilson had a large quantity of contraband goods at his house, persuaded a number of men to accompany him; and they seized the goods, and safely lodged them (as they thought) in the custom-house: but Wilson being a man of an enterprising spirit, and conceiving himself injured, went, in company with one Robertson, and some more of his gang, to the custom-house, where, breaking open the doors, they recovered their goods, which they brought off in carts, in defiance of all opposition.

Mr. Stark, hearing that such a daring insult had been committed, dispatched an account thereof to the barons of the Exchequer, who immediately applying to the Lord Justice Clerk, his lordship issued his warrant to the sheriff of Fife, commanding him to assemble all the people in his jurisdiction to seize the delinquents, and replace the goods.

In consequence of the above order many were apprehended, but all discharged again for want of evidence, except Wilson and Robertson, who were both found guilty, and sentenced to die.

A custom prevailed in Scotland, at that time, of taking the condemned criminals to church every Sunday, under the care of three or four of the city guards. The above two criminals were accordingly taken to one of the churches on the Sunday before they were to suffer; when, just getting within the door, Wilson, though handcuffed, assisted in his companion's escape, by seizing hold of one soldier with his teeth, and keeping the others from turning upon him, while he cried out to Robertson to run.

Robertson accordingly took to his heels, and, the streets being crowded with people going to church, he passed uninterrupted, and got out at one of the city gates just as they were going to shut it, a custom constantly observed during divine service.

The city being now alarmed, Porteous was immediately dispatched in search of him, but all in vain; Robertson, meeting with a friend who knocked off his handcuffs and procured him a horse, got the same evening on board a vessel at Dunbar, which landed him safely in Holland.

We are informed that, in the year 1756, he was living, and kept a public house with great credit near the bridge at Rotterdam.

On the following Wednesday a temporary gallows was erected in the Grass-market for the execution of Wilson, who was ordered to be conducted there by fifty men, under the command of Porteous.

Porteous, being apprehensive an attempt would be made to rescue the prisoner, represented to the provost the necessity there was for soldiers to be drawn up ready to preserve the peace: on which five companies of the Welsh Fuzileers, commanded by a major, were ordered to be in readiness in the Lawn-market, near the place of execution.

No disturbance arising, the prisoner finished his devotions, ascended the ladder, was turned off, and continued hanging the usual time; at the expiration of which, the hangman going up the ladder to cut him down, a stone struck him on the nose, and caused it to bleed. This stone was immediately followed by many others; at which Porteous was so much exasperated, that he instantly called out to his men, 'Fire, and be damned!' discharging his own piece at the same time, and shooting a young man, who was apprentice to a confectioner, dead on the spot.

Some of the soldiers, more humanely, fired over the heads of the people, but unfortunately killed two or three who were looking out at the windows. Others of the soldiers wantonly fired amongst the feet of the mob, by which many were so disabled as to be afterwards obliged to suffer amputation.

Porteous now endeavoured to draw off his men, as the mob grew exceedingly outrageous, throwing stones, with every thing else they could lay their hands on, and continuing to press on the soldiers; on which Porteous, with two of his men, turned about and fired, killing three more of the people, which amounted to nine in the whole that were left dead on the spot, besides many wounded.

A sergeant was sent by the major of the Welsh Fuzileers to inquire into the cause of the disturbance, but the mob was so outrageous that he could gain no intelligence. Porteous, being assisted by the Fuzileers, at last conducted his men to the guard, when, being sent for by the provost, he passed a long examination, and was committed to prison in order to take his trial for murder.

On the 6th of July, 1736, the trial came on before the lords of justiciary, previously to which Porteous made a judicial confession that the people were killed as mentioned in the indictments; but pleaded self-defence. His counsel then stated the following point of law, to be determined by the judges previously to the jury being charged with the prisoner:—

'Whether a military officer, with soldiers under his command, who, being assaulted by the populace, should fire, or order his men to fire, was not acting consistently with the nature of self-defence, according to the laws of civilized nations?'

The counsel for the prosecution being ordered to plead to the question by the Court, they pronounced, as their opinion, 'That if it was proved that Captain Porteous either fired a gun, or caused one or more to be fired, by which any person or persons was or were killed, and if the said firing happened without orders from a magistrate properly authorized, then it would be murder in the eye of the law.'

Thus the question being decided against him, and the jury empanelled, forty-four witnesses were examined for and against the prosecution.

The prisoner being now called on for his defence, his counsel insisted that the magistrates had ordered him to support the, execution of Wilson, and repel force by force, being apprehensive of a rescue; that powder and ball had been given them for the said purpose, with orders to load their pieces.

They insisted, also, that he only meant to intimidate the people by threats, and actually knocked down one of his own men for presenting his piece; that, finding the men would not obey orders, he drew off as many as he could; that he afterwards heard a firing in the rear, contrary to his directions. That, in order to know who had fired, he would not suffer their pieces to be cleaned till properly inspected; and that he never attempted to escape, though he had the greatest opportunity, and might have effected it with the utmost ease.

They farther insisted, that, admitting some excesses had been committed, it could not amount to murder, as he was in the lawful discharge of his duty; neither could it be supposed to be done with premeditated malice.

In answer to this the counsel for the crown argued, that the trust reposed in the prisoner ceased when the execution was over; that he was then no longer an officer employed for that purpose for which the fire-arms had been loaded; and that the reading of the Riot Act only could justify their firing, in case a rescue had been actually attempted.

The prisoner's counsel replied, that the magistrates, whose duty it was to have read the act, had deserted the soldiery, and taken refuge in a house for their own security;

and that it was hard for men to suffer themselves to be knocked on the head when they had lawful weapons put into their hands to defend themselves.

The charge being delivered to the jury, they retired for a considerable time, when they brought him in guilty, and he received sentence of death.

The king being then at Hanover, and much interest being made to save the prisoner, the queen, by the advice of her council, granted a respite till his majesty's return to England. The respite was only procured one week before his sentence was to be put in execution, of which when the populace were informed, such a scheme of revenge was meditated as is perhaps unprecedented.

On the 7th of September, between nine and ten in the evening, a large body of men entered the city of Edinburgh, and seized the arms belonging to the guard: they then patrolled the streets, crying out, 'All those who dare avenge innocent blood, let them come here.' They then shut the gates, and placed guards at each.

The main body of the mob, all disguised, marched in the mean time to the prison; when, finding some difficulty in breaking open the door with hammers, they immediately set fire to it, taking great care that the flames should not extend beyond their proper bounds. The outer door was hardly consumed before they rushed in, and, ordering the keeper to open the door of the captain's apartment, cried out, 'Where is the villain, Porteous?' He replied, 'Here I am; what do you want with me?' To which they answered, that they meant to hang him in the Grassmarket, the place where he had shed so much innocent blood.

His expostulations were all in vain; they seized him by the legs and arms, and dragged him instantly to the place of execution.

On their arrival they broke open a shop, to find a rope suitable to their purpose, which they immediately fixed round his neck; then, throwing the other end over a dyer's pole, hoisted him up; when he, endeavouring to save himself, fixed his hands between the halter and his neck, which being observed by some of the mob, one of them struck him with an axe, and this obliging him to quit his hold, they soon put an end to his life.

When they were satisfied he was dead, they immediately dispersed to their several habitations, unmolested themselves, and without molesting any one else.

Upon this circumstance being made known, a royal proclamation was issued, offering a large reward for the apprehension of the offenders; and the magistrates of Edinburgh, the scene of the murder, were summoned to answer for their neglect in not quelling the riot, fined, and rendered incapable of acting again in any judicial capacity. In such a mob as that which seized Porteous, it was difficult to fix upon individuals; and the deceased having rendered himself very obnoxious to the whole people, the affair there rested.

Thus ended the life of Captain John Porteous, a man possessed of qualifications which, had they been properly applied, would have rendered him an ornament to his country, and made him exceedingly useful in a military capacity. His uncommon spirit and invincible courage would have done honour to the greatest hero of antiquity; but, when advanced to power, he became intoxicated with pride, and, instead of being the admiration of, he became despised and hated by, his fellow-citizens. The fate of this unhappy man, it is hoped, will be a caution to those in power not to abuse it; but, by an impartial distribution of justice, to render themselves worthy members of society.

He was put to death at Edinburgh, September 7, 1736.

PRICE STRANGLING HIS WIFE ON HOUNSLOW HEATH.

GEORGE PRICE

Convicted of murder, but who died in Newgate.

———

THIS malefactor was a native of the Hay, in Brecknock-shire, where he lived as servant to a widow-lady, who was so extremely partial to him that the neighbours circulated reports to their mutual prejudice. Having lived in this station seven years, he repaired to London, where he got places in two respectable families, and then returned to his former service in Wales; when his mistress treated him with such distinction, that the country people became even more severe in their censures than before.

On his quitting this lady a second time, she made him a present of a valuable watch, which he brought to London, and then engaged in the service of—Brown, esq. of Golden Square, who used to make frequent excursions to Hampstead, attended by his servant.

Price now became acquainted with Mary Chambers, servant in a public house at Hampstead, whom he married at the expiration of a fortnight from his first paying his addresses to her; but Mr. Brown, disapproving of the match, dismissed Price from his service.

Soon after this he took his wife into Brecknockshire, and imposed her on his relations as the daughter of a military officer, who would become entitled to a large fortune. He was treated in the most friendly manner by his relations; and the young couple returning to London, the wife went to lodge at Hampstead, while Price engaged in the service of a gentleman in New Broad Street.

Mrs. Price, being delivered of twins, desired her husband to buy some medicines to make the children sleep, which he procured; and the children dying soon afterwards, a report was circulated that he had poisoned them; but this circumstance he denied to the last moment of his life.

In a short time Price's master removed into Kent, whither he attended him; and, in the interim, his wife was again brought to bed, a circumstance that greatly chagrined him, as he had now made other connexions, and was grown weary of the support of his own family. Mrs. Price having afterwards become a third time pregnant, he told her he could not support any more children, and recommended her to take medicines to procure abortion; which was accordingly done, and the horrid intention was answered.

Price now paid his addresses to a widow in Kent; and, considering his wife as an obstacle between him and his wishes, he formed the infernal resolution of murdering her.

Having been bruised by a fall from his horse, and his master having business in London, he was left behind, to take his passage in a Margate as soon as his health would permit; and on his arrival at Billingsgate his wife was waiting to receive him, in the hope of obtaining some money towards her present support.

Price no sooner beheld her than he began to devise the plan of the intended murder; on which he told her that he had procured the place of a nursery-maid for her in the neighbourhood of Putney, and that he would attend her thither that very day. He then directed her to clean herself, and meet him at the Woolpack, in Monkwell Street.

In her way to her lodgings she called at the house of her husband's master, where the servants advised her not to trust herself in her husband's company; but she said she had no fear of him, as he had treated her with unusual kindness. Accordingly she went home and dressed herself (having borrowed some clothes of her landlady), and met her husband, who put her in a chaise, and drove her out of town towards Hounslow.

As they were riding along, she begged he would stop while she bought some snuff, which he, in a laughing manner, refused to do, saying she would never want any again. When he came on Hounslow Heath, it being near ten o'clock at night, he suddenly stopped the chaise, and threw the lash of the whip round his wife's neck; but drawing it too hastily, he made a violent mark on her chin: immediately finding his mistake, he placed it lower; on which she exclaimed, 'My dear! my dear! for God's sake—if this is your love, I will never trust you more?!'

Immediately on her pronouncing these words, which were her last, he pulled the ends of the whip with great force; but, the violence of his passion abating, he let go before she was quite dead: yet, resolving to accomplish the horrid deed, he once more put the thong of the whip about her neck, and pulled it with such violence that it broke; but not till the poor woman was dead.

Having stripped the body, he left it almost under a gibbet, where some malefactors hung in chains, having first disfigured it to such a degree that he presumed it could not be known. He brought the clothes to London, some of which he cut in pieces, and dropped in different streets; but, knowing that the others were borrowed of the landlady, he sent them to her; a circumstance that materially conduced to his conviction.

He reached London about one o'clock in the morning; and, being interrogated why he came at such an unseasonable hour, he said that the Margate had been detained in the river by contrary winds.

On the following day the servants, and other people, made so many inquiries respecting his wife, that, terrified at the idea of being taken into custody, he immediately fled to Portsmouth, with a view of entering on board a ship; but no vessel was then ready to sail.

While he was drinking at an alehouse in Portsmouth, he heard the bellman crying him as a murderer, with such an exact description of him, that he was apprehensive of being seized; and, observing a window which opened to the water, he jumped out and swam for his life.

Having gained the shore, he travelled all night till he reached a farm-house, where he inquired for employment. The farmer's wife said he did not appear as if he had been used to country work; but he might stay till her husband's arrival.

The farmer regarded him with great attention, and said he wanted a ploughman, but that he was certain he would not answer his purpose, as he had the appearance of a person who had absconded for debt, or possibly there might be some criminal prosecution against him.

Price expressed his readiness to do any thing for an honest subsistence; but the farmer refused to employ him, though he said he would give him a supper and a lodging. But, when bed-time came, the. farmer's men refused to sleep with Price, in the fear of his robbing them of their clothes; in consequence of which he was obliged to lie on some straw in the barn.

On the following day he crossed the country towards Oxford, where he endeavoured to get into service, and would have been engaged by a physician; but, happening to read a newspaper in which he was advertised, he immediately decamped from Oxford, and travelled into Wales.

Having stopped at a village a few miles from Hay, at the house of a shoemaker to whom his brother was apprenticed, the latter obtained permission to accompany George home; and, while they were on their walk, the malefactor recounted the particulars of the murder which had obliged him to seek his safety in flight.

The brother commiserated his condition; and, leaving him at a small distance from their father's house, went in, and found the old gentleman reading an advertisement describing the murderer. The younger son bursting into tears, the father said he hoped his brother was not come; to which the youth replied, 'Yes, he is at the door; but, being afraid that some of the neighbours were in the house, he would not come in till he had your permission.'

The offender, being introduced, fell on his knees, and earnestly besought his father's blessing; to which the aged parent said, 'Ah! George, I wish God may bless you, and that what I have heard concerning you may be false.' The son said, 'It is false; but let me have a private room: make no words; I have done no harm; let me have a room to myself.'

Being accommodated agreeably to his request, he produced half a crown, begging that his brother would buy a lancet, as he was resolved to put a period to his miserable existence: but the brother declined to be in any way aiding to the commission of the crime of suicide; and the father, after exerting every argument to prevent his thinking of such a farther violation of the laws of God, concealed him for two days.

It happened that the neighbours observing a fire in a room where none had been for a considerable time before, a report was propagated that Price was secreted in the house of his father; whereupon he thought it prudent to abscond in the night; and, having reached Gloucester, he went to an inn, and procured the place of an ostler.

The terrors of his conscience now agitated him to such a degree, that the other servants could not help asking what ailed him; to which he replied, that a girl he had courted having married another man, he had never been able to enjoy any peace of mind since.

During his residence at Gloucester, two of the sons of the lady with whom he had first lived as a servant happened to be at a school in that city; and Price behaved to them with so much civility that they wrote to their mother, describing his conduct; in reply to which she informed them that he had killed his wife, and desired them not to hold any correspondence with him.

The young gentlemen mentioning this circumstance, one of Price's fellow-servants said to him, 'You are the man that murdered his wife on Hounslow Heath. I will not betray you; but, if you stay longer, you will certainly be taken into custody.'

Stung by the reflections of his own conscience, and agitated by the fear of momentary detection, Price knew not how to act; but at length he resolved to come to London, and surrender to justice and calling on his former master, and being apprehended, he was committed to Newgate.

At the following sessions at the Old Bailey he was brought to his trial, and convicted on almost the strongest circumstantial evidence that was ever adduced against any offender. He had prepared a written defence; but declined reading it, as he found it was so little likely to operate with any effect in his favour.

He was sentenced to death, but died of the gaol fever,[4] in Newgate, before the law could be executed on him, on the 22d of October 1738.

------

[4] THE GAOL FEVER.—Our readers may be gratified by an account of this malignant die temper, which was so fatal and frequent in old Newgate, and other county gaols in different parts of England, the death of Price, being the first caused by it which we have had occasion to mention, affords us an opportunity; and agreeably thereto we proceed with the best accounts we have been able to collect of the fatality which, in former times, resulted from a want of cleanliness and the free admission of air into prisons.

It always was attended with a degree of malignity, in proportion to the closeness and stench of the place. It is, therefore, of the highest importance for gaolers to keep clean every part of their prison, the neglect of which has often proved fatal to every person in-haling the pestiferous air.

The assize held at Oxford in the year 1577, called the 'Black Assize,' was a, dreadful instance of the deadly effects of the gaol fever. The judges, jury, witnesses, nay, in fact every person, except the prisoners, women, and children, in Court, were killed by a foul air, which at first was thought to have arisen out of the bowels of the earth; but that great philosopher, Lord Bacon, proved it to have come from the prisoners, taken out of a noisome gaol, and brought into Court to take their trials; and they alone, being subject in the inhaling foul air, were not injured by it.

'Baker's Chronicle,' a work of the highest authenticity, thus speaks of the Black Assize:—

'The Court were surprised with a pestilent savour, whether arising from the noisome smell of the prisoners, or from the damp of the ground, is uncertain; but all that were present within forty hours died, except the prisoners, and the women and children; and the contagion went no farther. There died Robert Bell, lord chief baron, Robert de Olie, Sir William Babington, the high sheriff of Oxfordshire, some of the most eminent lawyers the jurors, and three hundred others, more or less.'

In the year 1730, the Lord Chief Baron Pengelly, with several of his officers and servants; Sir James Sheppard, sergeant-at-law; and John Pigot, Esq. high sheriff for Somersetshire, died at Blandford, on the Western circuit of the Lent assize, from the infected stench brought with the prisoners from Ilchester gaol to their trials at Taunton, in which town the infection afterwards spread, and carried off some hundred persons.

In 1754 and 1755 this distemper prevailed in Newgate to a degree which carried off more than one-fifth of the prisoners.

Others attributed the cause of the sudden mortality at Oxford to witchcraft, the people in those times being very superstitious. In 'Webster's Display of Witchcraft,' a work of some authenticity is to the relation of circumstances as they occurred, we find the following account of the Black Assize, which we insert as a matter of curiosity:—

The 4th and 5th days of July, 1559, were holden the assizes at Oxford, where was arraigned and condemned one Rowland Jenkes, for his seditious tongue, at which time there arose such a damp, that almost all were smothered. Very few escaped that were not taken at that instant. The jurors died presently; shortly after, died Sir Robert Bell, lord chief baron, Sir Robert De Olie, Sir Wm. Babington, Mr. Weneman, Mr. De Olie, high sheriff, Mr. Davers, Mr. Harcoutt, Mr. Kirle, Mr. Pheteplace, Mr. Greenwood, Mr. Foster, Sergeant Baram, Mr. Stevens, &c. There died in Oxford three hundred person; and sickened there, but died in other places, two hundred and odd, from the 6th of July to the 12th of August, after which day died not one of that sickness, for one of them infected not another, nor any one woman or child died thereof. This is the punctual relation according to our English annals, which relate nothing of what should be the cause of the arising of such a damp just at the conjuncture of time when Jenkes was condemned, there being none before, and so it could not be a prison infection; for that would have manifested itself by smell, or operating sooner. But to take away all scruple and to assign the true cause it was thus: It fortuned that a manuscript fell into my hands, collected by an ancient gentleman of York, who was a great observer and garter, of strange things and facts, who lived about live time of this accident happening at Oxford, wherein it is related thus; That Rowland Jenkes, being imprisoned for treasonable words spoken against the queen, and being a popish recusant, had, not with standing during the time of his restraint, liberty sometime to walk abroad with the keeper; and that one day he came to an apothecary, and showed' him a receipt which, he desired him to make up; but the apothecary, upon viewing of it, told him that it was a strong and dangerous receipt, and required some time to prepare it; also asking to what use he would apply it. He answered, 'To kill the rats, that since his imprisonment spoiled his books'; so being satisfied, he promised to make it ready. After a certain time he Cometh

We are taught, in the case of this unhappy wretch and his wife, some very useful lessons of instruction. Price was guilty of murder in a complicated sense. He first advised his wife to take medicines to procure abortion; and then actually murdered her who could be base enough to follow such pernicious advice: thus she, as is but too commonly the case in instances of departure from the laws of God, fell a sacrifice to the passions of her seducer.

What must have been the thoughts of this unhappy wretch, when, after having murdered his wife, he deposited her body almost under the gibbet on Hounslow Heath! What the terrors of his conscience when he heard his person minutely described by the bellman at Portsmouth! What must have been his feelings when he discovered his guilt to his brother, and when he met the eye of his offended parent! How agonized must his mind have been when he desired his brother to buy a lancet, that he might add suicide to murder! In a word, what terror! must this most unhappy wretch have felt in his peregrinations through the country, from his commission of the crime to his Surrender to justice, and thence to the moment of his exit!

If ever any man could, well might he say, in the words of Scripture, 'A wounded spirit who can bear?'

---

to know if it were ready, but the apothecary said the ingredients were so hard to procure that he had not done it, and so gave him the receipt again, of which he had taken a copy, which mine author had there precisely written down, but did, seem horribly poisonous, that I cut It forth, lest it might fall into the hands of wicked persons. But after, it seems, he had it prepared, and, against the day of his trial, had made a wick of it (for so is the word, that is, so fitted, that like a candle it might be fired) which, as soon as ever he was condemned, he lighted, having provided himself a tinder-box, and steel to strike fire. And whosoever should know the ingredients of that wick, or candle, and the manner of the composition, will easily be persuaded of the virulency and venomous effect of it.'"

TURPIN PLACING AN OLD WOMAN ON THE FIRE, TO COMPEL THE DISCOVERY
OF HER TREASURE.

RICHARD TURPIN

Executed for horse-stealing.

———

THIS man was the son of John Turpin, a farmer at Thackstead, in Essex; and, having received a common school education, was apprenticed to a butcher in Whitechapel; but was distinguished from his early youth for the impropriety of his behaviour, and the brutality of his manners.

On the expiration of his apprenticeship he married a young woman of East Ham, in Essex, named Palmer; but he had not been long married before he took to the practice of stealing his neighbours' cattle, which he used to kill and cut up for sale.

Having stolen two oxen belonging to Mr. Giles, of Plaistow, he drove them to his own house; but two of Giles's servants, suspecting who was the robber, went to Turpin's, where they saw the carcasses of two beasts of such size as had been lost; but, as the hides were stripped from them, it was impossible to say that they were the same: learning, however, that Turpin used to dispose of his hides at Waltham Abbey, they went thither, and saw the hides of the individual beasts that had been stolen.

No doubt now remaining who was the robber, a warrant was procured for the apprehension of Turpin; but, learning that the peace officers were in search of him, he made his escape from the back window of his house at the very moment they were entering at the door.

Having retreated to a place of security, he found means to inform his wife where he was concealed: she accordingly furnished him with money, with which he travelled into the hundreds of Essex, where he joined a gang of smugglers, with whom he was for some time successful; till a set of the Customhouse officers, by one fortunate stroke, deprived him of all his ill-acquired gains.

Thrown out of this kind of business, he connected himself with a gang of deer-stealers, the principal part of whose depredations were committed on Epping Forest, and the parks in its neighbourhood: but, this business not succeeding to the expectation of the robbers, they determined to commence housebreakers.

Their plan was, to fix on houses that they presumed contained any valuable property; and, while one of them knocked at the door, the others, were to rush in, and seize whatever they might deem worthy of their notice.

The first attack of this kind was at the house of Mr. Strype, an old man who kept a chandler's shop at Watford, whom they robbed of all the money in his possession, but did not offer him any personal violence.

Turpin now acquainted his associates that there was an old woman at Loughton who was in possession of seven or eight hundred pounds; whereupon they agreed to rob her; and when they came to the door one of them knocked, and the rest, forcing their way into the house, tied handkerchiefs over the eyes of the old woman and her maid.

This being done, Turpin demanded what money was in the house; and the owner hesitating to tell him, he threatened to set her on the fire if she did not make an immediate discovery. Still, however, she refused to give the desired information: on which the villains actually placed her on the fire, where she sat till the tormenting pains compelled her to discover her hidden treasure; so that the robbers possessed themselves of above four hundred pounds, and decamped with the booty.

Some little time after this they agreed to rob the house of a farmer near Barking; and, knocking at the door, the people declined to open it: on which they broke it open; and having bound the farmer, his wife, his son-in-law, and the servant-maid, they robbed the house of above seven hundred pounds; which delighted Turpin so much, that he exclaimed, 'Ay, this will do, if it would always be so!' and the robbers retired with their prize, which amounted to above eighty pounds for each of them.

This desperate gang, now flushed with success, determined to attack the house of Mr. Mason, the keeper of Epping Forest; and the time was fixed when the plan was to be carried into execution: but Turpin, having gone to London to spend his share of the former booty, intoxicated himself to such a degree, that he totally forgot the appointment.

Nevertheless, the rest of the gang resolved, that the absence of their companion should not frustrate the preposed design; and having taken a solemn oath to break every article of furniture in Mason's house, they set out on their expedition.

Having gained admission, they beat and kicked the unhappy man with great severity. Finding an old man sitting by the fire-side they permitted him to remain uninjured; and Mr. Mason's daughter escaped their fury, by running out of the house, and taking shelter in a hog-sty.

After ransacking the lower part of house, and doing much mischief, they went up stairs, where they broke every thing that fell in their way, and, among the rest, a china punch-bowl, from which dropped one hundred and twenty guineas, which they made prey of, and effected their escape. They now went to London in search of Turpin, with whom they shared the booty, though he had not taken part in the execution of the villainy.

On the 11th of January, 1735, Turpin and five of his companions went to the house of Mr. Saunders, a rich farmer at Charlton, in Kent, between seven and eight in the evening, and, having knocked at the door, asked if Mr. Saunders was at home. Being answered in the affirmative, they rushed into the house, and found Mr. Saunders, with his wife and friends, playing at cards in the parlour. They told the company that they should remain uninjured if they made no disturbance. Having made prize of a silver snuff-box which lay on the table, part of the gang stood guard over the rest of the company, while the others attended Mr. Saunders through the house, and, breaking open his escritoires and closets, stole above a hundred pounds, exclusive of plate.

During these transactions the servant-maid ran up stairs, barred the door of her room, and called out 'Thieves!' with a view of alarming the neighbourhood; but the robbers broke open the door, secured her, and then robbed the house of all the valuable property they had not before taken. Finding some mince-pies, and some bottles of wine, they sat down to regale themselves; and, meeting with a bottle of brandy, they compelled each of the company to drink a glass of it.

Mrs. Saunders fainting through terror, they administered some drops, in water, to her, and recovered her to the use of her senses. Having staid in the house a considerable time, they packed up their booty and departed, having first declared that if any of the family gave the least alarm within two hours, or advertised the marks of the stolen plate, they would return and murder them at a future time.

Retiring to a public house at Woolwich, where they had concerted the robbery, they crossed the Thames to an empty house in Ratcliffe Highway, where they deposited the stolen effects till they found a purchaser for them.

The division of the plunder having taken place, they, on the 18th of the same month, went to the house of Mr. Sheldon, near Croydon, in Surrey, where they arrived about seven in the evening. Having got into the yard, they perceived a light in the stable, and, going into it, found the coachman attending his horses. Having immediately bound him, they quitted the stable, and, meeting Mr. Sheldon in the yard, they seized him, and compelled him to conduct them into the house, whence they stole eleven guineas, with jewels, plate, and other things of value, to a large amount. Having committed this robbery, they returned Mr. Sheldon two guineas, and apologized for their conduct.

This being done, they hastened to the Black Horse, in the Broadway, Westminster, where they concerted the robbery of Mr. Lawrence, of Edgware, near Stanmore, in Middlesex, for which place they set out on the 4th of February, and arrived at a public house in that village about five o'clock in the evening. From this place they went to Mr. Lawrence's house, where they arrived about seven o'clock, just as he had discharged some people who had worked for him.

Having left their horses at the outer gate, one of the robbers, going forwards, found a boy who had just returned from folding his sheep: the rest of the gang following, a pistol was presented, and instant destruction threatened if he made any noise. They then took off his garters, tied his hands therewith, and told him to direct them to the door, and, when they knocked, to answer, and bid the servants open it, in which case they would not hurt him: but, when the boy came to the door, he was so terrified that he could not speak; on which one of the gang knocked, and a man-servant, imagining it was one of the neighbours, opened the door, whereupon they all rushed in, armed with pistols.

Having seized Mr. Lawrence and his servant, they threw a cloth over their faces, and, taking the boy into another room, demanded what fire-arms were in the house; to which he replied, only an old gun, which they broke in pieces. They then bound Mr. Lawrence and his man, and made them sit by the boy; and Turpin, searching the gentleman, took from him a guinea, a Portugal piece, and some silver; but, not being satisfied with this booty, they forced him to con-duct them up stairs, where they broke open a closet, and stole some money and plate: but that not being sufficient to satisfy them, they threatened to murder Mr. Lawrence, each of them destining him to a different death, as the sav-ageness of his own nature prompted him. At length one of them took a kettle of water from the fire, and threw it over him; but it providentially happened not to be hot enough to scald him.

In the interim, the maidservant who was churning but-ter in the dairy, hearing a noise in the house, apprehended some mischief; on which she blew out her candle to screen herself; but being found in the course of their search, one of the miscreants compelled her to go up stairs, where he gratified his brutal passion by force. They then robbed the house of all the valuable effects they could find, locked the family in the parlour, threw the key into the garden, and took their ill-gotten plunder to London.

The particulars of this atrocious robbery being represented to the king, a proclamation was issued for the apprehension of the offenders, promising a pardon to any one of them who would impeach his accomplices; and a reward of fifty pounds was offered, to be paid on conviction. This, however, had no effect; the robbers continued their depredations as before; and, flushed with the success they had met with, seemed to bid defiance to the laws.

On the 7th of February, six of them assembled at the White Beat Inn, in Drury-lane, where they agreed to rob the house of Mr. Francis, a farmer near Marylebone. Arriving at the place, they found a servant in the cow-house, whom threatening to murder if he was not perfectly silent, they bound fast. This being done, they led him into the stable, where, finding another of the servants, they bound him in the same manner.

In the interim Mr. Francis happening to come home, they presented their pistols to his breast, and threatened instant destruction to him if he made the least noise opposition.

Having bound the master in the stable with his servants, they rushed into the house, tied Mrs. Francis, her daughter, and the maid-servant, and beat them in a most cruel manner. One of the thieves stood as a sentry while the rest rifled the house, in which they found a silver tankard, a medal of Charles I, a gold watch, several gold rings, a considerable sum of money, and a variety of valuable linen and other effects, which they conveyed to London.

Hereupon a reward of one hundred pounds was offered for the apprehension of the offenders; in consequence of which two of them were taken into custody, tried, convicted on the evidence of an accomplice, and hanged in chains: and the whole gang being dispersed, Turpin went into the country to renew his depredations on the public.

On a journey towards Cambridge, he met a man genteelly dressed, and well mounted; and, expecting a good
booty, he presented a pistol to the supposed gentleman, and
demanded his money. The party thus stopped happened to
be one King, a famous highwayman, who knew Turpin;
and, when the latter threatened instant destruction if he
did not deliver his money, King burst into a fit of laughter,
and said, 'What, dog cat dog?—Come, come, brother Turpin, if you don't know me I know you, and shall be glad of
your company.'

These brethren in iniquity soon struck the bargain, and,
immediately entering on business, committed a number of
robberies; till at length they were so well known that no
public house would receive them as guests. Thus situated,
they fixed on a spot between the King's Oak and the Loughton road, on Epping Forest, where they made a cave which
was large enough to receive them and their horses.

This cave was enclosed within a sort of thicket of
bushes and brambles, through which they could look and
see passengers on the road, while themselves remained
unobserved.

From this station they used to issue, and robbed such
a number of persons, that at length the very pedlars who
travelled the road carried fire-arms for their defence: and,
while they were in this retreat, Turpin's wife used to supply them with necessaries, and frequently remained in the
cave during the night.

Having taken a ride as far as Bungay, in Suffolk, they
observed two young countrywomen receive fourteen pounds
for corn, on which Turpin resolved to rob them of the money.
King objected, saying it was a pity to rob such pretty girls:
but Turpin was obstinate, and obtained the booty.

Upon their return home, on the following day, they
stopped a Mr. Bradle, of London, who was riding in his
chariot with his children. The gentleman, seeing only one

robber, was preparing to make resistance, when King called to Turpin to hold the horses. They took from the gentleman his watch, money, and an old mourning-ring; but returned the latter, as he declared that its intrinsic value was trifing; yet he was very unwilling to part with it.

Finding that they readily parted with the ring, he asked them what he must give for the watch: on which King said to Turpin, 'What say you, Jack? Here seems to be a good honest fellow; shall we let him have the watch?' Turpin replied, 'Do as you please'; on which King said to the gentleman, 'You must pay six guineas for it: we never sell for more, though the watch should be worth six-and-thirty.' The gentleman promised that the money should be left at the Dial, in Birchin Lane.

On the 4th of May, 1737, Turpin was guilty of murder, which arose from the following circumstance:—A reward of a hundred pounds having been offered for apprehending him, one Thomas Morris, a servant of Mr. Thompson, one of the keepers of Epping Forest, accompanied by a higgler, set off in order to apprehend him. Turpin seeing them approach near his dwelling, Mr. Thompson's man having a gun, he mistook them for poachers; on which he said there were no hares near that thicket. 'No,' said Morris; 'but I have found a Turpin'; and, presenting his gun, required him to surrender.

Hereupon Turpin spoke to him as in a friendly manner, and gradually retreated at the same time, till, having seized his own gun, he shot him dead on the spot, and the higgler ran off with the utmost precipitation.

This murder being represented to the secretary of state, the following proclamation was issued by government, which we give a place to, from its describing the person of this notorious depredator:

'It having been represented to the king that Richard Turpin did, on Wednesday, the 4th of May last, barbarously

murder Thomas Morris, servant to Henry Thompson, one
of the keepers of Epping Forest, and commit other notorious felonies and robberies near London, his majesty is
pleased to promise his most gracious pardon to any of his
accomplices, and a reward of two hundred pounds to any
person or persons, that shall discover him, so that he may
be apprehended and convicted. Turpin was born at Thackstead, in Essex, is about thirty, by trade a butcher, about five
feet nine inches high, very much marked with the small-
pox, his cheek-bones broad, his face thinner towards the
bottom, his visage short, pretty upright, and broad about
the shoulders.'

Turpin, to avoid the proclamation, went farther into the
country in search of his old companion, King; and in the
mean time sent a letter to his wife, to meet him at a public house at Hertford. The woman attended according to
this direction; and her husband coming into the house soon
after she arrived, a butcher to whom he owed five pounds,
happened to see him; on which he said, 'Come, Dick, I know
you have money now; and, if you will pay me, it will be of
great service.'

Turpin told him that his wife was in the next room; that
she had money, and that he should be paid immediately;
but, while the butcher was hinting to some of his acquaintance that the person present was Turpin, and that they
might take him into custody after he had received his debt,
the highwayman made his escape through a window, and
rode off with great expedition.

Turpin having found King, and a man named Potter,
who had lately connected himself with them, they set off
towards London in the dusk of the evening; but, when they
came near the Green Man, on Epping Forest, they overtook
a Mr. Major, who riding on a very fine horse, and Turpin's
beast being jaded he obliged the rider to dismount, and
exchange horses.

The robbers now pursued their journey towards London; and Mr. Major going to the Green Man, gave an account of the affair; on which it was conjectured that Turpin had been the robber, and that the horse which he exchanged must have been stolen.

It was on a Saturday evening that this robbery was committed; but, Mr. Major being advised to print handbills immediately, notice was given to the landlord of the Green Man, that such a horse as Major had lost, had been left at the Red Lion, in Whitechapel. The landlord going thither, determined to wait till some person came for it; and, at about eleven at night, King's brother came to pay for the horse, and take him away: on which he was immediately seized, and conducted into the house.

Being asked what right he had to the horse, he said he had bought it; but the landlord, examining a whip which he had in his hand, found a button at the end of the handle half broken off, and the name of Major on the remaining half. Hereupon he was given into the custody of a constable; but, as it was not supposed that he was the actual robber, he was told, that he should have his liberty, if he would discover his employer.

Hereupon he said, that a stout man, in a white duffel coat, was waiting for the horse in Red Lion-street; on which the company going thither, saw King, who drew a pistol, attempted to fire it, but it flashed in the pan; he then endeavoured to draw out another pistol, but he could not, as it got entangled his pocket.

At this time Turpin was watching at a small distance, and, riding towards the spot, King cried out, 'Shoot him, or we are taken'; on which Turpin fired, and shot his companion, who called out, 'Dick, you have killed me!' which the other hearing, rode off at full speed.

King lived a week after this affair, and gave information that Turpin might be found at a house near Hackney

Marsh; and, on inquiry, it was discovered that Turpin had been there on the night that he rode off, lamenting that he had killed King, who was his most faithful associate.

For a considerable time did Turpin skulk about the forest, having been deprived of his retreat in the cave since he shot the servant of Mr. Thompson. On the examination of this cave there were found two shirts, two pair of stockings, a piece of ham, and part of a bottle of wine.

Some vain attempts were made to take this notorious offender into custody; and, among the rest, the huntsman of a gentleman in the neighbourhood went in search of him with bloodhounds. Turpin perceiving them, and recollecting that King Charles II evaded his pursuers under covert of the friendly branches of the oak, mounted one of those trees, under which the hounds passed, to his inexpressible terror, so that he determined to make a retreat into Yorkshire.

Going first to Long Sutton, in Lincolnshire, he stole some horses, for which he was taken into custody, but escaped from the constable as he was conducting him before a magistrate, and hastened to Welton, in Yorkshire, where he went by the name of John Palmer, and assumed the character of a gentleman.

He now frequently went into Lincolnshire, where he stole horses, which he brought into Yorkshire, and either sold or exchanged them.

He often accompanied the neighbouring gentlemen on their parties of hunting and shooting; and one evening, on a return from an expedition of the latter kind, he wantonly shot a cock belonging to his landlord. On this Mr. Hall, a neighbour, said, 'You have done wrong in shooting your landlord's cock'; to which Turpin replied, that, if he would stay while he loaded his gun, he would shoot him also.

Irritated by this insult, Mr. Hall informed the landlord of what had passed; and, application being made to some magistrates, a warrant was granted for the apprehension of the offender, who being taken into custody, and carried before a bench of justices, then assembled at the quarter-sessions, at Beverley, they demanded security for his good behaviour, which being unable or unwilling to give, he was committed to Bridewell.

On inquiry, it appeared that he made frequent journeys into Lincolnshire, on his return always abounding in money, and that he was likewise in possession of several horses, so that it was conjectured that he was a horse-stealer and a highwayman.

On this the magistrates went to him on the following day, and demanded who he was, where he had lived, and what was his employment? He replied, in substance, 'That about two years ago he had lived at Long Sutton, in Lincolnshire, and was by trade a butcher; but that, having contracted several debts for sheep that proved rotten, he was obliged to abscond, and come to live in Yorkshire.'

The magistrates, not being satisfied with this tale, commissioned the clerk of the peace to write into Lincolnshire, to make the necessary inquiries respecting the supposed John Palmer. The letter was carried by a special messenger, who brought an answer from a magistrate in the neighbourhood, importing that John Palmer was well known, though he had never carried on trade there: that he had been accused of sheep-stealing, for which he had been in custody, but had made his escape from the peace-officers: and that there were several informations lodged against him for horse-stealing.

Hereupon the magistrates thought it prudent to remove him to York Castle, where he had not been more than a month when two persons from Lincolnshire came and claimed a mare and foal, and likewise a horse, which he had stolen in that county.

After he had been about four months in prison, he wrote the following letter to his brother in Essex:

'York, Feb. 6, 1739.

'Dear Brother,

'I am sorry to acquaint you that I am now under confinement in York Castle for horse-stealing. If I could procure an evidence from London to give me a character, that would go a great way towards my being acquitted. I had not been long in this country before my being apprehended, so that it would pass off the readier. For Heaven's sake, dear brother, do not neglect me; you will know what I mean when I say,

'I am yours,

'JOHN PALMER.'

This letter, being returned, unopened, to the post-office in Essex, because the brother would not pay the postage of it, was accidentally seen by Mr. Smith, a schoolmaster, who, having taught Turpin to write, immediately knew his hand, on which he carried the letter to a magistrate, who broke it open, and it was thus discovered that the supposed John Palmer was the real Richard Turpin.

Hereupon the magistrates of Essex dispatched Mr. Smith to York, who immediately selected him from all the other prisoners in the Castle. This Mr. Smith, and another gentleman, afterwards proved his identity on his trial.

On the rumour that the noted Turpin was a prisoner in York Castle, persons flocked from all parts of the country to take a view of him, and debates ran high whether he was the real person or not. Among others who visited him was a young fellow who pretended to know the famous Turpin, and, having regarded him a considerable time with looks of great attention, he told the keeper he would bet him half a guinea that he was not Turpin; on which the prisoner, whispering to the keeper, said 'Lay him the wager, and I'll go your halves.'

When this notorious malefactor was brought to trial, he was convicted on two indictments, and received sentence of death.

After conviction he wrote to his father, imploring him to intercede with a gentleman and lady of rank, to make interest that his sentence might be remitted, and that he might be transported. The father did what was in his power; but the notoriety of his character was such, that no persons would exert themselves in his favour.

This man lived in the most gay and thoughtless manner after conviction, regardless of all considerations of futurity, and affecting to make a jest of the dreadful fate that awaited him.

Not many days before his execution he purchased a new fustian frock and a pair of pumps, in order to wear them at the time of his death; and on the day before he hired five poor men, at ten shillings each, to follow the cart as mourners: he gave hatbands and gloves to several other persons; and also left a ring, and some other articles, to a married woman in Lincolnshire, with whom he had been acquainted.

On the morning of his death he was put into a cart, and being followed by his mourners, as above mentioned, he was drawn to the place of execution, in his way to which he bowed to the spectators with an air of the most astonishing indifference and intrepidity.

When he came to the fatal tree he ascended the ladder; and, on his right leg trembling, he stamped it down with an air of assumed courage, as if he was ashamed to be observed to discover any signs of fear. Having conversed with the executioner about half an hour, he threw himself off the ladder, and expired in a few minutes. Turpin suffered at York, April 10, 1739.

The spectators of the execution seemed to be much affected at the fate of this man, who was distinguished by the comeliness of his appearance. The corpse was brought to the Blue Boar, in Castle Gate, York, where it remained till the next morning, when it was interred in the churchyard of St. George's parish, with an inscription on the coffin, bearing the initials of his name, and his age. The grave was made remarkably deep, and the people who acted as mourners took such measures as they thought would secure the body: yet, about three o'clock on the following morning, some persons were observed in the churchyard, who carried it off; and the populace, having an intimation whither it was convoyed, found it in a garden belonging to one of the surgeons of the city.

Hereupon they took the body, laid it on a board, and having carried it through the streets in a kind of triumphal manner, and then filled the coffin with unslacked lime, buried it in the grave where it had been before deposited.—It is difficult to conceive the reason of all this concern and sympathy; for surely a more heartless and depraved villain than Turpin never existed. Independently of the brutal murders perpetrated by him, it was impossible to overlook the mean rascality of his robbing the two country girls (which even his fellow-thief objected to), or the barbarity of placing an old woman on the fire, because she refused directing his gang to the little board which had probably been laid by as the support of her declining years.

Lympus stopping the Post-Boy on the Highway.

LYMPUS STOPPING THE POST-BOY ON THE HIGHWAY.

THOMAS LYMPUS

Executed for robbing the mail.

———

FROM serving some years as a messenger to the General Post-office, this man formed the dangerous resolution of robbing the mails. At this time the vast property in circulation by means of the post was not, as at present, secured from being plundered by any lurking thief upon the road. Since the adoption of Mr. Palmer's plan of regulations it is nearly an impossibility to rob the mail.

On the 21st of February, 1738, this public plunderer began his depredations by stopping the post-boy bringing the Bath and Bristol mails, about seven o'clock in the evening, at the end of Sunning Lane, two miles north of Reading, in Berkshire.

For the apprehension of the robber the postmaster-general offered a reward of two hundred pounds, over and above the sum allowed by act of parliament for apprehending highwaymen; or, if any accomplice in the said robbery should make a discovery of the person who committed the fact, such accomplice should be entitled to the reward of two hundred pounds, and also receive his majesty's most gracious pardon. The advertisement described the robber to be a middle-sized man, wearing a great riding-coat, with a white velvet or plush cape.

No sooner had Lympus rifled the bags of their most valuable contents than he determined upon attempting to make his escape to France. For this purpose he hastened to the nearest sea-port, and actually landed there, but not before the officers of justice got information of his flight. They pursued him to France, and demanded him to be delivered up to them as a national robber; but, flying to the sanctuary of the church, and declaring himself a Roman Catholic, he received protection, and for a while evaded the offended laws of his own country.

There is often to be found in such as fly for a heinous crime, after some time passed abroad in safety, a desire to return, which in vain they struggle to suppress. Instances of this nature present themselves, where, after many years have expired since the commission of their crime, men have returned, and either surrendered, or placed themselves so as to favour their apprehension; which would really seem as though their minds would not permit them any peace in this world. So it was, in some measure, with the malefactor now recorded, who could not rest with his booty in France, but returned in a short time for farther plunder, and immediately committed another mail robbery, for which he was apprehended and brought to trial.

It appeared, by the evidence of the post-boy, that he was stopped between the towns of Crewkherne and Sherborne by the prisoner, on horseback, who compelled him to dismount, then bound him hand and foot, and rode off with the mail, containing twenty-four bags, from as many post-towns.

Having taken out the bank-notes, he again contemplated an escape to France, and for that purpose once more embarked; but the winds were no longer propitious to his hopes, for the vessel was driven back, and obliged to put into Dart mouth. Here he offered one of the stolen notes in payment, which being endorsed by one Follet, of Topsham, as described in the account of the robbery, he was suspected of being the robber. Apprehending himself to be in danger, he immediately decamped, and was making the best of his way towards Kingsbridge, but was pursued by seven men, who took him on a warrant being granted for that purpose. He was convicted of this robbery, and, after much equivocation, confessed, since sentence of death, having robbed the Bristol mail a little more than a year before, and impeached one Patrick, a dealer in hops, as his accomplice.

He was executed on the top of Dunkit Hill, within a mile of Wells, in Somersetshire, September 21, 1739, and affected to die professing the religion he had adopted in France.

The security now given to our mail-coaches rendering an open attempt on them impracticable, unless sustained by a whole band of robbers, recourse has been frequently had to artifice in order to get possession of the mail. One of these tricks was thus played off with success.

It was customary to deposit the mail-bags at a private house in Castle Street, Reading, near to which the horses belonging to the mail were changed. The guard announced the approach of the mail to the inn by sounding his horn, and, whilst the horses were putting to, he went to the receiving-house to exchange his bags. A horn was sounded in the street, quite late in the evening of the 26th of January, 1806, and soon after a man called for the downward bag, which was delivered to him, as usual, out of a window, and in return for which he gave a bag, which was afterwards found to contain shavings. The robbery was discovered soon after by the arrival of the mail, but not till the villains had effected their escape.

Bradford, going to murder his Guest, finds the Deed already accomplished.

BRADFORD, GOING TO MURDER HIS GUEST, FINDS THE DEED
ALREADY ACCOMPLISHED.

JONATHAN BRADFORD

Executed for a supposed murder.

JONATHAN BRADFORD kept an inn at the city of Oxford.
A gentleman, (Mr. Hayes), attended by a man-servant, put
up one evening at Bradford's house; and in the night, the
former being found murdered in his bed, the landlord was
apprehended on suspicion of having committed the barbarous and in-hospitable crime.

The evidence given against him was to the following
effect:—Two gentlemen who had supped with Mr. Hayes,
and who retired at the same time to their respective

chambers, being alarmed in the night with a noise in his room, and soon hearing groans, as of a wounded man, got up in order to discover the cause, and found their landlord, with a dark lantern, and a knife in his hand, standing, in a state of astonishment and horror, over his dying guest, who almost instantly, expired.

On this evidence, apparently conclusive, the jury convicted Bradford, and he was executed; but the fate of this man may serve as an additional lesson to jurymen to be extremely guarded in receiving circumstantial evidence. On a trial at Nisi Prius, and between personal right and wrong, the jury are often directed by the judge to take into consideration presumptive evidence where positive proof is wanting; but, in criminal charges, it seldom should, unsupported by some oral testimony, or ocular demonstration, be sufficient to find a verdict against the accused.

The facts attending the above dreadful tragedy were not fully brought to light until the death-bed confession of the real murderer, a time when we must all endeavour to make our peace with God.

Mr. Hayes was a man of considerable property, and greatly respected. He had about him, when his sad destiny led him under the roof of Bradford, a considerable sum of money; and the landlord, knowing this, determined to murder and rob him. For this horrid purpose, he proceeded with a dark lantern and a carving-knife, intending to cut the throat of his guest while yet sleeping; but what must have been his astonishment and confusion to find his intended victim already murdered, and weltering in his blood?

The wicked and unworthy servant had also determined on the murder of his master; and had just committed the bloody deed, and secured his treasure, a moment before the landlord entered for the same purpose!!!

Mrs. Branch and her Daughter cruelly beating Jane Buttersworth.

MRS. BRANCH AND HER DAUGHTER CRUELLY BEATING JANE BUTTERSWORTH.

ELIZABETH and MARY BRANCH

Executed for murder.

———

THESE cruel women were born at Philips-Norton, in Somersetshire. The mother was distinguished from her childhood by the barbarity of her disposition, which increased with her years, and discovered itself on various occasions, particularly in fomenting divisions among her father's servants, to render whom unhappy appeared to be one of the greatest pleasures of her life.

Her parents, observing with regret this ferocity of temper, told her that she would never get a husband unless she changed her conduct. This seemed for a while to have some influence on her, which gave great satisfaction to her parents; but it will appear from the following narrative that this influence was not lasting.

Being addressed by a neighboring farmer, named Branch, a marriage took place; but the husband soon found what an unfortunate choice he had made; for his wife no sooner came into possession of her matrimonial power than she began to exercise her tyranny on her servants, whom she treated with undeserved and unaccountable cruelty, frequently denying them the common necessaries of life, and sometimes turning them out of doors at night, in the midst of winter; but their wages in these cases were sent them by Mr. Branch, who was as remarkable for his humanity and justice as his wife was for the opposite qualities. Mary Branch, the daughter, was an exact resemblance of her mother in every part of her diabolical temper.

Mr. Branch dying, and leaving an estate of about three hundred pounds a year, he was no sooner buried than all the servants quitted the family, determined not to live with so tyrannical a mistress; and her character became so notorious that she could obtain no servants but poor creatures who were put out by the parish, or casual vagrants who strolled the country.

It is needless to mention the particulars of the cruelties of this inhuman mother and daughter to such servants as they could procure, at whom they used to throw plates, knives, and forks, on any offence, real or supposed; we shall therefore proceed to an account of their trial and execution for the murder of Jane Buttersworth, a poor girl who had been placed with them by the parish officers.

At the assizes held at Taunton, in Somersetshire, in March, 1740, Elizabeth Branch, and Mary, her daughter, were indicted for the wilful murder of Jane Buttersworth;

the principal evidence against them being in substance as follows:

Ann Somers, the dairy-maid, deposed that the deceased, having been sent for some yeast, and staying longer than was necessary, excused herself to her old mistress, on her return, by telling a lie; on which the daughter struck her violently on the head with her fist, and pinched her ears. Then both of them threw her on the ground, and the daughter kneeled on her neck, while the mother whipped her with twigs till the blood ran on the ground; and the daughter, taking off one of the girl's shoes, beat her with it in a cruel manner. The deceased cried for mercy, and, after some struggles, ran into the parlour, whither they followed her, and beat her with broomsticks till she fell down senseless; after which the daughter threw a pail of water on her, and used her with other circumstances of cruelty too gross to mention.

Somers now went out to milk the cows, and on her return, at the expiration of half an hour, found her mistress sitting by the fire, *and* the girl lying dead on the floor; but she observed that a clean can had been put on her head since she went out, and that the blood had run through it.

Saying she believed the girl was dead, the old mistress gave her abusive language; and the deceased being put to bed, Somers was ordered to lie with her; which she was obliged to comply with, in the fear of being treated in a manner equally cruel. Somers was not suffered to go out on the following day; and at night the body was privately buried.

This transaction, added to the character of the mistress, having raised a suspicion in the neighborhood, a warrant was issued by the coroner to take up the body; and, an inquest being made into the cause of the girl's death, Mr. Salmon, a surgeon, declared that she had received several wounds, almost any one of which would have proved mortal.

The defence made by the prisoners on their trial was, that the prosecution was malicious; for that the deceased had been subject to fits, in one of which she fell down, and received the bruises which occasioned her death; but, bringing no proofs in support of this allegation, the jury found them guilty, and they were sentenced to die.

After conviction they entertained great hopes of pardon, and presented a petition to the judge; but all the favour they could obtain was a respite for five weeks, in consideration that Mrs. Branch might have some temporal affairs to settle.

The mother appeared for some one little concerned under misfortunes but the daughter saw her unhappy fate, and begged the prayers of every one whom she saw.

A sermon was preached to them on the night before their execution, which seemed to have a great effect on the mother, who now began seriously to reflect on her approaching exit; and both of them made due preparation for death.

As the country people were violently enraged against them, they were conducted to Ivelchester (the place of execution) between three and four in the morning of May 3, 1710, attended only by the gaoler and about six people, lest they should have been torn in pieces.

When they came to the spot, it found that the gibbet had been cut down; on which a carpenter was sent for, who immediately put up another; and they were executed before six o'clock, to the disappointment of thousands of people who had come from all parts of the country to witness the death of two such unworthy wretches.

Just before they were turned off Mrs. Branch made the following speech:—

'Good people,

'You who are masters and mistresses of families, to you I speak in a more particular manner. Let me advise you never to harbour cruel, base, and mean thoughts of your servants, as that they are your slaves and drudges, and that any sort of usage, be it ever so bad, is good enough for them. These, and such like, were the thoughts that made me use my servants as slaves, vagabonds, and thieves; it was these that made me spurn at and despise them, and led me *on* from one degree of cruelty to another.

'Keep your passions within due bounds; let them not get the mastery over you, lest they bring you to this ignoble end. I am fully punished for all my severities; and it is true I did strike my maid, but not with a design to kill her, and so far I think the sentence about to be executed upon me is unjust; but the Lord forgive my prosecutors, and all those who have maliciously and falsely sworn against me.

'Another caution I would give to you who are parents; namely, to suppress in your children the first appearance of cruelty and barbarity. Nothing grieves me so much, under this shock, as that I have, by my example, and by my commands, made my daughter guilty with me of the same follies, cruelties, and barbarities, and thereby have involved her in the same punishment with myself.

'I declare I had no design of killing the deceased, as the Lord is my judge, and before whom I must shortly appear. I beg of you to pray for me unto God that my sins may be forgiven me, and that I may be received to mercy.'

After this the daughter spoke these few words:—

'Good people, pity my unhappy case, who, while young, was trained up in the paths of cruelty and barbarity; and let all present take warning by my unhappy end, so as to avoid the like crimes. You see I am cut off in the prime of life, in the midst of my days.—Good people, pray for me!'

MARTHA TRACY ROBBING MR. HUMPHREYS NEAR NORTHUMBERLAND HOUSE,
IN THE STRAND.

MARTHA TRACY

Executed for a street robbery.

———

THIS woman was a native of Bristol, and descended from poor parents, who educated her in the best manner in their power. Getting a place in the service of a merchant when she was sixteen years of age, she lived with him three years, and then came to London.

Having procured a place in a house where lodgings were let to single gentlemen, and being a girl of an elegant appearance, and fond of dress, she was liable to a variety of temptations.

Her vanity being even more than equal to her beauty, she at length conceived that she had made a conquest of one of the gentlemen-lodgers, and was foolish enough to think he would marry her.

With a view of keeping alive the passion she thought she had inspired, she sought every pretence of going into his chamber; and he, having some designs against her virtue, purchased her some new clothes, in which she went to church on the Following Sunday, where she was observed by her mistress.

On their return from church, the mistress strictly inquired how she came to be possessed of such fine clothes; and, having learnt the real state of the case, she was discharged from her service on the Monday morning.

As she still thought the gentleman intended marriage, she wrote to him, desiring he would meet her at a public house; and, on his attending, she wept incessantly, and complained of the treatment she had met with from her mistress, which she attributed to the presents she had received from him.

The seducer advised her to calm her spirits, and go into lodgings, which he would immediately provide for her, and where he could securely visit her till the marriage should take place.

Deluded by this artifice, she went that day to lodge at a house in the Strand, which he said was kept by a lady who was related to him. In this place he visited her on the following, and several successive days; attending her to public places, and making her presents of elegant clothes, which effectually flattered her vanity, and lulled asleep the small remains of her virtue.

It is needless to say that her ruin followed. After a connexion of a few months, she found him less frequent in his visits; and, informing him she was with child, demanded that he would make good his promise of marriage: on which he declared that he had never intended to marry her, and that he would not maintain her any longer; and hinted that she should seek another lodging.

On the following day the mistress of the house told her she must not remain there any longer, unless she would pay for her lodgings in advance, which being unable to do or, perhaps, unwilling to remain in a house where she had been an unworthily treated, she packed up her effects, and removed to another.

When she was brought to bed, the father took away the infant and left the wretched mother in a very distressed situation. Having subsisted for some time by pawning her clothes, she was at length on reduced as to listen to the advice of a woman of the town, who persuaded her to procure a subsistence by the casual wages of prostitution.

Having embarked in this horrid course of life, she soon became a common street-walker, and experienced all those calamities incident to so deplorable a situation. Being sometimes tempted to pick pockets for a subsistence, she became an occasional visitor at Bridewell, where her mind grew only the corrupt by the conversation of the abandoned wretches confined in that place.

We now come to speak of the fact, the commission of which forfeited her life to the violated laws of her country.

At the sessions held at the old Bailey, in the month of January, 1745, she was indicted for robbing William Humphreys of a guinea on the king's highway.

The fact was, that being passing, at midnight, near Northumberland House, in the Strand, she accosted Mr. Humphreys, who declining to hold any correspondence with her, two fellows with whom she was connected came up, and one of them knocking him down, they both ran away; when she robbed him of a guinea, which she concealed in her mouth; but Mr. Humphreys seizing her, and two persons coming up, she was conducted to the watch-house, where the guinea was found in her mouth, as above mentioned, by the constable of the night.

At her trial it was proved that she had called the men, one of whom knocked down the prosecutor; so that there could be no doubt of her being an accomplice with them; whereupon the jury brought her in guilty.

After conviction she appeared to have a proper idea of her former guilt, and the horrors of her present situation. In fact she was a sincere penitent, and lamented that pride of heart which had first seduced her to destruction.

Martha Tracy was hanged at Tyburn, on the 16th of February, 1745, behaving with the greatest decency and propriety to the last moment of her life.

The fate of this woman affords a striking lesson to girls against them taking pride in those personal charms which, the more brilliant they are, will be only the more likely to lead them to destruction. The idea she had formed of making a conquest of a man in a rank of life superior to her own served only to assist towards her ruin; but we cannot help thinking that he who could be base enough to seduce her under solemn promises of marriage was still more guilty than herself, and in some degree an accessory to all the crimes she afterwards committed.

It seems strangely unnatural that the father should take away the child, and leave the mother to perish, or to subsist only in a most infamous manner, for which she had been qualified by the gratification of his passions.

In the gay hours of festivity men may triumph in the advantages they have gained over women in their unguarded moments; but surely Reflection must come, with all her attendant train of horrors. Conscience will assert her rights; and the misery the wicked seducer suffers in this life he ought to consider only as a prelude to the more aggravated torments he has to expect in the next.

If any one of the readers of this narrative has been guilty of the enormous crime we are now reprobating, it will become him to think seriously of the great work of reformation; and to repent, in the most unfeigned manner, while Providence yet permits him the opportunity of repentance. It ought to be remembered, by offenders of every class, that the God of mercy is also a God of justice.

SIMMS AND OTHER YOUNG THIEVES REGALING AT A BRICK-KILN NEAR
TOTTENHAM COURT ROAD.

HENRY SIMMS

Executed for highway robbery.

———

HENRY SIMMS was born in the parish of St. Martin's-in-
the-Fields, London, and, losing his father while very young,
his grandmother, who was a Dissenter, sent him first to a
school kept by a clergyman of her own persuasion; but, as
he frequently ran away, she placed him at an academy in
St. James's parish, where he became a proficient in writing and arithmetic, and was likewise a tolerable Latin and
French scholar.

Before the boy had completed his tenth year he gave a specimen of his dishonest disposition. His grandmother taking him with her on a visit to a tradesman's house, he stole twenty shillings from the till in the shop; which being observed by the maid-servant, she informed her master; and, the money being found on the youth, he was severely punished.

He now began to lie from home on nights, and associated with the vilest of company in the purlieus of St. Giles's. His companions advising him to rob his grandmother, he stole seventeen pounds from her, and, taking his best apparel, repaired to St. Giles's, where his new acquaintances made him drunk, put him to bed, and then robbed him of his money and clothes. On his waking he covered himself with some rags he found in the room and, after strolling through the streets in search of the villains, went into an ale-house, the landlord of which, hearing his tale, interceded with his grandmother to take him again under her protection. To this, after some hesitation, she consented; and, buying a chain with a padlock, she had him fastened, during the day-time, to the kitchen grate, and at night he slept with a man who was directed to take care that he did not escape.

After a month of confinement he had his liberty granted him and new clothes purchased, with which he immediately went among some young thieves who were tossing up for money, in St Giles's. On the approach of night they took him to a brick-kiln near Tottenham Court Road, where they broiled some steaks, and supped in concert; and were soon joined by some women, who brought some geneva, with which the whole company regaled themselves.

Simms, falling asleep, was robbed of his clothes; and when the brickmakers came to work in the morning they found him in his shirt only. While they were conducting him towards town he was met by his grandmother's servant, who was in search of him, and conveyed him to her house. Notwithstanding his former behaviour the old lady received him kindly, and placed him with a breeches-maker. He having corrected him for his ill behaviour, he ran away, and taking his best clothes from his grandmother's house, in her absence, sold them to a Jew, and spent the money in extravagance.

The old gentlewoman now went to live at the house of Lady Stanhope, whither the graceless boy followed her, and being refused admittance he broke several of the windows. This in some measure compelled his grandmother to admit him; but that very night he robbed the house of as many things as produced him nine pounds, which he carried to a barn in Marylebone Fields, and spent among his dissolute companions. For this offence he was apprehended, and, after some hesitation, confessed where he had sold the effects. From this time his grandmother gave him up as incorrigible. Soon afterwards he was apprehended as a pickpocket, but he was discharged for want of evidence.

Simms now associated with the worst of company; but after a narrow escape on a charge of being concerned in sending a threatening letter to extort money, and two of his companions being transported for other offences, he seemed deterred from continuing his evil courses; and thereupon wrote to his grandmother, entreating her further protection. Still anxious to save him from destruction, she prevailed on a friend to take him into his house, where for some time he behaved regularly; but, getting among his old associates, they robbed a gentleman of his watch and money, and threw him into a ditch in Marylebone Fields; when only some persons accidentally coming up prevented his destruction.

Two more of Simms' companions being now transported, he hired himself to an innkeeper as a driver of a post-chaise; and after that lived as postilion to a nobleman, but was soon discharged on account of his irregular conduct. Having received some wages, he went again among the thieves, who dignified him with the title of "Gentleman Harry," on account of his presumed skill, and the gentility of his appearance. Simms now became intimately acquainted with a woman who lived with one of his accomplices, in revenge for which the fellow procured both him and the woman to be taken into custody on a charge of felony, and they were committed to Newgate; but, the Court paying no regard to the credibility of the witnesses, the prisoners were acquitted.

Soon after his discharge Simms robbed a gentleman of his watch and seventeen pounds on Blackheath, and likewise robbed a lady of a considerable sum near the same spot. Being followed to Lewisham, he was obliged to quit his horse, when he presented two pistols to his pursuers, by which he so intimidated them as to effect his escape, though with the loss of his horse.

Repairing to London he bought another horse, and travelling into Northamptonshire, and putting up at an inn at Towcester, learned that a military gentleman had hired a chaise for London; on which he followed the chaise the next morning, and kept up with it for several miles. At length the gentleman, observing him, said: "Don't ride so hard, Sir, you'll soon ride away your whole estate"; to which Simms replied: "Indeed I shall not, for it lies in several counties"; and, instantly quitting his horse, he robbed the gentleman of one hundred and two guineas.

He now hastened to London, and, having dissipated his ill-acquired money at a gaming-table, rode out towards Hounslow, and meeting the postilion who had driven the above-mentioned gentleman in Northamptonshire gave him five shillings, begging he would take no notice of having seen him. A reward being at length offered for apprehending Simms, he entered on board a privateer; but being soon weary of a seafaring life he deserted, and enlisted for a soldier. While in this station he knocked out the eye of a woman at a house of ill-fame, for which he was apprehended and lodged in New Prison. Soon after this, Justice de Veil admitted him an evidence against some felons, his accomplices, who were transported, and Simms regained his liberty.

Being apprehended for robbing a baker's shop, he was convicted, and being sentenced to be transported was, accordingly, shipped on board one of the transport vessels. As this sailed round to the Isle of Wight he formed a plan for seizing the captain, and effecting an escape; but as a strict watch was kept on him it was not possible for him to carry this plan into execution. The ship arriving at Maryland, Simms was sold, for twelve guineas, but he found an early opportunity of deserting from the purchaser. Having learned that his master's horse was left tied to a gate at some distance from the dwelling-house, he privately decamped in the night, and rode thirty miles in four hours, through extremely bad roads: so powerfully was he impelled by his fears.

He now found himself by the seaside, and, turning the horse loose, he hailed a vessel just under sail, from which a boat was sent to bring him on board. As hands were very scarce, the captain offered him six guineas, which were readily accepted, to work his passage to England. There being at this time a war between England and France, the ship was taken by a French privateer, but soon afterwards ransomed, and Simms entered on board a man of war, where his diligence promoted him to the rank of a midshipman; but the ship had no sooner arrived at Plymouth than he quitted his duty, and, travelling to Bristol, spent the little money he possessed in the most dissipated manner.

His next step was to enter himself on board a coasting vessel at Bristol; but he had not been long at sea, before, on a dispute with the captain, he threatened to throw him overboard, and would have carried his threat into execution if the other seamen had not prevented him. Simms asked for his wages when the ship returned to port; but the captain threatening imprisonment for his ill behaviour at sea, he decamped with only eight shillings in his possession.

Fertile of contrivances, he borrowed a saddle and bridle, and, having stolen a horse in a field near the city, he went once more on the highway, and, taking the road to London, robbed the passengers in the Bristol coach, those in another carriage, and a lady and gentleman travelling singly, and repaired to London with the booty he had acquired.

Having put up the stolen horse at an inn in Whitechapel, and soon afterwards seeing it advertised, he was afraid to fetch it; on which he stole another horse; but, as he was riding through Tyburn turnpike, the keeper, knowing the horse, brought the rider to the ground.

Hereupon Simms presented a pistol, and threatened the man with instant death if he presumed to detain him. By this daring mode of proceeding he preserved his liberty, and, having made a tour round the fields, re-entered London by another road.

On the following day he went to Kingston-upon-Thames, where he stole a horse, and robbed several people on his return to London; and the day afterwards he robbed seven farmers of eighteen pounds. His next depredations were on Epping Forest, where he committed five robberies in one day, but soon spent what he thus gained among women of ill fame.

Thinking it unsafe to remain longer in London, he set out with a view to go to Ireland, but had rode only to Barnet when he crossed the country to Harrow-on-the-Hill, where he robbed a gentleman, named Sleep, of his money and watch, and would have taken his wig; but the other said it was of no value, and hoped, as it was cold weather, his health might not be endangered by being deprived of it.

The robber threatened Mr. Sleep's life unless he would swear never to take any notice of the affair; but this that gentleman absolutely refused. Hereupon Simms said, that, if he had not robbed him, two other persons would, and told him to say 'Thomas' if he should meet any people on horseback.

Soon after this Mr. Sleep, meeting two men whom he presumed to be accomplices of the highwayman, cried out 'Thomas'; and the travellers paying no regard to him, he was confirmed in his suspicions, and rode after them; and, on his arrival at Hoddesdon Green, he found several other persons, all of them in pursuit of the highwayman.

In the mean time Simms rode forwards, and robbed the St. Albans stage; after which he went as far as Hockliffe; but, being now greatly fatigued, he fell asleep in the kitchen of an inn, whither he was pursued by some light horsemen from St. Albans, who took him into custody.

Being confined for that night, he was carried in the morning before a magistrate, who committed him to Hedford gaol. By an unaccountable neglect his pistol had not been taken from him, and on his way to prison he attempted to shoot one of his guards; but, the pistol missing fire, his hands were tied behind him, and, when he arrived at the prison, he was fastened to the floor, with an iron collar round his neck.

Being removed to London by a writ of habeas corpus, he was lodged in Newgate, where he was visited, from motives of curiosity, by numbers of people, whom he amused with a narrative of his having been employed to shoot the king.

On this he was examined before the Duke of Newcastle, then secretary of state; but, his whole story bearing evident marks of fiction, he was remanded to Newgate, to take his trial at the ensuing Old Bailey sessions.

Ten indictments were preferred against him, but, being convicted for the robbery of Mr. Sleep, it was not thought necessary to arraign him on any of the others.

After conviction he behaved with great unconcern, and, in some instances, with insolence. Having given a fellow-prisoner a violent blow, he was chained to the floor. Simms appeared shocked when the warrant for his execution arrived; but soon resuming his former indifference, he continued it even to the moment of execution, when he behaved in the most thoughtless manner.

He was hanged at Tyburn on the 16th of November, 1746.

WILLIAM YORK, AGED TEN YEARS, MURDERING SUSAN MAHEW, AGED FIVE YEARS.

WILLIAM YORK

Convicted of child murder.

———

THIS unhappy child was but just turned of ten years of age when he committed the dreadful crime of which he was convicted. He was a pauper in the poorhouse. Belonging to the parish of Eye, in Suffolk, and was committed, on the coroner's inquest, to Ipswich gaol, for the murder of Susan Mahew, another child, of five years of age, who had been his bedfellow. The following is his confession, taken and attested by a justice of the peace, and which was, in part, proved on the trial, with many corroborating circumstances of his guilt. Criminal laws are supposed to have arrived at a greater degree of perfection than any other?

This is an important inquiry, interesting in the highest degree to every member of the body politic.

If, in pursuing such an inquiry, the situation of Holland, Flanders, and several of the northern states on the Continent, be examined, it will be found that this terrific evil had (we allude to the situation of those states previously to the late wars) there scarcely an existence; and that even the precaution of bolting doors and windows during the night was seldom used: although, in those countries, from the opulence of many of the inhabitants, there were great temptations to plunder.

This security did not proceed from severer punishments, for in very few countries are they more sanguinary than in England. It is to be attributed to a more correct and energetic system of police, joined perhaps to an early and general attention to the employment, education, and morals, of the lower orders of the people: a habit of industry and sobriety is thus acquired, which, imbibed in early life, 'grows with their growth and strengthens with their strength.'

Houses intended to be entered during the night are, in general, previously reconnoitered and examined for days preceding. If one or more of the servants are not already associated with the gang, the most artful means are used to obtain their assistance; and, when every previous arrangement is made, the mere operation of robbing a house becomes a matter of little difficulty. By the connivance and assistance of immediate or former servants, the villains are led to the place where the most valuable, as well as the most portable, articles are deposited, and the object is speedily attained.

In this manner do the principal burglars and housebreakers proceed: and let this information serve as a caution to every person in the choice both of their male and female servants; since the latter as well as the former are not seldom accomplices in very atrocious robberies.

It frequently happens that the burglars make their contracts with the receivers on the evening before the plunder is obtained, so as to secure a ready admittance immediately afterwards, and before daybreak, for the purpose of effectual concealment, by melting plate, obliterating marks, and securing all other articles, so as to place them out of the reach of discovery. This has long been reduced to a regular system, which is understood and followed as a trade. Even hackney-coachmen have been known to promote, in an eminent degree, the perpetration of burglaries and other felonies: bribed by a high reward, many of these have eagerly entered into the pay of nocturnal depredators, waiting in the neighborhood until the robbery is completed, and then drawing up at the moment the watchmen are going their rounds, or off their stands, for the purpose of conveying the plunder to the house of the receiver, who is generally waiting the issue of the enterprise.

THE SMUGGLERS MURDERING CHATER AT HARRIS'S WELL.

BENJAMIN TAPNER, JOHN COBBY, JOHN HAMMOND WILLIAM JACKSON, WILLIAM CARTER, RICHARD MILLS THE ELDER, and RICHARD MILLS THE YOUNGER (FATHER and SON)

Executed for murder.

———

—Oh! What are these?
Death's ministers, not men, who thus deal death
Inhumanly to man, and multiply
Ten thousand fold the sin of him who slew
His brother; for of whom such massacre
Make they, but of their brethren—men of men

PARADISE LOST.

WHILE London and its environs were, about this time, beset with gangs of highwaymen, pickpockets, and swindlers, the country was infested with leagues of villains not less dangerous, and much more cruel. These were fellows who preyed upon the public by defrauding the revenue, in landing goods without a regular entry and payment of the duty. All mercantile nations have regulations of this nature; and indeed they are, in some measure, necessary for the regulation and protection of commerce, which in Britain is a main spring of the commonweal.

The smugglers on the sea-coast formerly went in parties sufficiently strong to oppose the officers of the excise, and sometimes even to menace parties of the military sent to apprehend them. Whenever a custom-house officer misfortunately fell into their hands, he was barbarously tortured, and often murdered. A more cruel murder than this we are about to detail is not to be found in these volumes; and we much question whether the judicial annals of Europe can furnish any more diabolical.

The two unfortunate sufferers who were murdered by this desperate gang were William Galley the elder, a custom-house officer of Southampton, and Daniel Chater, a shoemaker of Fording-bridge. These men having been sent to give information respecting some circumstances attending the daring burglary at the custom-house at Poole, and not returning to their respective homes, a suspicion arose that they had been waylaid and murdered by the smugglers, and a search for them was therefore instituted.

Those employed for this purpose, after every inquiry, could hear no certain tidings of them, fear of the smugglers' resentment silencing such inhabitants on the road over which they had carried the unfortunate men as were not in connexion with them. At length a Mr. Stone, following his hounds, came to a spot which appeared to have been dug not long before, and, from the publicity of the circumstance of the men above mentioned being missed, he conjectured that there they might have been buried, and thereof gave immediate information. Upon digging there, nearly seven feet in the earth, the remains of Galley were found, but in so putrid a state as not to be known, except by the clothes. The search after Chater was now pursued with redoubled vigilance, and his body was found in a well (six miles distant from the burial-place of Galley) in Harris's Wood, near Lady Holt Park, with a quantity of stones, wooden rails, and earth, upon it.

At a special commission held at Chichester, on the 16th of January, 1749, Benjamin Tapner, John Cobby, John Hammond, William Carter, Richard Mills the elder, and Richard Mills the younger, were indicted for the murder of Daniel Chater; the three first as principals, and the others as accessories before the fact: and William Jackson and William Carter were indicted for the murder of William Galley.

Benjamin Tapner was a native of Aldington, in Sussex, and worked for some time as a bricklayer; but, being of an idle disposition, he soon quitted his business, and associated with a gang of smugglers, who had rendered themselves formidable to the neighborhood by their lawless depredations.

John Cobby was an illiterate country fellow, the son of James Cobby, of the county of Sussex, labourer, and joined the smugglers a little time before he was thirty years of age.

John Hammond was a labouring man, born at Berstead, in Sussex, and had been a smuggler sometime before he was apprehended for the above-mentioned murders, which was when he was almost forty years old.

William Jackson was a native of Hampshire, and had a wife and large family. He was brought up to the business of husbandry; but the hope of acquiring more money in an easier way induced him to engage with the smugglers, which at length ended in his ruin.

William Carter, of Rowland's Castle, in Hampshire, was the son of William Carter, of Eastmean, in the same county, thatcher. He was about the age of thirty-nine, and had practised smuggling a considerable time before the perpetration of the fact which led to his destruction.

Richard Mills, the elder, was a native of Trotton, in Sussex, and had been a horse-dealer by profession; but it is said that a failure in that business induced him to commence smuggler; and he had been long in that illicit practice to become one of the most hardened of the gang.

Richard Mills, the younger, lived at Stedham, in Sussex, and for some time followed his father's profession of hore-dealing; but unfortunately making a connexion with the smugglers, he came to the same ignominious end as his companions, in the thirty-seventh year of his age.

The two men, Galley and Chater, were proceeding on Sunday, February 14, 1748, to Major Battine, a justice of the peace, at Stanstead, in Sussex, with a letter written by Mr. Shearer, collector of the customs at Southhampton, requesting him to take an examination of Chater concerning one Diamond of Dymar, who was committed to Chichester gaol on suspicion of being one who broke the king's warehouse at Poole. Chater was engaged to give evidence, but with some reluctance, declaring that he saw Diamond, and shook hands with him, who, with many others, was coming from Poole, loaded with tea, of which he threw him a bag. Having passed Havant, and come to the New Inn, at Leigh, they inquired their way, when George Austin, his brother, and brother-in law, said that they were going the same road, and would accompany them to Rowland's Castle, where they might get better directions, it being just by the major's residence.

A little before noon they came to the White Hart, at Rowland's Castle, kept by Elizabeth Payne, widow, who had two sons, blacksmiths, in the same village. After some talk she told George Austin, privately, she was afraid that these two strangers were come to hurt the smugglers. He said, 'No, sure; they were only carrying a letter to Major Battine.' Upon this she sent one of her sons for William Jackson and William Carter, who lived near her house. Meanwhile Chater and Galley wanted to be going, and asked for their horses; but she told them that the major was not then at home, which, indeed, was true.

As soon as Jackson and Carter came, she told them her suspicions, with the circumstance of the letter. Soon after she advised George Austin to go away, lest he should come to some harm; he did so, leaving his brothers.

Payne's other son went and fetched in William Steele, Samuel Downer, otherwise Little Samuel, Edmund Richards, and Henry Sheerman, otherwise Little Harry, all smugglers, belonging to the same gang.

After they had drank a little while, Carter, who had some knowledge of Chater, called him into the yard, and asked him where Diamond was. Chater said he believed he was in custody, and that he was going to appear against him, which he was sorry for, but could not help it. Galley came into the yard to them, and, asking Chater why he would stay there, Jackson, who followed him, said, with a horrid imprecation, 'What is that to you?' and immediately struck him a blow in the face, which knocked him down, and set his nose and mouth bleeding. Soon after they all came into the house, when Jackson, reviling Galley, offered to strike him again, but one of the Paynes interposed.—Galley and Chater now began to be very uneasy, and wanted to be going; but Jackson, Carter, and the rest of them, persuading them to stay and drink more rum, and make it up, (for they were sorry for what had happened), they sat down again; Austin and his brother-in-law being present. Jackson and Carter desired to see the letter, but they refused to show it. The smugglers then drank about plentifully, and made

Galley and Chater fuddled; afterwards persuading them to lie down on a bed, which they did, and fell asleep: the letter was then taken away, read, and, the substance of it greatly exasperating them, it was destroyed.

One John Royce, a smuggler, now came in; and Jackson and Carter told him the contents of the letter, and that they had got the old rogue, the shoemaker of Fording-bridge, who was going to give information against John Diamond, the shepherd, then in custody at Chichester. Here William Steele proposed to take them both to a well, about two hundred yards from the house, and to murder and throw them in.

This proposal was not taken, as they had been seen in their company by the Austins, Mr. Garnet, and one Mr. Jenks, who was newly come into the house to drink. It was next proposed to send them to France; but that was objected against, as there was a possibility of their coming over again. Jackson's and Carter's wires, being present, cried out 'Hang the dogs, for they come here to hang you!' It was then proposed and agreed to keep them confined till they could know Diamond's fate, and, whatever it was, to treat these in the same manner; and each to allow three-pence a week towards keeping them.

Galley and Chater continuing asleep, Jackson went in, and began the first scene of cruelty; for, having put on his spurs, he got upon the bed, and spurred their foreheads, to wake them, and afterwards whipped them with a horse-whip, so that when they came out they were both bleeding. The abovesaid smugglers then took them out of the house; but Richards returned with a pistol, and swore he would shoot any person who should mention what had passed.

Meanwhile the rest put Galley and Chater on one horse, tied their legs under the horse's belly, and then tied the legs of both together. They now set forward, all but Royce, who had no horse. They had not gone above two hundred yards before Jackson called out 'Whip 'em, cut 'em, slash 'em, damn 'em!' upon which all began to whip except Steele, who led the horse, the roads being very bad. They whipped them for half a mile, till they came to Woodash, where they fell off, with their heads under the horse's belly; and their legs, which were tied, appeared over the horse's back. Their tormentors soon set them upright again, and continued whipping them over the head, face, shoulders, &c. till they came to Dean, upwards of half a mile farther: here they both fell again as before, with their heads under the horse's belly, which were struck at every step by the horse's hoofs.

Upon placing them again in the saddle, they found them so weak that they could not sit; upon which they separated them, and put Galley before Steele, and Chater before Little Sam; and then whipped Galley so severely, that, the lashes coming upon Steele, at his desire they desisted. They then went to Harris's well, near Lady Holt Park, where they took Galley off the horse, and threatened to throw him into the well: upon which he desired them to dispatch him at once, and put an end to his misery. 'No,' says Jackson, cursing, 'if that's the case, we have more to say to you'; then put him on a horse again, and whipped him over the Downs, till he was so weak that he fell off; when they laid him across the saddle, with his breast downwards, and Little Sam got up behind him; and as they went on he squeezed Galley's testicles so, that he groaned with the agony, and tumbled off. Being then put astride, Richards got up behind him; soon the poor man cried out 'I fall, I fall, I fall!' and Richards, pushing him, said, 'Fall and be damned!' Upon which he fell down and expired; and the villains, taking up the body, laid it again on the horse, and proposed to go to some proper place where Chater might be concealed till they heard the fate of Diamond.

Jackson and Carter called at one Pescod's house, desiring admittance for two sick men; but he absolutely refused it.

Being now one o'clock in the morning, they agreed to go to one Scardefield at the Red Lion, at Hake, which was not far. Here Carter and Jackson got admittance, after many refusals. While Scardefield went to draw liquor, he heard more company come in; but, though they refused to admit him into the room, he saw one man stand up very bloody, and another lie as dead. They said they had engaged some officers, lost their tea, and several of them were wounded, if not killed.

Jackson and Little Harry now carried Chater down Old Mills's, which was not far off, and chained him in a turf-house; and Little Harry staying to watch him, Jackson returned again to the company. After they had drank gin and rum they all went out, taking the body of Galley with them. Carter compelled Scardefield to show them a place before used to bury smuggled tea, and to lend them spades, and a candle and lantern: there they began to dig, and, it being very cold, he helped to make a hole, where they buried 'something that lay across a horse like a dead man.'

They continued at Scardefield's, drinking, all that day, and in the night went to their own homes, in order to be seen on Tuesday, agreeing to meet again on Thursday at the same house, and bring more of their associates. They met accordingly, and brought old Richard Mills, and his sons Richard and John, Thomas Stringer, John Cobby, Benjamin Tapner, and John Hammond, who, with the former, made fourteen. They consulted now what was to be done with Chater;—it was unanimously agreed that he must be destroyed. Richard Mills, junior, proposed to load a gun, clap the muzzle to his head, tie a long string to the trigger, then all to pull it, that all might be equally guilty of his murder. This was rejected, because it would put him out of his pain too soon; and at length they came to a resolution to carry him up to Harris's well, which was not far off, and to throw him in.

All this while Chater was in the utmost horror and misery, being visited by one or other of them, who abused him both with words and blows. At last they all came, and, Tapner and Cobby going into the turf-house, the former pulled out a clasp-knife, and said, with a great oath, 'Down on your knees, and go to prayers, for with this knife I'll be your butcher!' The poor man knelt down; and, as he was at prayers, Cobby kicked him, calling him 'informing villain.' Chater asking what they had done with Mr. Galley, Tapner, slashing the knife across his eyes, almost cut them out, and the gristle of his nose quite through: he bore it patiently, believing they were putting an end to his misery. Accordingly Tapner struck at him again, and made a deep cut in his forehead. Upon this old Mills said, 'Do not murder him here, but somewhere else.' Accordingly they placed him upon a horse, and all set out together for Harris's well, except Mills and his sons, they having no horses ready, and laying, in excuse, 'That there were enough without them to murder one man.' All the way Tapner whipped him till the blood came; and then swore that, if he blooded the saddle, he would torture him the more! which, as he could not stop his wounds from bleeding, was an incredible instance of barbarity.

When they were come within two hundred yards of the well, Jackson and Carter stopped, saying to Tapner, Cobby, Stringer, Steele, and Hammond, 'Go on and do your duty on Chater, as we have ours upon Galley.' In the dead of the night of the 18th they brought him to the well, which was nearly thirty feet deep, but dry, and paled close round. Tapner having fastened a noose round Chater's neck, they bade him get over the pales to the well. He was going through a broken place; but though he was covered with blood, and fainting with the anguish of his wounds, they forced him to climb up, having the rope about his neck, one end of which being tied to the pales, they pushed him into the well; but, the rope being short, he hung no farther within it than his thighs, and, leaning against the edge, he hung above a quarter of an hour, and was not strangled. They then untied him, and threw him head foremost into the well. They tarried some time, and, hearing him groan, they concluded to go to one William Comleah's, a gardener, to borrow a rope and ladder, saying they wanted to relieve one of their companions who had fallen into Harris's well. He said they might take them; but they could not manage the ladder, in their confusion, it being a long one.

They then returned to the well; and, still hearing him groan, and fearful that the sound thereof might lead to a discovery, the place being near the road, they threw upon him some of the rails and gateposts fixed about the well; also great stones; when, finding him silent, they left him.

Their next consultation was how to dispose of their horses; when they killed Galley's, which was grey, and, taking his bridle off, cut it into small pieces, and hid them so as to prevent any discovery; but a bay horse that Chater had rode on got from them.

On their return home these execrable murderers stopped at the house of one of their acquaintance to drink, where they were hardened enough to boast of the outrage they had committed, and even spoke of it as a circumstance that merited praise.

After a long and diligent search for the perpetrators of these crimes, some of the smugglers were taken up on suspicion, and, being examined in presence of the commissioners of the customs, were admitted evidences for the crown, on discovering all they knew of the horrid transaction.

In consequence hereof the prisoners were brought to trial at the time and place above mentioned; when Sir Michael Foster presided in Court.

The judge's charge to the grand jury was full of good sense, and highly reprobated the practice of smuggling, by which the fair trader is defrauded, and the revenue greatly injured.

When the trial came on, the evidence was very full and circumstantial against the prisoners; and the jury, after being out of Court about a quarter of an hour, brought in a verdict of guilty against all the prisoners: whereupon the judge pronounced sentence on the convicts in one of the most pathetic addresses that was ever heard; representing the enormity of their crime, and exhorting them to make immediate preparation for the awful fate that awaited them; adding, 'Christian charity obliges me to tell you that your time in this world will be very short.'

The heinousness of the crime of which these men had been convicted rendering it necessary that their punishment should be exemplary, the judge ordered that they should be executed on the following day: and the sentence was accordingly carried into execution against all but Jackson, who died in prison on the evening that he was condemned. They were attended by two ministers; and all, except Mills and his son (who took no notice of each other, and though themselves not guilty because they were not present at the finishing of the inhuman murder), showed great marks of penitence, Tapner and Carter gave good advice to the spectators, desired diligence might be used to apprehend Richards, whom they charged as the cause of their being brought to this wretched end. Young Mills smiled several times at the executioner, who was a discharged marine, and, having ropes too short for some of them, was puzzled to fit them. Old Mills, being forced to stand tip-toe to reach the halter, desired that he might not be hanged by inches. The Mills's were so rejoiced at being told that they were not to be hanged in chains after execution, that death seemed to excite in them no terror; while Jackson was so struck with horror at being measured for his irons, that he soon expired.

They were hanged at Chichester on the 18th of January, 1749, amidst such a concourse of spectators as is seldom seen on occasions of a public execution.

Carter was hung in chains near Rake, in Sussex; Tapner on Rook's Hill, near Chichester; and Cobby and Hammond at Cesley Isle, on the beach where they sometimes landed their smuggled goods, and where they could be seen at a great distance east and west.

Jackson had lived some years a Roman Catholic; and, from the following popish relic found in his pocket, there is little doubt but he died such, as far as such a scoundrel could be to belong to any religion:

'Saneti tres reges,
Gaspar, Melchior, Balthazar,
Orate pro nobis, nunc et in hora
Mortis nostræ.
Ces billets ont touché aux trios
tetes de
S.S. Rois a Cologne.
Ils sont pour des voyageurs, contre
les malheurs de chemins, maux
de tete, mal caduque, fievres,
socellerie, toute sorte de malefice,
et mort subite.'

The English of which is,

'Ye three holy kings,
Gaspar, Melchior, Balthazar,
Pray for us now, and in the hour of death.
These papers have touched the three heads of
The holy kings of Cologne.
They are to preserve travellers from accidents on the
road, head-aches, falling sickness, fevers, witchcraft,
all kinds of mischief, and sudden death.'

The body of the above-mentioned Jackson was thrown into a hole near the place of execution; as were, those of Mills, the father and son, who had no friends to take them away: and at a small distance from this spot is erected a stone, on which is the following inscription:

'Near this place was buried the body of William Jackson, who, upon a special commission of Oyer and Terminer, held at Chichester on the 16th day of January, 1748-9, was, with William Carter, attainted for the murder of William Galley, custom-house officer; and who likewise was, together with Benjamin Tapner, John Cobby, John Hammond, Richard Mills the elder, Richard Mills the younger, his son, attainted for the murder of Daniel Chater; but, dying in a few hours after sentence of death was pronounced upon him, he thereby escaped the punishment which the heinousness of his complicated crimes deserved, and which was, the next day, most justly inflicted upon his accomplices.

'As a memorial to posterity, and a warning to this and
succeeding generations,
This stone is erected,
A. D. 1749.'

To comment upon these odious and loathsome transactions is impossible; the imagination is glad to escape from scenes of such unrivalled atrocity and horror. We would rather contemplate the wretched victims of undeserved ferocity at length relieved by the friendly hand of Death; while the still more wretched victims of their own evil passions are, by the memorial stone above described, held up by name to the scorn and detestation of posterity.

MILLS AND HIS COMPANIONS WHIPPING HAWKINS TO DEATH.

JOHN MILLS

Executed for murder.

———

THIS monster was another son of Richard Mills, whose execution has already appeared; and the sequel will show that he was in the habits of cruelty and villainy 'worthy of his sire.'

He also was concerned in the murder of the custom-house officers, but escaped a little longer the hand of justice. He was likewise one of that gang of villains who most daringly broke open the custom-house at Poole; and yet was he reserved to make atonement for a fresh murder, equally cruel as that for which his father and brother had forfeited their lives.

John Mills, and some associates, travelling over Hind Heath, saw the judges on their road to Chichester, to try the murderers of Chater and Galley; on which young Mills proposed to rob them; but the other parties refused to have any concern in such an affair.

Soon after his father, brother, and their accomplices, were hanged, Mills thought of going to Bristol, with a view of embarking for France; and, having hinted his intentions to some others, they resolved to accompany him; and, stopping at a house on the road, they met with one Richard Hawkins, whom they asked to go with them; but the poor fellow hesitating, they put him on horseback behind Mills, and carried him to the Dog and Partridge, on Slendon Common, which was kept by John Reynolds.

They had not been long in the house when complaint was made that two bags of tea had been stolen, and Hawkins was charged with the robbery. He steadily denied any knowledge of the affair; but this not satisfying the villains, they obliged him to pull off his clothes; and, having likewise stripped themselves, they began to whip him with the most unrelenting barbarity; and Curtis, one of the gang, said he did know of the robbery, and, if he would not confess, he would whip him till he did; for he had whipped many a rogue, and washed his hands in his blood.[5]

---

[5] ON THE 11TH of December, 1750, John Wathing, nicknamed Peter Jack, a smuggler of Horsey, in Norfolk, was hanged. This villain, among the numerous enormities which he committed, at the head of eleven more smugglers, went in the night to the house of Abraham Bailey, who had been a custom-house watchman, pulled him out of bed, whipped him with their whips until the blood trickled down his body, then hung him by the neck to a tree, but let him down before he was dead. When he recovered his senses they obliged him to answer their

These bloodthirsty villains continued whipping the poor wretch till their breath was almost exhausted: while he begged them to spare his life, on account of his wife and child. Hawkins drawing up his legs, to defend himself in some measure from their blows, they kicked him on the groin in a manner too shocking to be described; continually asking him what was become of the tea. At length the unfortunate man mentioned something of his father and brother; on which Mills and one Curtis said they would go and fetch them; but Hawkins expired soon after they had left the house.

Rowland, one of the accomplices, now locked the door; and, putting the key in his pocket, he and Thomas Winter (who was afterwards admitted evidence) went out to meet Curtis and Mills, whom they saw riding up a lane leading from an adjacent village, having each a man behind him. Winter desiring to speak with his companions, the other men stood at a distance, while he asked Curtis what he meant to do with them, who replied, to confront them with Hawkins.

Winter now said that Hawkins was dead, and begged that no more mischief might be done; but Curtis replied, 'By G—we will go through it now'; but at length they permitted them to go home, saying that when they were wanted they should be sent for.

The murderers now coming back to the public house, Reynolds said 'You have ruined me'; but Curtis replied that he would make him amends. Having consulted how they should dispose of the body, it was proposed to throw it into a well in an adjacent park; but this being objected to, they carried it twelve miles and, having tied stones to it, in order to sink it, they threw it into a pond in Parham Park,

---

questions, and made him swear to his own damnation if he revealed what they had done to him.

belonging to Sir Cecil Bishop; and in this place it lay more than two months before it was discovered.

This horrid and unprovoked murder gave rise to a royal proclamation, in which a pardon was offered to any persons, even outlawed smugglers, except those who had been guilty of murder, or concerned in breaking open the custom-house at Poole, on the condition of discovering the persons who had murdered Hawkins, particularly Mills, who was charged with having had a concern in the horrid transaction.

Hereupon William Pring, an outlawed smuggler, who had not had any share in either of the crimes excepted in the proclamation, went to the secretary of state, and informed him that he would end Mills if he could be ascertained of his own pardon; adding that he believed he was either at Hath or Bristol.

Being assured that he need not doubt of the pardon, he set out for Bristol, where he found Mills, and with him Thomas and Lawrence Kemp, brothers; the former of whom had broken out of Newgate, and the other was outlawed by proclamation. Having consulted on their desperate circumstances, Pring offered them a retreat at his house near Beckenham, in Kent, hence they might make excursions, and commit robberies on the highway.

Pleased with this proposal, they set out with Pring, and arrived in safety at his house; where they had not and been long before he pretended that his horse being an indifferent, and theirs remarkably good he would go and procure another, and then they would proceed on the intended expedition.

Thus saying, he set out, and they agreed to wait for his return; but, instead of going to procure a horse, he went to the house of Mr. Rackster, an officer of the excise at Horsham, who, taking with him seven or eight armed men, went to Beckenham at night, where they found Mills and the two brothers Kemp just going to supper on a breast of veal. They immediately-secured the brothers by tying their arms; but Mills, making resistance, was cut with a hanger before he would submit.

The offenders, being taken, were conducted to the county gaol for Sussex; and, being secured till the assizes, were removed to East Grinstead, where the brothers Kemp were tried for highway robberies, convicted, sentenced, and executed.

Mills, being tried for the murder of Hawkins, was capitally convicted, and received sentence of death, and to be hung in chains near the place where the murder was committed.

After conviction he mentioned several robberies in which he had been concerned, but refused to tell the names of any of his accomplices; declaring that he thought he should merit damnation if he made discoveries by means of which any of his companions might be apprehended and convicted.

The country being at that time filled with smugglers, a rescue was feared; wherefore he was conducted to the place of execution by a guard of soldiers; and, when there, prayed with a clergyman, confessed that he had led a bad life, acknowledged the murder of Hawkins, desired that all young people would take warning by his untimely end, humbly implored the forgiveness of God, and professed to die in charity with all mankind.

He was executed on Slendon Common on the 12th of August, 1749, and afterwards hung in chains near the same spot.

CAPTAIN INNIS KILLED IN A DUEL BY CAPTAIN CLARKE.

CAPTAIN CLARKE, R. N.

Convicted of murder.

———

THE Captains Innis and Clarke were commanders under Admiral Knowles (the first of the Warwick, and the latter of the Canterbury, line-of-battle ships, sixty-four guns each), when he obtained a victory over a Spanish fleet of equal force, and, taking from them the Conquestadore, ran their vice-admiral on shore, where she blew up, the rest escaping under favour of the night. It was the general opinion that, had the admiral availed himself of an opportunity, which at one time presented itself, of bringing up his fleet to bear at once upon the enemy, the whole might have been taken.

The issue of this battle was, therefore, unsatisfactory to the nation; and the admiral was called to account for his conduct before a court-martial, held on board the royal yacht the Charlotte, at Deptford, which sat during nine days.

The decision of the Court, being unfavorable to the admiral, caused a divided opinion among the officers. It did not, however, affect the personal bravery of that commander; on the contrary, it appeared in evidence that he displayed the greatest intrepidity, exposing his person to imminent danger after his ship was disabled; but it also appeared that in manœuvring, previous to the engagement, he had not availed himself of an advantage, by which neglect the battle was begun by four of his vessels when six might have been brought up. The Court therefore determined that he fell under the 14th and 23rd articles of war, namely, the offence of 'negligence'; for which they sentenced him to be reprimanded.

This sentence caused much ill blood among the officers. The admiral had already been called out twice in duels with his captains, and had received more challenges of the same kind; but government, being apprized of the outrages, put a stop to them, by taking the challengers into custody.

Captain Clarke, it appears, had given evidence on the trial of the admiral, which displeased Captain Innis to so great a degree, that he called him a 'perjured rascal,' and charged him in all companies, gave him with giving false evidence. This was certainly language worse to be borne by an officer than ranking wounds, or even death. Captain Clarke being apprized that Innis, in this way, traduced and vilified him a verbal challenge, which the other accepted.

On the 12th of August, 1749, early in the morning, these gentlemen, attended by their seconds, met in Hyde Park. The pistols of Captain Clarke were screw-barrelled, and about seven inches long; those of Captain Innis were common pocket pistols, three inches and a half in the barrel.

They were not more than five yards distant from each other, when they turned about, and Captain Clarke fired before Captain Innis had levelled his pistol. The ball took effect in the breast, of which wound Captain Innis expired at twelve o'clock the same night.

The coroner's jury found a verdict of wilful murder against Captain Clarke, on which he was apprehended, brought to trial at the Old Bailey, found guilty, and sentenced to death. The king, in consideration of his services, and the bravery he displayed in fighting his ship under Admiral Knowles, was pleased to grant him a free pardon.

There were other circumstances in this unfortunate rencontre which were favorable to Captain Clarke; his firing on turning round, and the fact of his pistol being larger than that of Captain Innis not being deemed unfair by the sanguinary rules of duelling, since Captain Innis might have provided himself with a large pair, had he pleased. But what pleaded powerfully in his behalf was the expression of the dying man, who acquitted and forgave him. When a soldier seized Captain Clarke, the former asked the wounded man what he should do with him, to which he faintly answered, 'Set him at liberty, for what he has done was my own seeking.'

On the 1st of June, 1750, being the last day of the sessions of the Old Bailey, Captain Clarke, among the other convicts, was brought up to receive sentence of death, when he pleaded his majesty's pardon, which had been then lately sent him, and which being recorded, he was discharged.

From the necessity of the esteem of others have arisen single combats. They are thought to have been unknown to the ancients, perhaps because they did not assemble in their temples, in their theatres, or with their friends, suspiciously armed with swords; and, perhaps, because single combats were a common spectacle exhibited to the people by gladiators, who were slaves, and whom freemen disdained to imitate.

In vain have the laws endeavored to abolish this custom by punishing the offenders with death. A man of honour, deprived of the esteem of others, foresees that he must be reduced either to a solitary existence, insupportable to a social creature or become the object of perpetual insult; considerations sufficient to overcome the fear of death.

It may not be without its use to repeat here what has been mentioned by other writers, *viz.* that the best method of preventing this crime is to punish the aggressor; that is, the person who gave occasion to the duel; and to acquit him who, without any fault on his side, is obliged to defend that which is not sufficiently secured to him by the laws.

EVERETT SEIZED BY A DOG WHILE ATTEMPTING TO ROB A GENTLEMAN.

JOHN EVERETT, alias GEORGE ANDERSON

Executed for robbery.

———

THIS man was a native of Hertford, in which town he served his apprenticeship to a baker. The young men in the neighborhood declined associating with him, and held him in universal abhorrence, so ungracious were his manners, and so strong his propensity to wickedness. Upon the expiration of his apprenticeship he connected himself with a gang of notorious gamblers, and other dissolute wretches, in conjunction with whom he perpetrated a great number of villainies, but for several years escaped the vengeance of the law.

By persuasions, and the promise of a sum of money, Everett, and a man named Wright, induced a young woman to exhibit a charge of felony against two innocent men, who were put on their trial, but happily acquitted, as the perjured evidence was not able to authenticate her accusation. In revenge for their failing to supply the girl with the money they had promised, she lodged an information against Everett and Wright, who were in consequence indicted for subornation of perjury, and sentenced to stand on the pillory at the end of Chancery Lane, where they received very severe treatment from the populace.

Soon after the above punishment had been inflicted, Everett was tried at Hicks's Hall, and sentenced again to stand on the pillory, for having fraudulently obtained a thirty-six shilling piece. He was afterwards convicted of having circulated counterfeit Portugal coin, and ordered to be imprisoned for two years in Newgate.

Soon after Everett's trial a company of gentlemen went to Newgate to visit a criminal, and in a short time they discovered that they had been robbed of their handkerchiefs. The circumstance being mentioned to Everett, he pretended to be much surprised, and intimated that there was but little probability of the property being recovered. However, in a little time he produced the handkerchiefs, and received some money from the gentlemen, as a reward for his supposed honesty.

While he remained in Newgate he picked the pocket of almost every person who came to visit the prisoners: he was continually uttering the most reprobate speeches, and seemed to delight in the practice of every species of wickedness. Upon the expiration of the time he was sentenced to remain in prison he found sureties for his good behaviour for two years, and was discharged.

Having stopped a young gentleman in Fleet Street, he was asked if a robbery was intended; upon which he knocked the gentleman down, but a large dog belonging to the injured party immediately seized the villain, who with great difficulty disengaged himself just time enough to escape being secured by the watch.

Everett and a woman of the town went to a small inn at Hoddesden, in Hertfordshire, which was kept by an ancient widow, and, being invited into a room behind the bar, after having each drank a glass of wine, the widow and her female guest went to walk in the garden: in the mean time Everett broke open a bureau, and stole sixty pounds in cash, and several gold rings. They kept the widow in conversation till the time of going to bed, in order to divert her from going to the bureau; and the next morning decamped with their booty.

They took the road to Nottingham, whence they crossed the country to Newmarket, and then returned to London. Everett's numerous villainies had rendered his name so notorious, that he was fearful of being apprehended; and therefore he went under the denomination of George Anderson, and lived in a very private manner till the money he had so wickedly obtained was expended.

He now procured a knife eighteen inches long, and determined to levy contributions on passengers on the highway. In the road between Kentishtown and Hampstead, he attempted to rob a countryman, who, being of an intrepid temper, a desperate contest ensued, in which Everett proved the conqueror, and dangerously wounded his antagonist, from whom he, however, obtained but a small booty.

At length he was detected in stealing a quantity of riband in a shop in London, and was apprehended, but not without making a vigorous resistance, in doing which he dangerously wounded the shopkeeper in the face and hands.

For this crime he was tried at the Old Bailey, convicted, and received sentence of death. The night after the warrant for his execution arrived he laid a plan to escape. He was furnished with implements for this purpose, and for sawing off his fetters, by his wife and his kept mistress, who, on this occasion, agreed. Being discovered, the former was sent to one of the Compters, and his concubine to the other. On this he behaved so insolently and outrageously that it was necessary to chain him to the floor of his cell, where he remained blaspheming and threatening vengeance to the keeper and turnkeys.

A report being circulated that he meditated a design against the life of the gaoler, his cell was carefully searched, but no suspicious instruments were found.

Whether he really harbored the design of murdering the keeper is a matter of doubt. He denounced vengeance against the man who gave the information, declaring, with horrid imprecations, that, if he could procure a pistol, or any other offensive weapon, he would put him to death.

He joined in prayer with the Ordinary of Newgate at the place of execution, but declined addressing the populace; and, a little time before being turned off, said he considered death as too severe a punishment for the crime he had committed.

On the 31st of December, 1750, this offender was executed at Tyburn.

Everett's propensity to wickedness was apparent in his earliest years; and, though he found himself universally despised by all who were not abandoned like himself, he neglected to effect a reformation in his manners, whereby he might have removed all prejudices against him, and have become a respectable member of the community. He had lived without regard either to religious or moral obligations: but the utmost distraction of mind was occasioned by the upbraidings of a guilty conscience, and the terrible approach of death. The miserable situation of this man exhibits a striking proof of the justice with which Shake-speare has put the following lines into the mouth of a man oppressed with guilt:—

'—Pray I cannot,
Though inclination be as sharp as 'twill;
My stronger guilt defeats my strong intent;
And, like a man to double business bound,
I stand in pause where I shall first begin,
And both neglect.
—O wretched state! O bosom black as death!
O limed soul, that, struggling to get free, Art more engaged!'

PARSONS IMPLORING HIS FATHER'S FORGIVENESS.

WILLIAM PARSONS, ESQ.

Executed for returning from transportation.

———

THE unhappy subject of this narrative was the eldest son of Sir William Parsons, Bart., of the county of Nottingham, and was born in London in the year 1717. He was placed under the care of a pious and learned divine at Pepperharrow, in Surrey, where he received the first rudiments of education. In a little more than three years he was removed to Eton College, where it was intended that he should qualify himself for one of the universities.

While he was a scholar at Eton he was detected in stealing a volume of Pope's of Homer in the shop of a bookseller named Pote. Being charged with the fact, he confessed that he had stolen many other books at different times. The case being represented to the master, Parsons underwent a very severe discipline.

Though he remained at Eton nine years, his progress in learning was very inconsiderable. The youth was, indeed, of so unpromising a disposition, that Sir William determined to send him to sea, as the most probable means to prevent his destruction; and soon procured him to be appointed midshipman on board a man of war then lying at Spithead, under sailing orders for Jamaica, there to be stationed for three years.

Some accident detaining the ship beyond the time when it was expected she would sail, Parsons applied for leave of absence, and went on shore; but, having no intention to return, he immediately directed his course towards a small town about ten miles from Portsmouth, called Bishop's Waltham, where he soon ingratiated himself into the favour of the principal inhabitants.

His figure being pleasing, and his manner of address easy and polite, he found but little difficulty in recommending himself to the ladies.

He became greatly enamoured of a beautiful and accomplished young lady, the daughter of a physician of considerable practice, and prevailed upon her to promise she would yield him her hand in marriage.

News of the intended alliance coming to the knowledge of his father, Sir William, and his uncle, the latter hastened to Waltham, to prevent a union which he apprehended would inevitably produce the ruin of the contracting parties.

With much difficulty the uncle prevailed upon. Parsons to return to the ship, which in a few days afterwards proceeded on her voyage.

The ship had not been long arrived at the place of destination when Parsons resolved to desert, and return to

England, and soon found an opportunity of shipping himself on board the Sheerness man of war, then preparing to sail on her return home.

Immediately after his arrival in England he set out for Waltham, in order to visit the object of his desires; but his uncle, being apprized of his motions, repaired to the same place, and represented his character in so unfavorable, but at the same time in so just a light, as prevented the renewal of his addresses to the physician's daughter.

He went home with his uncle, who observed his conduct with a most scrupulous attention, and confined him as much as possible within doors. This generous relation at length exerted his interest to get the youth appointed midshipman on board his majesty's ship the Romney, which was ordered on the Newfoundland station.

Upon his return from Newfoundland, Parsons learnt, with infinite mortification, that the Duchess of Northumberland, to whom he was related, had revoked a will made in his favour, and bequeathed to his sister a very considerable legacy, which he had expected to enjoy. He was repulsed by his friends and acquaintance, who would not in the least countenance his visits at their houses; and his circumstances now became exceedingly distressed.

Thus situated, he applied to a gentleman named Bailey, with whom he had formerly lived on terms of intimacy, and whose humanity induced him to invite Parsons to reside in his house, and to furnish him with the means of supporting the character of a gentleman. Mr. Bailey was also indefatigable in his endeavours to effect a reconciliation between young Parsons and his father, in which he at length succeeded.

Sir William having prevailed upon his son to go abroad again, and procured him an appointment under the governor of *James Fort*, on the river Gambia, he embarked on board a vessel in the service of the Royal African Company.

Parsons had resided at James Fort about six months, when a disagreement took place between him and Governor Aufleur; in consequence of which the former signified a resolution of returning to England. Hereupon the governor informed him that he was commissioned to engage him as an indented servant for five years. Parsons warmly expostulated with the governor, declaring that his behaviour was neither that of a man of probity nor a gentleman, and requested permission to return. But, so far from complying, the governor issued orders to the sentinels to be particularly careful lest he should effect an escape.

Notwithstanding every precaution, Parsons found means to get on board a homeward-bound vessel, and being followed by Mr. Aufleur, he was commanded to return, but cocking a pistol, and presenting it to governor, he declared he would fire upon any man who should presume to molest him. Here upon the governor departed, and in a short time the ship sailed for England.

Soon after his arrival in his native country he received an invitation to visit an uncle who lived at Epsom, which he gladly accepted, and experienced a most cordial and friendly reception.

He resided with his uncle about three months, and was treated with all imaginable kindness and respect. At length one of the female servants in the family swore herself to be pregnant by him, which so incensed the old gentleman, that he dismissed Parsons from his house.

Reduced to the most deplorable state of poverty, he directed his course towards the metropolis; and, three half-pence being his whole stock of money, he subsisted four days upon the bread purchased with that small sum, quenching his thirst at the pumps he casually met with in the streets. He lay four nights in a hay-loft in Chancery Lane, belonging to the Master of the Rolls, by permission of the coachman, who pitied his truly deplorable case.

At length he determined to apply for redress to an ancient gentle-woman with whom he had been acquainted in his more youthful days, when she was in the capacity of companion to the Duchess of Northumberland. Weak and emaciated through want of food, his appearance was rendered still more miserable by the uncleanliness and disorder of his apparel; and, when he appeared before the old lady, she tenderly compassionated his unfortunate situation, and recommended him to a decent family in Cambridge Street, with whom he resided some time in a very comfortable manner, the old gentlewoman defraying the charge of his lodging and board; and a humane gentleman, to whom she had communicated his case, supplying him with money for common expenses.

Sir William came to town at the beginning of the winter, and received an unexpected visit from his son, who dropped upon his knees, and supplicated forgiveness with the utmost humility and respect. His mother-in-law was greatly enraged at his appearance, and upbraided her husband with being foolishly indulgent to so graceless a youth, at the same time declaring that she would not live in the house where he was permitted to enter.

Sir William asked him what mode of life he meant to adopt; and his answer was, that he was unable to determine, but would cheerfully pursue such measures as so indulgent a parent should think proper to recommend. The old gentleman then advised him to enter as a private man in the horse-guards; which he approved of, saying he would immediately offer himself as a volunteer.

Upon mentioning his intention to the adjutant, he was informed that he must pay seventy guineas for his admission into the corps. This news proved exceedingly afflicting, as he had but little hope that his father would advance the necessary sum. Upon returning to his father's lodgings, he learnt that he had set out for the country, and left him a present of only five shillings.

Driven now nearly to a state of distraction, he formed the desperate resolution of putting an end to his life, and repaired to St. James's Park, intending to throw himself in Rosamond's Pond. While he stood on the brink of the water, waiting for an opportunity of carrying his impious design into effect, it occurred to him that a letter he had received, mentioning the death of an aunt, and that she had bequeathed a legacy to his brother, might be made use of to his own advantage; and he immediately declined the thoughts of destroying himself.

He produced the letter to several persons, assuring them that the writer had been misinformed respecting the legacy, which in reality was left to himself. Under the pretext of being entitled to the above legacy, he obtained money and effects from different people to a considerable amount; and, among those who were deceived by the above stratagem, was a tailor in Devereux Court, in the Strand, who gave him credit for several genteel units of clothes.

The money and other articles thus fraudulently obtained enabled him to engage in scenes of gaiety and dissipation; and he seemed to entertain no idea that his happiness would be but of short duration.

Accidentally meeting the brother of the young lady to whom he had made professions of love at Waltham, he intended to renew his acquaintance with him, and his addresses to his sister: but the young gentleman informed Parsons that his sister died suddenly a short time after his departure from Waltham.

Parsons endeavored as much as possible to cultivate the friendship of the above young gentleman, and represented his case in so plausible a manner as to obtain money from him at different times to a considerable amount.

Parsons's creditors now became exceedingly importunate; and he thought there was no probability of relieving himself from his difficulties but by connecting himself in marriage with a woman of fortune.

Being eminently qualified in those accomplishments which are known to have a great influence over the female world, Parsons soon ingratiated himself into the esteem of a young lady possessed of a handsome independence bequeathed her by her lately deceased father. He informed his creditors that he had a prospect of an advantageous marriage; and, as they were satisfied that the lady had a good fortune, they supplied him with every thing necessary for prosecuting the amour, being persuaded that, if the expected union took place, they should have no difficulty in recovering their respective demands.

The marriage was solemnized on the 10th of February, 1740, in the twenty-third year of our malefactor's age. On occasion of this event the uncle who lived at Epsom visited him in London, and gave him the strongest assurances that he would exert every possible endeavour to promote his interest and happiness, on condition that he would avoid such proceedings as would render him unworthy of friendship and protection. His relations in general were perfectly satisfied with the connexion he had made, and hoped that his irregular and volatile disposition would be corrected by the prudent conduct of his bride, who was a justly esteemed young lady of great sweetness of temper, virtue, and discretion.

A few weeks after his marriage his uncle interceded in his behalf with the Right Honourable Arthur Onslow; and, through the interest of the gentleman, he was appointed an ensign in the, thirty-fourth regiment of foot.

He now discharged all his debts, which proved highly satisfactory to his relations; and this conduct was the means of his obtaining further credit in times of future distress.

He hired a very handsome house in Poland Street, where he resided two years, in which time he had two children, one of whom died very young. From Poland Street he removed to Panton Square; and the utmost harmony subsisted between he and his wife, who were much respected by their relations acquaintances.

But it must be observed, that, though his conduct in other respects had been irreproachable from the time of his marriage, he was guilty of unpardonable indiscretion as to the manner of his living; for he kept three saddle-horses, a chaise and pair, several unnecessary servants, and engaged in many other superfluous expenses that his income could not afford.

Unfortunately Parsons became acquainted with an infamous gambler, who seduced him to frequent gaming-houses, and to engage in play. He thus lost considerable sums, which were shared between the pretended friend of Parsons and his wicked accomplices.

Parsons was now promoted to a lieutenancy in a regiment that was ordered into Flanders, and he was accompanied to that country by the abandoned miscreant whom he considered as his most valuable friend. The money he lost by gaming, and the extravagant manner in which he lived, in a short time involved him in such difficulties, that he was under the necessity of selling his commission, in order to discharge his debts contracted in Flanders. The commission being sold, Parsons and his treacherous companion returned to England.

His arrival was no sooner known than his creditors were extremely urgent for the immediate discharge of their respective claims; which induced him to take a private lodging in Gough Square, where he passed under the denomination of Captain Brown. He pretended to be an unmarried man, and saw his wife only when appointments were made to meet at a public house. While he lodged in Gough Square he seduced his landlord's daughter, who became pregnant by him; and her imprudence in yielding to the persuasions of Parsons proved the means of involving her in extreme distress.

His creditor having discovered the place of his retreat, he deemed it prudent to remove; and at this juncture an opportunity offered by which he hoped to retrieve his fortune; and he therefore embarked as captain of marines on board the Dursley privateer.

Soon after the arrival of the ship at Deal, Parsons went on shore, provided with pistols, being determined not to submit to an arrest, which he supposed would be attempted. He had no sooner landed on the beach than he was approached by five or six men, one of whom attempted to seize him; but Parsons, stepping aside, discharged one of his pistols, and lodged a ball in the man's thigh. He then said he was well provided with weapons, and would fire upon them if they presumed to give him further molestation. Hereupon the officers retreated; and Parsons returned to the ship, which sailed from Deal the following morning.

They had been in the Channel about a week, when they made a prize of a French privateer, which they carried into the port of Cork. Parsons, being now afflicted with a disorder that prevailed among the French prisoners, was sent on shore for the recovery of his health. During his illness the vessel sailed on another cruise; and he was no sooner in a condition to permit him to leave his apartment, than he became anxious to partake of the fashionable amusements.

In order to recruit his finances, which were nearly exhausted, he drew bills of exchange on three merchants in London, on which he raised sixty pounds; and, before advice could be transmitted to Cork that he had no effects in the hands of the persons on whom he had drawn the bills, he embarked on board a vessel bound for England.

He landed at Plymouth, where he resided some time under a military character, to support his claim to which

he was provided with a counterfeit commission. He frequented all places of public resort, and particularly where
gaming was permitted. His money being nearly expended,
he obtained a hundred pounds from a merchant of Plymouth, by means of a false draft upon an alderman of London.
Some time after the discovery of the fraud the injured party
saw Parsons a transport prisoner on board a ship bound to
Virginia, lying in Catwater Bay, where he assured him of
entire forgiveness, and made him a present of a guinea.

From Plymouth Parsons repaired to London, and, his
money being nearly spent, he committed the following
fraud, in conjunction with a woman of the town:—Taking his accomplice to a tavern in the Strand (where he was
known), he represented her as an heiress who had consented
to a private marriage, and requested the landlord to send
immediately for a clergyman. The parson being arrived,
and about to begin the ceremony, Parsons pretended to recollect that he had forgotten to provide a ring, and ordered
the waiter to tell a shopkeeper in the neighborhood to bring
some plain gold rings. Upon this the clergyman begged to
recommend a very worthy man, who kept a jeweller's shop
in the neighborhood; and Parsons said it was a matter of
indifference with whom he laid out his money, adding, that,
as he wished to compliment his bride with some small present, the tradesman might also bring some diamond rings.

The rings being brought, and one of each chosen, Parsons produced a counterfeit draft, saying the jeweller might
either give him change then, or call for payment after the
ceremony; on which the jeweller retired, saying he would
attend again in the afternoon. In a little time the woman
formed a pretence for leaving the room, and, upon her not
returning soon, our hero affected great impatience, and,
without taking his hat, quitted the apartment, saying he
would inquire of the people of the house whether his bride
had not been detained by some unforeseen accident.

After waiting a considerable time, the clergyman called the landlord; and, as neither Parsons nor the woman could be found, it was rightly concluded that their whole intention was to perpetrate a fraud. In the mean time our hero and his accomplice met at an appointed place, and divided their booty.

Soon after the above transaction Parsons intimated to a military officer that, on account of the many embarrassments he was under, he was determined to join the rebel army, as the only expedient by which he could avoid being lodged in prison. The gentleman represented the danger of engaging in such an adventure, and, lest his distress should precipitate him to any rash proceeding, generously supplied him with forty guineas, to answer present exigencies.

He soon after borrowed the above gentleman's horse, pretending that he had occasion to go a few into the country on a matter of business; but he immediately rode to Smithfield, where he sold the horse at a very inadequate price.

That he might escape the resentment of the gentleman whom he had treated, in so unworthy a manner, he lodged an information against him, as being disaffected to the government: In consequence of which he was deprived of his commission, and suffered an imprisonment of six months. He exhibited information of a similar nature against two other gentlemen, who had been most liberal benefactors to him, in revenge for refusing any longer to supply him with the means of indulging his extravagant and profligate disposition.

In the year 1745 he counterfeited a draft upon one of the collectors of the excise, in the name of the Duke of Cumberland, for five hundred pounds. He carried the draft to the collector, who paid him fifty pounds in part, being all the cash that remained in his hands.

He went to a tailor, saying he meant to employ him on the recommendation of a gentleman of the army whom he had long supplied with clothes; adding, that a captain's commission was preparing for him at the War-office. The tailor furnished him with several suits of clothes, but, not being paid according to agreement, he entertained some suspicion as to the responsibility of his new customer; and therefore inquired at the War-office respecting Captain Brown, and learnt that a commission was making out for a gentleman of that name. Unable to get any part of the money due to him, and determined to be no longer trilled with, he instituted a suit at common law, but was non-suited, having laid his action in the fictitious name of Brown, and it appearing that Parsons was the defendant's real name.

Parsons sent a porter from the Ram Inn, in Smithfield, with a counterfeit draft upon Sir Joseph Hankey and Company for five hundred pounds. Parsons followed the man, imagining that, if he came out of Sir Joseph's house alone, he would have received the money; but that, if he was accompanied by any person, it would be a strong proof of the forgery being discovered. Upon observing Sir Joseph, therefore, get into a hackney-coach with the porter, he resolved not to return to the inn.

He next went to a widow named Bottomley, who lived near St. George's church, and, saying he had contracted to supply the regiment to which he belonged with hats, gave her an order to the amount of a hundred and sixty pounds. He had no sooner got possession of these hats than he sold them to a Jew for one half of the sum he had agreed to pay for them.

Being strongly apprehensive that he could not long avoid arrest from some of his numerous and highly exasperated creditors, by means of counterfeit letters he procured himself to be taken into custody as a person disaffected to the king and government; and he was supported, without expense, in the house of one of the king's messengers, for the space of eighteen months.

Being released from the messenger's house, he revolved in his mind a variety of schemes for eluding the importunity of his creditors, and at length embarked for Holland, where he remained a few months; and, when his money was nearly expended, returned to England. A few days after his arrival in London he went to a masquerade, where he engaged in play to the hazard of every shilling he possessed, and was so fortunate as to obtain a sufficient sum for his maintenance for several months.

His circumstances being again distressed, he wrote in pressing terms to his brother-in-law, who was an East India director, entreating that he would procure him a commission in the company's service, either by land or sea. The purport of the answer was, that a gentleman in the Temple was authorized to give the supplicant a guinea, but that it would be fruitless for him to expect further favours.

Having written a counterfeit draft, he went to Ranelagh on a masquerade night, where he passed the draft to a gentleman who had won some small sums of him. The party who received the draft offered it for payment in a day or two afterwards, when it was proved to be a counterfeit, in consequence of which Parsons was apprehended, and committed to Wood Street Compter.

As no prosecutor appeared, Parsons was necessarily acquitted; but a detainer being lodged, charging him with an offence similar to the above, he was removed to Maidstone gaol, in order for trial at the Lent assizes at Rochester.

Mr. Carey, the keeper of the prison, treated Parsons with great humanity, allowing him to board in his family, and indulging him in every privilege that he could grant without a manifest breach of the duties of his office. But such was the ingratitude of the culprit, that he meditated a plan, which, had it taken effect, would have utterly ruined the man to whom he was indebted in such great obligations. His intention was privately to take the keys from

Mr. Carey's apartment; and not only to escape himself, but even to give liberty to every prisoner in the gaol; and this scheme he communicated to a man accused of being a smuggler, who reported the matter to Mr. Carey, desiring him to listen at an appointed hour at night, when he would hear a conversation that would prove his intelligence to be authentic. Mr. Carey attended at the appointed time; and, being convinced of the ingratitude and perfidy of Parsons, he abridged him of the indulgences he had before enjoyed, and caused him to be closely confined.

Being convicted at the assizes at Rochester, he was sentenced to transportation for seven years; and in the following September he was put on board the Thames, Captain Dobbins, bound for Maryland, in company with upwards of a hundred and seventy other convicts, fifty of whom died on the voyage. In November, 1749, Parsons was landed at Annapolis, in Maryland; and, having remained in a state of slavery about seven weeks, a gentleman of considerable property and influence, who was not wholly unacquainted with his family, compassionating his unfortunate situation, obtained his freedom, and received him at his house in a most kind and hospitable manner.

Parsons had not been in the gentleman's family many days before he rode off with a horse which was lent him by his benefactor, and proceeded towards Virginia; on the borders of which country he stopped a gentleman on horseback, and robbed him of five pistoles, a moidore, and ten dollars.

A few days after, he stopped a lady and gentleman in a chaise, attended by a negro servant, and robbed them of eleven guineas and some silver: after which he detected his course to Potomack river, where, finding a ship nearly ready to sail for England, he embarked, and after a passage of twenty-five days landed at Whitehaven.

He now produced a forged letter, in the name of one of his relations, to a capital merchant of Whitehaven, signifying that he was entitled to the family estate, in consequences of his father's decease, and prevailed upon him to discount a false draft upon a banker in London seventy-five pounds.

Upon his arrival in the metropolis he hired a handsome lodging at the west end of the town; but he almost constantly resided in houses of ill fame, where the money he had so unjustifiably obtained was soon dissipated.

Having hired a horse, he rode to Hounslow Heath, where, between ten and eleven o'clock at night, he stopped a postchaise in which were two gentlemen, whom he robbed of five guineas, some silver, and a watch.

A short time afterwards he stopped a gentleman near Turnham Green, about twelve o'clock at night, and robbed him of thirty shillings and a gold ring. The gentleman requested that the ring might be returned, as he valued it, being his wife's wedding-ring. Parsons complied with this request, and voluntarily returned the gentleman five shillings, telling him at the same time that nothing but the most pressing necessity could have urged him to the robbery: after which the gentleman shook hands with the robber, assuring him that, on account of the civility of his behaviour, he would not appear to prosecute if he should hear of his being apprehended.

He attempted to rob a gentleman in a coach and four near Kensington, but, hearing some company on the road, he proceeded towards Hounslow, and on his way thither overtook a farmer, and robbed him of between forty and fifty shillings. He then took the road to Coln-brook, and robbed a gentleman's servant of two guineas and a half, and a silver watch. After this he rode to Windsor, and returned to London by a different road.

His next expedition was on the Hounslow road; and at the entrance of the Heath he stopped two gentlemen, and robbed them of seven guineas, some silver, and a curiously wrought silver snuff-box.

Returning to his lodgings near Hyde Park Corner one evening, he overtook a footman in Piccadilly, and, joining company with him, a familiar conversation took place, in the course of which Parsons learnt that the other was to set out early on the following Sunday with a portmanteau, containing cash and notes to a considerable value, the property of his master, who was then at Windsor.

On the Sunday morning he rode towards Windsor, intending to rob the footman. Soon after he had passed Turnham Green he overtook two gentlemen, one of whom was Mr. Fuller, who had prosecuted him at Rochester, and who, perfectly recollecting his person, warned him not to approach. However, he paid no attention to what Mr. Fuller said, but still continued sometimes behind and sometimes before them, though at a very inconsiderable distance.

Upon coming into the town of Hounslow, the gentlemen alighted, and commanded Parsons to surrender, adding that, if he did not instantly comply, they would alarm the town. He now dismounted, and earnestly entreated that the gentlemen would permit him to speak to them in private, which they consented to; and the parties being introduced to a room at an inn, Parsons surrendered his pistols, which were loaded and primed, and supplicated for mercy in the most pathetic terms.

In all probability he would have been permitted to escape, had not Mr. Day, then landlord of the Rose and Crown, at Hounslow, come into the room, and advised that he might be detained, as he conceived him very nearly to answer the description of a highwayman by whom the roads in that part of the country had been long infested. He was secured at the inn till the next day, and then examined by a magistrate, who committed him to Newgate.

Parsons was now arraigned for returning from transportation before the expiration of the term of his sentence; nothing therefore remained to convict him but the identifying his person. This done, he received sentence of death. His distressed father and wife used all their interest to obtain for him a pardon, but in vain: he was an old offender, and judged by no means a fit object for mercy.

While Parsons remained in Newgate, his behaviour was such that it could not be determined whether he entertained a proper idea of his dreadful situation. There is, indeed, but too much reason to fear that the hopes of a reprieve (in which he deceived himself even to the last moments of his life) induced him to neglect the necessary preparation for eternity.

His taking leave of his wife afforded a scene extremely affecting: he recommended to her parental protection his only child, and regretted that his misconduct had put it in the power of a censorious world to reflect upon both the mother and son.

At the place of execution he joined in the devotional exercises with a fervency of zeal that proved him to be convinced of the necessity of obtaining the pardon of his Creator.

William Parsons, Esq. suffered at Tyburn, on the 11th of February, 1751.

In tracing the depraved and melancholy course of this ill-fated man, the humane reader cannot but be struck with the apparent hollow-heartedness and apathy of his father. It is, no doubt, difficult to tell the precise degree of provocation Sir William had received; but we see that young Parsons was befriended, long after his natural protector had abandoned him, by an uncle, and several other more distant connexions; and it should be recollected that, if the child owes affection and patient forbearance towards its parent, the latter is no less bound to exercise similar duties towards the being whom he has been instrumental in bringing into the world. Nothing but the most hopeless and resolute depravity (if even that) should extinguish a father's tenderness; and it certainly does not appear to us that the wretched subject of the preceding narrative had reached that point at the period of his utter desertion by the baronet. If, at their last recorded interview, instead of advising his penitent son to enter the horse-guards as a private, (for which purpose, too, he left him altogether unprovided), Sir William Parsons had extended to him the feelings of real kindness and reconciliation, it is possible that his own name might have been saved from ignominy, and the youthful prodigal (who was then at an age, perhaps, the most susceptible of moral improvement) restored to his family, to himself, and to his God.

COLLEY AND THE MOB DUCKING OSBORNE AND HIS WIFE FOR REPUTED
WITCHCRAFT.

THOMAS COLLEY

Executed for murder.

———

THIS is not the only case which we shall be able to present arising out of the dregs of the superstition of witchcraft. In the days of the immortal Shakespeare this imbecility of the people was at its height. His writings, to suit the temper of the times, abound with ideal events. The scene in 'Macbeth,' of the Weird Sisters, is still represented in that inimitable tragedy.

The Ghost of Hamlet's father is made a principal speaking character in the magnificent play of 'Hamlet'; and, indeed, is absolutely necessary to the admirable plot which the work contains.

The 'Tempest' of the great bard has its spirits, and the 'Comus' of Milton its enchantment. But it is hoped those times are past, and, Reason asserting her right in the mind of man, things supernatural have long been nearly disbelieved.

But not alone in Britain, and the then separate kingdom of Scotland, did this superstition prevail; all the civilized parts of Europe were tinctured with the same absurdity.

By the fanatics who first inhabited New England, in America, it was planted in all its terrors; and, before we proceed, we shall show that our brethren across the vast Atlantic put each other to death, under the forms of a court of law founded on the constitution of England, on charges of witchcraft.

The following copy of an indictment, furnished us by a friend who took it from the American Court record, must prove a matter of curiosity to the reader at the present enlightened era:—

'Essex, ss. (a town in the colony of Massachusetts Bay, in New England).

'The jurors of our sovereign lord and lady, the king and queen (King William and Queen Mary), present, that George Burroughs, late of Falmouth, in the province of Massachusetts Bay, clerk (a Presbyterian minister of the Gospel), the ninth day of May, and divers other days and times, as well before as after, certain detestable arts, called witchcraft and sorceries, wickedly and feloniously hath used, practised, and exercised, at and in the town of Salem, in the county aforesaid, upon and against one Mary Walkot, single woman, by which said wicked arts the said Mary, on the day aforesaid, and divers other days and times, as well before as after, was, and is, tortured, afflicted, pined, consumed, wasted, and tormented, against the peace, &c.'

A witness, by name Ann Putnam, deposed as follows: 'On the 8th of May, 1692, I saw the apparition of George Burroughs, who grievously tormented me, and urged me to write in his book, which I refused. He then told me that his two first wives would appear to me presently, and tell me a great many lies, but I must not believe them. Then immediately appeared to me the forms of two women in winding-sheets, and napkins about their heads; at which I was greatly affrighted. They turned their faces towards Mr. Burroughs, and looked red and angry, and told him that he had been very cruel to them, and that their blood called for vengeance against him; and they also told him that they should be clothed with white robes in Heaven when he should be cast down into hell; and he immediately vanished away. And as soon as he was gone the women turned their faces towards me, and looked as pale as a white wall; and told me they were Mr. Burroughs's two wives, and that he had murdered them. And one told me she was his first wife, and he stabbed her under the left breast, and put a piece of sealing-wax in the wound; and she pulled aside the winding-sheet, and showed me the place: she also told me that she was in the house where Mr. Daris, the minister of Danvers, then lived, when it was done. And the other told me that Mr. Burroughs, and a wife that he hath now, killed her in the vessel as she was coming to see her friends from the eastward, because they would have one another. And they both charged me to tell these things to the magistrates before Mr. Burroughs's face; and, if he did not own them, they did not know but they should appear this morning. This morning, also, appeared to me another woman in a winding-sheet, and told me that she was Goodman Fuller's first wife, and Mr. Burroughs killed her, because there was a difference between her husband and him. Also, the ninth day of May, during his examination, he did most grievously torture Mary Walkot, Mercy Lewis, Elizabeth Hubbard, and Abigail Williams, by pinching, pricking, and choking them.'

Upon the above, and some other such evidence, was this unfortunate man condemned; and, horrible to relate, executed! Many other unhappy wretches suffered at the gallows on similar charges.

Having shown the mischief of this gross superstition in a world newly discovered, let us, before we proceed upon the trial of Colley, take a slight retrospect of the state of society in this respect, in the 16th century, on the more enlightened continent of Europe.

We find it asserted that, in the year 1562, a countrywoman, named Michelle Chaudron, of the little territory of Geneva, met the devil in her way from the city! The devil gave her a kiss, received a homage, and imprinted on her upper lip and on her right breast the mark which he was wont to bestow upon his favorites. This seal of the devil was described to be a little sign upon the skin, which renders it insensible, as we are assured by all the demonographical civilians of those times.

The devil ordered Michelle Chaudron to bewitch two young girls. She obeyed her master punctually. The parents of the two girls accused her of dealing with the devil. The young women themselves, being confronted with the criminal, declared that they felt a continual prickling in some parts of their bodies, and that they were possessed. Physicians were called—at least men who passed for physicians in those days. They visited the girls. They sought for the seal of the devil on the body of Michelle, which seal is called, in the verbal process, the satanical mark. Into one of these marks they plunged a long needle, which was itself no small torture. Blood issued from the wound, and Michelle testified by her cries that the part was not insensible. The judges, not yet finding sufficient evidence that Michelle Chaudron was a witch, ordered her to be tortured, which infallibly produced the proof they wanted. The poor creature, overcome by pain, confessed at last every thing they desired.

The physicians sought again for the satanical mark, and found it in a little black spot on one of her thighs. Into this they plunged their needle. The poor creature, already exhausted, and almost expiring with the pain of the torture, was insensible to the needle, and did not cry out. She was instantly condemned to be burnt: but, the world beginning at this time to be a little more civilized, her murderers ordered her to be previously strangled.

In the year 1748, in the bishopric of Wurtsburg, an old woman was convicted of witchcraft, and burnt. This was an extraordinary phenomenon in the eighteenth century, particularly among a people who boasted of having trampled superstition under, their feet, and flattered themselves that they had brought their reason to perfection.

On the 18th of April, 1751, a man named Nichols went to William Dell, the crier of Hemel-Hempstead, in Hertfordshire, and delivered to him a piece of paper, with fourpence to cry the words written thereon; a copy of which is as follows:—

'This is to give notice that on Monday next a man and a woman are to be publicly ducked at Tring, in this county, for their wicked crimes.'

This notice was given at Winslow and Leighton-Buzzard, as well as at Hemel-Hempstead, on the respective market-days, and was heard by Mr. Barton, overseer of the parish of Tring, who being informed that the persons intended to be ducked were John Osborne, and Ruth his wife, and having no doubt of the good character of both the parties, he sent them to the workhouse, as a protection from the rage of the mob.

On the day appointed for the practice of the infernal ceremony an immense number of people, supposed to be not fewer than five thousand, assembled near the workhouse at Tring, vowing revenge against Osborne and his wife, as a wizard and a witch, and demanding that they should be delivered up to their fury: they likewise pulled down a wall belonging to the workhouse, and broke the windows and window-frames.

On the preceding evening the master of the workhouse, suspecting some violence from what he heard of the disposition of the people, had sent Osborne and his wife to the vestry-room belonging to the church, as a place the most likely to secure them from insult.

The mob would not give credit to the master of the workhouse that the parties were removed, but, rushing into the house, searched it through, examining the closets, boxes, trunks, and even the saltbox, in search of them. There being a hole in the ceiling which appeared to have been left by the plasterers, Colley, who was one of the most active of the gang, cried out 'Let us search the ceiling!' This being done by Charles Young with similar want of success, they swore they would pull down the house, and set fire to the whole town of Tring, except Osborne and his wife were produced.

The master of the workhouse, apprehensive that they would carry their threats into execution, informed them at length where the poor people were concealed; on which the whole mob, with Colley at their head, went to the church, and brought them off in triumph.

This being done, the merciless brutes conducted them to a pond called Marlston-Mere, where the man and woman, having been stripped, were separately tied up in a cloth; a rope was then bound round the body of the woman, under her arm-pits, and two men dragged her into the pond, and through it several times; Colley going into the pond, and, with a stick, turning her from side to side.

Having ducked her repeatedly in this manner, they placed her by the side of the pond, and dragged the old man in, and ducked him: then he was put by, and the woman ducked again as before, Colley making the same use of his stick. With this cruelty, the husband was treated twice over, and the wife three times; during the last of which the cloth in which she was wrapped came off, and she appeared quite naked.

Not satisfied with this barbarity, Colley pushed his stick against her breast. The poor woman attempted to lay hold of it; but, her strength being now exhausted, she expired on the spot. Then Colley went round the pond, collecting money of the populace for the *sport* he had shown them in ducking the old witch, as he called her.

The mob now departed to their several habitations; and the body, being taken out of the pond, was examined by Mr. Foster, a surgeon; and the coroner's inquest being summoned on the occasion, Mr. Foster deposed that, 'on examining the body of the deceased, he found no wound, either internal or external, except a little place that had the skin off on one of her breasts; and it was his opinion that she was suffocated with water and mud.'

Hereupon Colley was taken into custody, and, when his trial came on, Mr. Foster deposed to the same effect as above mentioned; and there being a variety of other strong proofs of the prisoner's guilt, he was convicted, and received sentence of death: previously to which, however, he made the following defence: 'I happened to be so unfortunate as to be at Marlston Green, among other people, out of curiosity to see what the mob would do with John Osborne and his wife; where, seeing that they used them very barbarously, I went into the pond as a friend, to save her if I could; for I knew both very well, and never had any occasion to fall out with them, but bore them good will. As for the money I collected by the pond-side, it was for the great pains I had taken in the pond to save both the man and the woman.'

This defence was artful enough; but, as he brought no witnesses to support any part of it, the Jury paid no regard to it.

After conviction this man seemed to behold his guilt in its true light of enormity. He became, as far as he judged, sincerely penitent for his sins, and made good use of the short time he had to live in a solemn preparation for eternity. On the day before his execution he received the sacrament, and then signed the following solemn declaration, which he requested might be dispersed through the several towns and villages in the county:—

'Good people,

'I beseech you all to take warning by an unhappy man's suffering, that you be not deluded into so absurd and wicked a conceit as to believe that there are any such beings upon earth as witches.

'It was that foolish and vain imagination, heightened and inflamed by the strength of liquor, which prompted me to be instrumental (with others as mad as myself) in the horrid and barbarous murder of Ruth Osborne, the supposed witch, for which I am now so deservedly to suffer death.

'I am fully convinced of my former error, and, with the sincerity of a dying man, declare that. I do not believe there is such a thing in being as a witch; and pray God that none of you, through a contrary persuasion, may hereafter be induced to think that you have a right in any shape to persecute, much less endanger the life of, a fellow-creature. I beg of you all to pray to God to forgive me, and to wash clean my polluted soul in the blood of Jesus Christ, my Saviour and Redeemer.

'So exhorteth you all,

'The dying

'THOMAS COLLEY.'

The day before his execution he was removed from the gaol of Hertford, under the escort of one hundred men of the Oxford Blues, commanded by seven officers; and, being lodged in the gaol of St. Albans, was put into a chaise at five o'clock the next morning, with the hangman, and reached the place of execution about eleven, where his wife and daughter came to take leave of him; and the minister of Tring assisted him in his last moments, when he died exhibiting all the marks of unfeigned penitence.

He was executed the 24th of August, 1751, and his body afterwards hung in chains at a place called Gubblecut, near where the offence was committed.

It is astonishing that any persons could be so stupid as to believe in the ridiculous doctrine of witchcraft. How absurd to suppose that the power of Heaven is delegated to a weak and frail mortal; and, of all mortals, to a poor decrepit old woman! for we never hear of a young witch, but through the fascination of the eyes. Just when a woman has been poor and old enough to obtain the pity and compassion of every one; when nothing has remained to her but her innocence, her piety, and her tabby cat; then has she, by the voice of superstition, been dignified with the presumed possession of a power which the God of Heaven alone could exert!

It is remarkable, in the story before us, that the insurgents, in search of the presumed witch and wizard, had recourse to the saltbox. What a strange madness of credulity must have inflamed their minds! The reflection of a moment would have told them that, if the old folks had possessed power to have contracted themselves within the compass of a salt-box, they would have been able to have disappeared entirely; or even to have destroyed their persecutors by a mere effort of the will.

Pity is it, for the honour of common sense and true religion, and for the sake of example throughout the kingdom, that others, as well as Colley, had not been punished for this atrocious murder. As it is, however, his death has been of public service. We have heard of no ducking of witches presumptive since that time.

Those who are acquainted with history will observe, that what would have been deemed meritorious in the reign of James the First became criminal in that of George the Second; thanks to the increasing good sense, knowledge, and learning of the age!

The first-mentioned monarch wrote a book on the subject of witchcraft, which he called 'Demonologia'; and the complaisant parliament of his days passed a bill to make it felony for any man or woman to be guilty of witchcraft! and in consequence thereof many innocent persons were murdered under the form of law: but this act has been repealed by the wisdom of later times.

MARY BLANDY CONFESSING HAVING POISONED HER FATHER.

MARY BLANDY

Executed for the murder of her father.

———

It has been a melancholy remark that two young ladies—Miss Jefferies and Miss Blandy—well educated, and of considerable expectations from the parents whom they murdered should, as it were, at the same moment contemplate the death of their protectors.

Yet, though Miss Blandy's crime was committed on blood nearest in she does not appear to have been that determined a murderer we find in Miss Jefferies.

Public conversation was long divided in fate, and in comparisons of their different degrees of crimes.

There is too much reason to fear that both had been seduced by villainous men: but Miss Jefferies, as will be seen, was a premeditated and determined murderess. Over the fate of the wretched Miss Blandy we may indulge somewhat of commiseration; for the profligate wretch who seduced her was a disgrace to the noble blood from which he derived existence; and what renders his crime more heinous was his being a married man.

It will appear that, had not this corrupt twig of the noble branch of the tree of genealogy from which he grew spread his insidious snares to entangle the heart and corrupt the mind of Miss Blandy, she would not have been guilty of the abominable and unnatural point of parricide.

In a moral point of view, though the law may not immediately overtake the villainy, we would appeal to the hearts of the readers of our own sex—may, we would ask the question, in cooler moments of youth—'Can there be a more destructive vice than the seduction of a virtuous female, under promise of marriage?' Will not your inflamed passions cool? and then what must be the stings of conscience when you find the too-willing sacrifice to your lust a wretched creature, neglected by her friends, the scorn of the virtuous part of her sex. And the prey of your own?

Thus are we led to acknowledge, with sorrow, the lines of the poet, on a seduced woman:—

> Man, the lawless libertine, may rove,
> Free and Unquestion 'd, thro' the paths of love
> But woman, sense and nature's easy fool—
> If poor weak woman swerve from virtue's rule—I
> If, strongly charmid, she tempt the flow'ry way,
> And in the softer paths of pleasure stray—
> Ruin ensues, remorse, and endless shame,

And one false step entirely damns her fame:
In vain with tears the loss she may deplore
In vain look back to what she was before;
She sets, like stars that fall, to rise no more,

Mary Blandy was the only daughter of a Mr. Francis Blandy, an eminent attorney at Henley-upon-Thames, and town-clerk of that place. She had been educated with the utmost tenderness; and every possible care *was* taken to impress her mind with sentiments of virtue and religion. Her person had nothing in it remarkably engaging, but she was of a sprightly and affable disposition, of polite manners, engaging in conversation, and was much distinguished by her good sense. She had read the best authors in the English language, and had a memory remarkably retentive of the knowledge she had acquired. In a word, she excelled most of her sex in those accomplishments which are calculated to grace and dignify the female mind.

The father being reputed to be rich, a number of young gentlemen courted his acquaintance, with a view to make an interest with his daughter: but, of all the visitors, none were more agreeable, both to father and daughter, than the gentlemen of the army; and the former was never better pleased than when he had some of them at his table.

Miss Blandy was about twenty-six years of age when she became acquainted with Captain William Henry Cranstoun, who was then about forty-six. He was the son of Lord Cranstoun, of an ancient Scotch family, which had made great alliances, by intermarriages, with the nobility of Scotland. Being a younger brother, his uncle, Lord Mark Keri, procured him a commission in the army, which, with the interest of fifteen hundred pounds, was all he had for his support.

Cranstoun married a Miss Murray in Scotland, in the year 1745, and received a handsome fortune with her; but he was defective in the great article of prudence. His wife was delivered of a son within a year after the marriage. About this period he received orders to join his regiment in England, and was afterwards sent on a recruiting party to Henley, which gave rise to the unhappy connexion which ended so fatally.

It may seem extraordinary, and is, perhaps, a proof of Cranstoun's art, that he could ingratiate himself into the affections of Miss Blandy; for his person was diminutive, he was so marked with the small pox his face was in seams, and he squinted very much: but he possessed that faculty of small-talk which is unfortunately too much esteemed by many of the fair sex.

Mr. Blandy, who was acquainted with Lord Mark Ker, was fond of being deemed a man of taste, and so open to flattery, that it is not to be wondered at that a man of Cranstoun's artifice ingratiated himself into his favour, and obtained permission to pay his addresses to the daughter.

Cranstoun, apprehending that Miss Blandy might discover that he had a wife in Scotland, informed her that he was involved in a disagreeable lawsuit in that country with a young lady, who claimed him as husband; and so sure was he of the interest he had obtained in Miss Blandy's affections, that he had the confidence to ask her if she loved him well enough to wait the issue of the affair. She told him that, if her father and mother approved of her staying for him, she had no objection.

This must be allowed to have been a very extraordinary declaration love, and as extraordinary a reply.

Cranstoun endeavored to conduct amour with all possible secrecy; notwithstanding which it came to the knowledge of Lord Mark Ker, who wrote to Mr. Blandy, informing him that the captain had a wife and children in Scotland, and conjuring him to preserve his daughter from ruin.

Alarmed by this intelligence, Mr. Blandy informed his daughter of it; but she did not seem equally affected, as Cranstoun's former declaration had prepared her to expect some such news; and, when the old gentleman taxed Cranstoun with it, he declared it was only an affair of gallantry, of which he should have no difficulty to free himself.

Mrs. Blandy appears to have been under as great a degree of infatuation as her daughter, for she forbore all farther inquiry, on the captain's bare assurance that the report of his marriage was false. Cranstoun, however, could not be equally easy, he saw the necessity of devising some Scheme to get his first marriage annulled, or of bidding adieu to all the gratifications he could promise himself by a second.

After revolving various schemes in his mind, he at length wrote to his wife, requesting her to disown him for a husband. The substance of this letter was, that, 'having no other way of rising to preferment but in the army, he had but little ground to expect advancement there, while it was known he was encumbered with a wife and family; but, could he once pass for a single man, he had not the least doubt of being quickly preferred, which would procure him a sufficiency to maintain her, as well as himself, in a genteeler manner than now he was able to do. All, therefore, (adds he) I have to request of you is, that you will transcribe the enclosed copy of a letter, wherein you disown me for a husband; put your maiden name to it, and send it by the post: all the use I shall make of it shall be to procure my advancement, which will necessarily include your own benefit. In full assurance that you will comply with my request, I remain, your most affectionate husband,

'W. H. CRANSTOUN.'

Mrs. Cranstoun, ill as she had been treated by her husband, and little hope as she had of more generous usage, was, after repeated letters had passed, induced to give up her claim, and at length sent him the requested paper, signed Murray, which was her maiden name.

The villainous captain, being possessed of this letter, made some copies of it, which he sent to his wife's relations, and his own: the consequence of which was that they withdrew the assistance, they had afforded the lady, which reduced her to an extremity she had never before known.

Exclusive of this, he instituted a suit before the lords of session, for the dissolution of the marriage; but when Mrs. Cranstoun was heard, and the letters read, the artful contrivance was seen through, the marriage was confirmed, and Cranstoun was adjudged to pay the expenses of the trial.

At the next sessions Captain Cranstoun preferred a petition desiring to be heard by counsel on new evidence, which it was pretended had arisen respecting Miss Murray. This petition, after some hesitation, was heard; but the issue was, that the marriage was again confirmed, and Cranstoun was obliged to allow his wife a separate maintenance.

Still, however, he paid his addresses to Miss Blandy with the same fervency as before; which coming to the knowledge of Mrs. Cranstoun, she sent her the decree of the Court of Session, establishing the validity of the marriage.

It is reasonable to suppose that that would have convinced Miss Blandy of the erroneous path in which she was treading. On this occasion she consulted her mother: and, Cranstoun having set out for Scotland, the old lady advised her to write to him, to know the truth of the affair.

Absurd as this advice was, she wrote to him; but, soon after the receipt of her letter, he returned to Henley, when he had impudence enough to assert that the cause was not finally determined, but would be referred to the House of Lords.

Mr. Blandy gave very little credit to this assertion; but his wife assented at once to all Cranstoun said, and treated him with as much tenderness as if he had been her own child; of which the following circumstance will afford ample proof.

Mrs. Blandy and her daughter being on a visit to Mrs. Pocock, of Turville Court, the old lady was taken so ill as to be obliged to continue there for some days. In the height of her disorder, which was a violent fever, she cried 'Let Cranstoun be sent for.' He was then with the regiment at Southampton; but, her request being complied with, she no sooner saw him than she raised herself on the pillow, and hung round his neck, repeatedly exclaiming 'My dear Cranstoun, I am glad you are come; I shall now grow well soon!' So extravagant was her fondness, that she insisted on having him as her nurse; and he actually administered her medicines.

On the following day she grew better; on which she said 'This I owe to you, my dear Cranstoun; your coming has given me new health and fresh spirits. I was fearful I should die, and you not here to comfort that poor girl. How like death she looks!'

It would be ungenerous to the memory of Mrs. Blandy to suppose that she saw Cranstoun's guilt in its true light of enormity; but certainly she was a most egregious dupe to his artifices.

Mrs. Blandy and her daughter having come to London, the former wanted forty pounds, to discharge a debt she had contracted unknown to her husband; and Cranstoun coming into the room while the father and the daughter were weeping over their distresses, he demanded the reason of their grief; of which being informed, he left them, and, soon returning with the requisite sum, he threw it into the said lady's lap. Charmed by this apparent generosity, she burst into tears, and squeezed his hand fervently; on which he embraced her, and said, 'Remember it is a son; therefore do not make yourself uneasy as you do not lie under any obligation to me.'

Of this debt of forty pounds, ten pounds had been contracted by the ladies while in London, for expenses in consequence of their pleasures; and the other thirty by expenses treats given to Cranstoun Henley, during Mr. Blandy's absence.

Soon after this Mrs. Blandy died; and Cranstoun now complaining of his fear of being arrested for the forty pounds, the young lady borrowed that sum, which she gave him, and made him a present of her watch: so that he was a gainer by his former apparent generosity.

Mr. Blandy began now to show evident dislike of Captain Cranstoun's visits: but he found means to take leave of the daughter, to whom he complained of the father's ill treatment; but insinuated that he had a method of conciliating his esteem; and that when he arrived in Scotland he would send her some powders proper for the purpose; on which to prevent suspicion, he would write, 'Powders to clean the Scotch pebbles.'

'It does not appear that the young lady had any idea that the powders he was to send her were of a poisonous nature. She seems rather to have been infatuated by her love; and this is the only excuse that can be made for her subsequent conduct, which appears otherwise totally inconsistent with that good sense for which she was celebrated.

Cranstoun sent her the powders, according to promise; and Mr. Blandy being indisposed on the Sunday Se'night before his death, Susan Gunnel, a maid-servant, made him some water-gruel, into which Miss Blandy conveyed some of the powder, and gave it to her father; and, repeating this draught on the following day, he was tormented with the most violent pains in his bowels.

When the old gentleman's disorder increased, and he was attended by a physician, his daughter came into the room, and, falling on her knees to her father, said, 'Banish me where you please; do with me what you please, so you do but forgive me; and, as for Cranstoun, I will never see him, speak to him, or write to him, as long as I live, if you will forgive me.'

In reply to this the father said, 'I forgive thee, my dear, and I hope God will forgive thee; but thou should have considered before thou attempted any thing against thy father; thou should have considered I was thy own father.'

Miss Blandy now acknowledged that she had put powder in his gruel, but that it was for an innocent purpose; on which the father, turning in his bed, said, 'O such a villain! to come to my house, eat of the best and drink of the best my house could afford; and, in return, take away my life, and ruin my daughter. O! my dear, thou must hate that man.'

The young lady replied, 'Sir, every word you say is like a sword piercing to my heart; more severe than if you were angry: I must kneel, and beg you will not curse me.' The father said, 'I curse thee, my dear! how couldst thou think I would curse thee? No, I bless thee, and hope God will bless thee, and amend thy life. Do, my dear, go out of the room; say no more, lest thou should say any thing to thy own prejudice. Go to thy uncle Stephens; and take him for thy friend: poor man! I am sorry for him.'

Mr. Blandy dying in consequence of his illness, it was suspected that the daughter had occasioned his death; whereupon she was taken into custody, and committed to the gaol at Oxford.

She was tried on the 3rd of March, 1752; and, after many witnesses had been called to give evidence of her guilt, she was desired to make her defence, which she did in the following speech:—

'My Lord,—It is morally impossible for me to lay down the hardships I have received.—I have been aspersed in my character. In the first place it has been said I spoke ill of my father; that I have cursed him, and wished him at hell; which is extremely false. Sometimes little family affairs have happened, and he did not speak to me so kindly as I could wish. I own I am passionate, my lord; and in those passions some hasty expressions might have dropped; but great care has been taken to recollect every word I have spoken at different times, and to apply them to such particular purposes as my enemies knew would do me the greatest injury. These are hardships, my lord, such as yourself must allow to be so. It was said too, my lord, that I endeavored to make my escape. Your lordship will judge from the difficulties I labored under:—I had lost my father;—I was accused of being his murderer;—I was not permitted to go near him;—I was forsaken by my friends—affronted by the mob—and insulted by my servants.—Although I begged to have the liberty to listen at the door where he died, I was not allowed it. My keys were taken from me; my shoe-buckles and garters too—to prevent me from making away with myself, as though I was the most abandoned creature. What could I do, my lord? I verily believe I must have been out of my senses. When I heard my father was dead, I ran out of the house, and over the bridge, and had nothing on but a half sack and petticoats, without a hoop—my petticoats hanging about me. The mob gathered round me. Was this a condition, my lord, to make my escape in? A good woman beyond the bridge, seeing me in this distress, desired me to walk in till the mob was dispersed: the town-sergeant was there. I begged he would take me under his protection, to have me home: the woman said it was not proper, the mob was very great, and that I had better stay a little. When I came home they said I used the constable ill. I was locked up for fifteen hours, with only an old servant of the family to attend me. I was not allowed a maid for the common decencies of my sex. I was sent to gaol, and was in hopes there at least this usage would have ended; but was told it was reported I was frequently drunk; that I attempted to make my escape; that I did not attend at chapel. A more abstemious woman, my lord, I believe, does not live.

'Upon the report of my making my escape, the gentleman who was high-sheriff last year (not the present) came and told me, by order of the higher powers, he must put an iron on me. I submitted as I always do, to the higher powers. Some time after he came again, and said he must put a heavier one upon me; which I have worn, my lord, will I have hither. I asked the sheriff why I was so ironed. He said he did it by the command of some noble peer, on his hearing that I intended making my escape. I told him I never had any such thought, and I would bear it with the other cruel usage I had received on my character. The Reverend Mr. Swinton, the worthy clergyman who attended me in prison, can testify I was regular at the chapel whenever I was well: sometimes I really was not able to come out, and then he attended me in my room they have likewise published, papers and depositions, which ought not to have been published, in order to represent me as the most abandoned of my sex, and to prejudice the world against me. I submit myself to your lordship, and to the worthy jury. I do assure his lordship, as I am to answer at the great tribunal where I must appear am as innocent as the child unborn of the death of my father. I would not endeavour to save my life at the expense of truth: I really thought the powder an innocent inoffensive thing; and I got it to procure his love (meaning towards Cranstoun). It has been mentioned, I should say, I was led. My lord, when a young woman loses her character, is not wide her ruin? Why, then, should this expression be construed in so wide a sense? Is it not ruining my character to have such a thing laid to my charge? And, whatever may be the event of this trial, I am ruined most effectually.'

The trial lasted eleven hours, and then the judge summed up the evidence, mentioning the scandalous behaviors of some people respecting the prisoner, in printing and publishing what they called depositions taken before the coroner relating to the affair before them: to which he added, 'I hope you have not seen them; but, if you have, I must tell you, as you are men of sense and probity, that you must divest yourselves of every prejudice that can arise from thence and attend merely to the evidence that has now been given.'

The judge then summed up the evidence with the utmost candour; and the jury, having considered the affair, found her guilty without going out of court.

After conviction she behaved with the utmost decency and resignation. She was attended by the Reverend Mr. Swinton, from whose hands she received the sacrament on the day before her execution, declaring that she did not know there was any thing hurtful in the powders she had given her father.

The night before her death she spent in devotion; and at nine in the morning of the 6th of April, 1752, she left her apartment, being dressed in a black bombazine, and having her arms bound with black rebinds.

The clergyman attended her to the place of execution, to which she walked with the utmost solemnity of deportment; and, when there, acknowledged her fault in administering the powders to her father; but declared that, as she must soon appear before the most awful tribunal, she had no idea of doing injury, nor any suspicions that the powders were of a poisonous nature.

Having ascended some steps of the ladder, she said 'Gentlemen, don't hang me high, for the sake of decency.' Being desired to go something higher, she turned about, and expressed her apprehensions that she should fall. The rope being put round her neck, she pulled her handkerchief over her face, and was turned off on holding out a book of devotions which she had been reading.

The crowd of spectators assembled on this occasion was immense; and when she had hung the usual time she was cut down, and the body, being put into a hearse, was conveyed to Henley, and interred with her parents, at one o'clock on the following morning.

It will now be proper to return to Cranstoun, who was the original contriver of this horrid murder. Having heard of Miss Blandy's commitment to Oxford gaol, he concealed himself some time in Scot. Land, and then escaped to Boulogne, in France. Meeting there with Mrs. Ross, who was distantly related to his family, he acquainted her with his situation, and begged her protection; on which she advised him to change his name for her maiden name of Dunbar.

Some officers in the French service, who were related to his wife, hearing of his concealment, vowed revenge, if they should meet with him, for his cruelty to the unhappy woman: on which he fled to Paris, from whence he went to Fumes, a town in Flanders, where Mrs. Ross had provided a lodging for his reception.

He had not been long at Fumes when he was seized with a severe fit of illness, which brought him to a degree of reflection to which he had been long a stranger. At length he sent for a father belonging to an adjacent convent, and received absolution from his hands, on declaring himself a convert to the Romish faith.

Cranstoun died on the 30th of November, 1752; and the fraternity of monks and friars looked on his conversion as an object of such importance, that solemn mass was sung on the occasion, and the body was followed to the grave not only by the ecclesiastics, but by the magistrates of the town.

His papers were then sent to Scotland, to his brother, Lord Cranstoun; his clothes were sold for the discharge of his debts; and his wife came into possession of the interest of the fifteen hundred pounds above mentioned.

ANN WILLIAMS BURNT AT THE STAKE.

ANN WILLIAMS

Executed for the murder of her husband.

———

THE behaviour of this fiend had long been a prelude
to the diabolical crime which she committed. She was in
her family turbulent and dictatorial; her husband the very
reverse. His mild and quiet disposition served only to nurse
her opposition and violence. He had long given way to her in
all things, and she, in return, ruled him with a rod of iron.

Before the commission of this horrid deed we have found
women make use of man's unqualified indulgence. Hence
arose the vulgar saying of 'the grey mare being the better

horse,' of 'hen-pecked husbands,' and many other irritating observations on men troubled with shrews.

One of the wisest of the ancient philosophers had his Xantippe: and the poet sings,

'When man to woman gives the sway, To what is right they oft say Nay.'

The pliancy of the more unfortunate man in question could not shield him from the consequence of the ascendency she had over him; it sunk into contempt, and she determined to rule alone. To effect this, her wicked heart suggested the death of her husband. For this horrid purpose she prevailed on their servant-man to purchase some white mercury, which she mixed in some gruel, and caused him to eat it. This mode of administering the poison, it was conjectured, was adopted in contempt of him; for it appeared the poor man did not like gruel. She then directed him to draw her some ale, of which he also drank; and was immediately seized with violent purgings and vomiting. She told the man, whom it seems she meant afterwards to share her bed, that she 'had given her husband the stuff he brought, and that it was operating purely.'

The dying man, in his agonies, said his wife was a wicked woman; that he was well until she made him eat some pap, which had done his business, and that he should be a dead man on the morrow; and, in spite of medical aid, he died next day, his body being in a state of mortification.

The horrid crime being fully proved against her, she received sentence to be burnt at the stake, which sentence was accordingly carried into execution at Gloucester, April 13, 1753, among a number of spectators, who showed little pity for her fate, and which became still more shocking from denying the fact, so incontrovertibly proved, to the very last moment of her existence.

BROWN, HOLDING HIS WIFE TO THE FIRE TILL HE CAUSED HER DEATH.

NICHOL BROWN

Executed for the murder of his wife.

————

In the account given of this man there is a savage ferocity which has not before come under our notice; for, though
we read in Captain Cook's, and other accounts of circum-
navigators, of their meeting with cannibals; and, further,
that even civilized men, by the dire dint of the excruciating
pains of hunger, have slain, and, with horrible compunction, eaten one of their companions, to support life in the
rest; yet where shall we find, except in this instance, a savage, in the land of civilization and of plenty, eat human

flesh? After this it no longer remains astonishingly horrible that such a brute could force his wife into the fire, and burn her to death.

This atrocious monster was a native of Cramond, a small town near Edinburgh, where he received a school education. At a proper age he was placed with a butcher in that city, and, when his apprenticeship was expired, went to sea in a man of war, and continued in that same four years. The ship being paid off, Brown returned to Edinson, and married the widow of a butcher, who had left her a decent fortune.

Soon after this marriage Brown commenced dealer in cattle, in which he met with such success, that, in the course of a few years, he became possessed of a considerable sum. His success, however, did not inspire him with sentiments of humanity. His temper was so bad, that he was shunned by all serious people of his acquaintance; for he delighted in fomenting quarrels among his neighbours.

Taking to a habit of drinking, he seldom came home sober at night; and, his wife following his sample, he used frequently to beat her for copying his own crime. This conduct rendered both parties obnoxious to their acquaintance; and the following story of Brown, which may be relied on as a fact, incontestably proves the unfeeling brutality of his nature.

About a week after the execution of Norman Ross for murder, Brown had been drinking with some company at Leith, till, in the height of their bully, they boasted what extravagant sections they could perform. Brown swore that he would cut off a place of flesh from the leg of the dead man, and eat it. His companions, drunk as they were, appeared shocked at the very idea; while Brown, to prove that he was reformed, procured a ladder, which he carried to the gibbet, and, cutting he a place of flesh from the leg of the suspended body of Ross, brought it back, broiled, and ate it.

The circumstance was much talked of, but little credit was given to it by the inhabitants of Edinburgh till Brown's companions gave the fullest testimony of its truth. It will be now proper that we recite the particulars of the shocking crime, for which this offender forfeited his life.

After having been drinking at an alehouse in the Cannongate, he went home about eleven at night, in a high degree of intoxication. His wife was also much in liquor; but, though equally criminal himself, he was so exasperated against her, that he struck her so violently that she fell from her chair. The noise of her fall alarmed the neighbours; but, as frequent quarrels had happened between them, no immediate notice was taken of the affair.

In about fifteen minutes the wife was heard to cry out 'Murder! help! fire! the rogue is murdering me! help, for Christ's sake!' The neighbours, now apprehending real danger, knocked at the door; but, no person being in the house but Brown and his wife, no admission was granted; and the woman was heard to groan most shockingly.

A person, looking through the key-hole, saw Brown holding his wife to the fire; on which he was called on to open the door, but refused to do so. The candle being extinguished, and the woman still continuing her cries, the door was at length forced open; and, when the neighbours went in, they beheld her a most shocking spectacle, lying half-naked before the fire, and her flesh in part broiled. In the interim Brown had got into bed, pretended to be asleep, and, when spoken to, appeared ignorant of the transaction. The woman, though so dreadfully burnt, retained her senses, accused her husband of the murder, and told in what manner it was perpetrated. She survived till the following morning, still continuing in the same tale, and then expired in the utmost agony.

The murderer was now seized, and, being lodged in the gaol of Edinburgh, was brought to trial, and capitally convicted.

After sentence he was allowed six weeks to prepare himself for a future state, agreeably to the custom in Scotland.

He was visited by several divines of Edinburgh, but steadily persisted in the denial of his guilt, affirming that he was ignorant of his wife being burnt till the door was broke open by the neighbours.

Among others who visited the criminal was the Reverend Mr. Kinloch, an ancient minister, who, urging him to confess his crime, received no other reply than that, 'if he was to die to-morrow, he would have a new suit of clothes, to appear decently at the gallows.' Mr. Kinloch was so affected by his declaration, that he shed tears over the unhappy convict.

On the following day, August the 14th, 1754, he was attended to the place of execution at Edinburgh by the Reverend Dr. Brown; but to the last he denied having been guilty of the crime for which he suffered.

After execution he was hung in chains; but the body was stolen from the gibbet, and thrown into a pond, where, being found, it was exposed as before. In a few days, however, it was again stolen; and, though a reward was offered for its discovery, no such discovery was made.

It is impossible to express sufficient horror at the crime of which this man was guilty; and it is therefore the less necessary to make any remarks on his case, as no one can be tempted to think of committing a similar crime till he is totally divested of all the feelings of humanity. From a fate so wretched as this may the God of infinite mercy deliver us!

MORGAN BURNING THE HOUSE, AFTER MURDERING ITS INHABITANTS.

EDWARD MORGAN

Executed for murder.

———

THOUGH we have shown the perpetrators of this foul crime under the cursed impulse of rage, jealousy, avarice, and revenge, yet have we to adduce one, resulting more from wantonness than a propensity to thieving—a murder marked with the basest ingratitude and perfidy.

The hospitality of the Welch is proverbial; and their Christmas feasts are open to all visitors. What villain could pollute the festive board? Where, we would ask, could be found the man, who would suck the blood of his generous

host and his family, and that host a near relation? Sorry are
we to acknowledge that such a monster have we found in a
Welchman.

The circumstances which came out on the trial of
Edward Morgan, at the assizes of Glamorgan, were these:—
According to annual custom, he had been invited by
Mr. Rees Morgan, of Lanvabon, his cousin, to spend the
Christmas holidays. He had partaken of the first day's festivity, and retired to bed along with a young man, apprentice to Mr. Rees Morgan. No sooner had he laid his head
upon the pillow, to use his own expression, than the devil
whispered him to get up, and murder the whole family, and
he determined to obey.

He first made an attempt on the apprentice, his bed-
fellow, but he struggled so far as to effect his escape, and
hid himself. The murderer then provided himself with a
knife, which he sharpened on a stone as deliberately as the
butcher uses his steel.

Thus prepared, he softly crept to the bedchamber of his
host and hostess, and cut their throats in their sleep; then
he proceeded to the bed of their beautiful daughter, with
whom the monster had but an hour before been sporting
and playing, and with equal expedition, and by the same
means, robbed her of life!

Not, however, satisfied with causing this inundation of
blood, he seized a firebrand, and proceeded to the barn and
outhouses, setting fire to them all; and, to complete the sum
of his crime, he fired the dwelling-house, after plundering
it of some articles.

'The Gloucester Journal,' of the year 1757, describes the
property consumed by fire on this melancholy occasion to
have been 'the dwelling-house, a barn full of corn, a beast-
house, with twelve head of cattle in it; and the farmer, his
wife, and daughter, were either murdered or perished in
the flames!'

It was at first conjectured that the unfortunate people had perished in the conflagration. Their murdered bodies, it is too true, were consumed to ashes, and the manner of their death was proved partly by what the concealed apprentice overheard, but chiefly from the murderer's own confession. He was executed at Glamorgan, April the 6th, 1757.

WHEATLEY DOING PENANCE IN CHURCH.

THE REVEREND MR. WHEATLEY

Sentenced to do public penance for adultery.

———

WE consider it a part of our duty to give our readers occasionally an account of the various modes of punishment, for the commission of crimes, in distant nations.

No guilt is more frequent than adultery, and none, in its progress, more tending to fatal consequences, involving whole families in ruin, and driving others to seek revenge in the blood of the spoilers of their honour.

That adultery is a crime which has been detested by all wise and good people, as scandalous in its nature, pernicious to society, and destructive of religion, appears by the various severe laws and punishments by which legislators and magistrates have endeavoured to restrain it.

The histories of the ancient heathens tell us that they thought it a crime so very black and abominable, that they have compared it to sacrilege, or to robbing of temples; and their philosophers judged it to be worse than perjury. The old Ethiopians ranked it with treason, as a crime of the like nature and guilt; and the Egyptians had a law that the man guilty of it should have a thousand stripes, and that the woman should lose her nose, as a mark of perpetual infamy.

The ancient Athenians punished all adulterers with death, and even those who were only suspected with some less penalty. It was the custom of the Persians to throw the adulteress down headlong into a deep well; for, as adultery was, at one time, a common crime among the nobility and gentry in the court of ancient Persia, it became the frequent cause of rebellions, murders, and other dreadful calamities, in that empire.

The tragedy of Mejistes and his whole family, occasioned by the adultery of his wife with Xerxes the emperor, is most horrible to relate; and the punishment of Appodines the physician, for debauching Amytis, the widow of Megabyzus, is also most shocking and terrible.

The old lawgivers of Greece punished this crime with death.

Among the Lybians it was the custom to treat married women guilty of adultery in the most severe manner, without mercy and without pardon.

In a certain city of Crete, when an adulterer was caught in the fact, and judicially convicted, he was first adjudged to be covered with a crown of wool, in derision of his soft and effeminate nature, signified by that material and the animal whence it was taken, then publicly to pay a heavy fine, and to be rendered incapable of bearing any office in the government.

The King of the Tenideans made a law that the adulterer should be beheaded with an axe; and commanded his own son, found guilty of this fact, to be put to death in that manner.

The Lepreans made a law that the men should be led round the city for three days together, and then burnt in the face with a brand of indelible infamy; and that the women should stand in the marketplace for eleven successive days, clothed only with a thin transparent garment, which should hang loose and untied, in order to expose them more to public shame, contempt, and laughter.

Hippomines, one of the kings of Athens, having caught an adulterer with his daughter Limona, ordered him to be tied to the wheel of a chariot, and her to one of the horses, and to be dragged about the streets till they died; a shameful and horrid spectacle to the whole city, but a public example of the most severe and impartial justice.

Dio the consul, the first King of the Romans, made a law that the faulty wife should be put to death after what manner her husband or relations thought fit; which law was afterwards confirmed, and continued in force many years. But the rigidly virtuous Cato allowed the husband to dispatch his wife immediately on finding her guilty, without staying for the forms of justice. Many also of the Roman emperors punished this crime with present death; though it must be confessed, indeed, that many others of them, with their empresses and daughters, and ladies of the highest quality, when Rome was declining, were notoriously guilty.

This vice soon after became very common among them in the days of their conquests, national influence, and prosperity; and yet, such diligence and labour had there been used to bring offenders to condign punishment, that Tacitus says, when he was a chief officer of Rome, he found in the public records the names of three thousand who had been put to death for committing adultery. Even the heathen Romans always punished malefactors convicted of this crime by banishment, and, in cases of the highest degree, with death.

The Hungarians, in those days when virtue was in more esteem than at present, made death the punishment, with dreadful infliction. The father was compelled to conduct and force his own daughter to the place of execution, the husband his wife, and the brother his sister.

In Old Saxony a woman convicted of this crime was punished precisely as the English law punished the murderer of her husband—strangled, and then burnt to ashes. The adulterer was then hung up over her grave; or else the chaste matrons of the town where the fact was committed had liberty to scourge him with whips and rods, from one village to another, until he died.

The Turks adopted the Levitical law, and stoned such offenders to death; though, before the law of Moses, the adulteress, when condemned, was burnt alive.

In holy writ, the prophet Jeremiah intimates that the King of Babylon was more cruel than any other monarch, for he roasted to death Zedekiah, the son of Maaseiah, and Ahad, the son of Kolaiah, because they had committed adultery with their neighbours' wives.

At this day, in Turkey, adulteries are often punished by drowning the guilty woman, and castrating the man.

The Spaniards and the Italians, by nature jealous and severe, wherever they suspect a man guilty with their wives, wait an opportunity of plunging a dagger secretly into his heart.

In France, five hundred years ago, two gentlemen of Normandy, who were brothers, were flayed alive, and hung upon gibbets, for adultery.

Modern writers have stigmatized this crime with the name it deserves—a most execrable villainy. Some of the old fathers of the Church have declared their minds with such sharpness and vehemence, as to pronounce it, in many cases, unpardonable.

If we look into the old books of the civil and canon laws we shall find that the several punishments made and ordained by them were either death by the sword or the loss of their noses, or some singular brand of infamy, or some large pecuniary mulct, or banishment; as we find by the old statutes of the Belgians and Hollanders. If a father caught his daughter in the fact, he might kill her and her and her gallant upon the spot; but a husband was empowered, in the like cases, to put the latter only to death, but the wife was reserved to the judgment of the law.

Adultery, from being more immediately an offence against the Church, has been generally excepted out of the acts of pardon and indemnity, as an evil in itself, or of that nature which kings themselves cannot or will not pardon.

It would be endless to recount the many kingdoms and republics, with all their different laws and customs, where this abominable crime hath been, and still is, chastised and exposed with very signal, infamous, painful, and terrible punishments. In England, we are sorry to say, its commission now too often goes unpunished, whether in the prince or the pickpocket.

Let, however, this short extract from eminent authors, contrasted with its barefaced commission in our own country, give the immoral and incontinent a specimen of the opinion of the wise and sober part of mankind; and let them dread the examples of the downfall of mighty empires from profligacy, lest its general adoption hurl their country into the like fate.

EARL FERRERS SHOOTING MR. JOHNSON, HIS STEWARD.

LAURENCE EARL FERRERS

Executed for murder.

———

FROM the royal blood of the Plantagenets was the house of Ferrers descended, and had been distinguished for ages. One of the family was slain, while fighting on behalf of the crown, at the memorable battle of Shrewsbury, in the beginning of the reign of Henry IV—a circumstance that is mentioned by the immortal Shakespeare.

Laurence Earl Ferrers was a man of an unhappy disposition. Though of clear intellects, and acknowledged abilities when sober, yet an early attachment to drinking greatly impaired his faculties; and, when drunk, his behaviour was that of a madman.

Lord Ferrers married the youngest daughter of Sir William Meridith, in the year 1752, but behaved to her with such unwarrantable cruelty that she was obliged to apply to Parliament for redress; the consequence of which was that an act passed for allowing her a separate maintenance, to be raised out of his estates.

The following will afford a specimen of the brutality of Lord Ferrers' behaviour: Some oysters had been sent from London, which not proving good, his lordship directed one of the servants to swear that the carrier had changed them; but the servant declining to take such an oath, the earl flew on him in a rage, stabbed him in the breast with a knife, cut his head with a candlestick, and kicked him on the groin with such severity, that he was incapable of a retention of urine for several years afterwards.

Lords Ferrers' brother and his wife paying a visit to him and his countess at Stanton-Harold, some dispute arose between the parties; and Lady Ferrers being absent from the room, the earl ran up stairs with a large clasp-knife in his hand, and asked a servant whom he met where his lady was. The man said, 'In her own room'; and, being directed to follow him thither, Lord Ferrers ordered him to load a brace of pistols with bullets. This order was complied with; but the servant, apprehensive of mischief, declined priming the pistols, which Lord Ferrers discovering, he swore at him, asked him for powder, and primed them himself. He then threatened that, if he did not immediately go and shoot his brother, the captain, he would blow his brains out. The servant hesitating, his lordship pulled the trigger of one of the pistols; but it missed fire. Hereupon the countess dropped on her knees, and begged him to appease his passions; but in return he swore at her, and threatened her destruction if she opposed him. The servant now escaped

from the room, and reported what had passed to his lordship's brother, who immediately called his wife from her
bed, and they left the house, though it was then two o'clock
in the morning.

The unfortunate Mr. Johnson, who fell a sacrifice to
the ungovernable passions of Lord Ferrers, had been bred
up in the family from his youth, and was distinguished for
the regular manner in which he kept his accounts, and his
fidelity as a steward.

When the law had decreed a separate maintenance for
the countess, Mr. Johnson was proposed as receiver of the
rents for her use; but he declined this office till urged to
take it on him by the earl himself. It appears that Johnson now stood high in his lordship's opinion: but a different scene soon ensued; for, the earl having conceived an
opinion that Johnson had combined with the trustees to
disappoint him of a contract for coal mines, he came to a
resolution to destroy the honest steward.

From this time he spoke of him in opprobrious terms,
said he had conspired with his enemies to injure him, and
that he was a villain. With these sentiments he gave him
warning to quit an advantageous farm which he held under
his lordship; but, finding that the trustees under the act of
separation had already granted him a lease of it, it having
been promised to him by the earl or his relations, he was
disappointed, and probably from that time he meditated a
more cruel revenge.

He thought proper, however, to dissemble his malice
to the man, as the most probable method to facilitate the
gratification of it; so that poor Johnson was deceived into
an opinion that he never was upon better terms with his
lord in his life than at the very time he was contriving to
destroy him.

His lordship at this time lived at Stanton, a seat about
two miles from Ashby de la Zouch, in Leicestershire,

and his family consisted of himself, Mrs. Clifford, a lady who lived with him, and her four natural daughters; and five servants—an old man and a boy, and three maids. Mr. Johnson lived at the house belonging to the farm, which he held under his lordship, called the Lount, about half a mile distant from Stanton.

On Sunday, the 13th of January, 1760, Lord Ferrers went to the Lount, and, after some discourse with Mr. Johnson, ordered him to come to him at Stanton on the Friday following, the 18th, at three o'clock in the afternoon. His lordship's hour of dinner was two; and soon after dinner, Mrs. Clifford being in the still-house, his lordship came to her, and told her that she and the children might fetch a walk. Mrs. Clifford, who seems to have considered this an order to go out, prepared herself and the young ladies immediately, and asked whether they might go to her father's which was not far off; to which he assented, and said they might stay till half an hour after five. The two men servants he also contrived to send out of the way, so that there was no one in the house but himself and the three maids.

In a very short time after the house was thus cleared Mr. Johnson came, and was let in by Elizabeth Burgeland, one of the maids. He asked if his lordship was within; and the girl replied Yes, he was in his room: Mr. Johnson immediately went, and knocked at the door; and the earl came to the door, and ordered him to wait in the still-house.

After he had been there about ten minutes his lordship came out again, and, calling him to his own room, went in with him, and immediately locked the door. When they were thus together, the earl first ordered him to settle an account, and, after a little time, produced a paper to him, purporting, as he said, to be a confession of his villainy, and required him to sign it. Johnson refused and expostulated, and his lordship then drawing a pistol, which he had charged and kept in his pocket for the purpose, presented it, and bid him kneel down. The poor man then knelt down upon one knee; but Lord Ferrers cried out, so loud as to be heard by one of the maids at the kitchen door, 'Down on your other knee; declare that you have acted against Lord Ferrers; your time is come—you must die'; and then immediately fired. The ball entered his body just below the last rib, yet he did not drop, but rose up, and expressed the sensations of a dying man both by his looks and by such broken sentences as are usually uttered in such situations. Lord Ferrers, though he at first intended to shoot him again, upon finding he did not drop, was yet forced out of that resolution by involuntary remorse, upon the complaints of the poor man, and the dreadful change that he perceived in his countenance: he then came out of the room, having been shut up in it with the unhappy victim about half an hour; and the report of the pistol having alarmed the women in the wash-house, he called out, 'Who is there?' One of them soon heard and answered him: he ordered her to send for one of the men, and another to assist in getting Mr. Johnson to bed.

At this time his lordship was perfectly sober; and, having dispatched a messenger for Mr. Kirkland, a surgeon, who lived at Ashby de la Zouch, he went back to the room where he had left Mr. Johnson with the maid, and asked him how he found himself. Johnson replied that he found himself like a dying man, and requested his lordship to send for his children: his lordship consented, and a messenger was dispatched to the Lount, to tell Miss Johnson that she must come to the hall directly, for that her father was taken very ill: upon coming to the hall she soon learned what had happened, and Lord Ferrers sent one of the maids with her up to the room into which her father had been removed, and immediately followed himself. Mr. Johnson was in bed, but did not speak to her: Lord Ferrers pulled down the clothes, and applied a pledget, dipped in arquebusade water, to the wound, and soon after left him. From the time the fact was committed Lord Ferrers continued to drink porter till he became drunk: in the mean time the messenger that had been sent for the surgeon, having at length found him at a neighboring village about five o'clock, told him that his assistance was wanted for Mr. Johnson at Stanton: he came immediately with the messenger, but in his way to Stanton called at the Lount, where he first heard that Mr. Johnson had been shot, the rumour of the accident having by that time reached all the neighboring parts.

When he came to the hall, Lord Ferrers told him that he had shot Johnson, but believed that he was more frightened than hurt; that he had intended to shoot him dead, for that he was a villain, and deserved to die; 'but,' says he, 'now I have spared his life, I desire you would do what you can for him.' His lordship at the same time desired that he would not suffer him to be seized, and declared, if any one should attempt it, he would shoot him.

Mr. Kirkland, who wisely determined to say whatever might keep Lord Ferrers, who was then in liquor, from any further outrages, told him that he should not be seized.

The patient complained of a violent pain in his bowels; and Mr. Kirkland preparing to starch the wound, the earl informed him of the direction of it, by showing him how he held the pistol when he fired it. Mr. Kirkland found the ball had lodged in the body, at which his lordship expressed great surprise, declaring that he had tried that pistol a few days before, and that it then carried a ball through a deal board near an inch and a half thick.

Mr. Kirkland then went down stairs to prepare some dressings, and Lord Ferrers soon after left the room. From this time, in proportion as the liquor, which he continued to drink, took effect, his passions became more tumultuous, and the transient fit of compassion, mixed with fear for himself, gave way to starts of rage, and the predominance of malice. He went up into the room where Johnson was dying, and pulled him by the wig, calling him villain, and threatening to shoot him through the head. The last time he went to him he was with great difficulty prevented from tearing the clothes off the bed, which he attempted with great fury, that he might strike him.

A proposal was made to the earl, by Mrs. Clifford, that Mr. Johnson should be removed to his own house; but he replied 'he shall not be removed; I will keep him here to plague the villain.' Many of these expressions were uttered in the hearing of Miss Johnson, whose sufferings in such a situation it is easier to conceive than express; yet, after his abuse of her father, he told her that if he died he would take care of her and of the family, provided they did not prosecute.

When his lordship went to bed, which was between eleven and twelve, he told Mr. Kirkland that he knew he could, if he would, set the affair in such a light as to prevent his being seized, desiring that he might see him before he went away in the morning, and declaring that he would rise at any hour.

Mr. Kirkland, for his own sake, was very solicitous to get Mr. Johnson removed, because, if he died where he was, contrary to the assurances he had given his lordship, he had reason to think his own life would be in danger. As soon as Lord Ferrers was in bed, therefore, he went and told Mr. Johnson that he would take care he should be removed with all expedition.

He accordingly went to the Lount, and, having fitted up an easy chair, with two poles, by way of a sedan, and procured a guard, he returned about two o'clock, and carried Mr. Johnson to his house, without much fatigue, where he languished till about nine the next morning, and then expired.

As soon as he was dead the neighbours set about seizing the murderer: a few persons, armed, set out for Stanton, and, as they entered the hall-yard, they saw him going towards the stable, as they imagined, to take a horse. He appeared to be just out of bed, his stockings being down, and his garters in his hand, having probably taken the alarm immediately on coming out of his room, and finding that Johnson had been removed.

One Springthorpe, advancing towards his lordship, presented a pistol, and required him to surrender; but his lordship putting his hand to his pocket, Springthorpe imagined he was feeling for a pistol, and stopped short, being probably intimidated, and suffered his lordship to escape back into the house, where he fastened the doors, and stood upon his defence.

The concourse of people who had come to apprehend him beset the house, and their number increased very fast. In about two hours his lordship appeared at the garret window, and called out 'How is Johnson?' Springthorpe answered 'He is dead'; upon which the earl insulted him, called him liar, and swore he would not believe anybody but Kirkland. Upon being again assured he was dead, he desired the people might be dispersed, and said he would surrender; yet, almost in the same breath, he desired the people might be let in, and have some victuals and drink; but the issue was, he went away from the window, swearing he would not be taken.

The people, however, still continued near the house; and, about two hours after his lordship had appeared at the garret window, he was seen by one Curtis, a collier, upon the bowling-green: his lordship was then armed with a blunderbuss, two or three pistols, and a dagger; but Curtis, so far from being intimidated, marched up boldly to him, in spite of his blunderbuss; and his lordship was so struck with the determined resolution that appeared in this brave fellow, that he suffered him to seize him without making the least resistance; yet, the moment he was in custody, declared he had killed a villain, and that he gloried in the act.

He was carried from Stanton to a public house, kept by one Kinsey, at Ashby De La Zouch, where he was kept till the Monday following, during which time the coroner had sat upon the body, and the jury had brought in their verdict—'Wilful murder.'

From Ashby De La Zouch he was sent to Leicester gaol; from thence, about a fortnight afterwards, he was brought in his own landau and six, under a strong guard, to London, where he arrived on the 14th of February, about noon, dressed like a jockey, in a close riding frock, jockey boots and cap, and a plain shirt.

Being carried before the House of Lords, he was committed to the custody of the Black Rod, and ordered to the Tower, where he arrived about six o'clock in the evening, having behaved, during the whole journey, and at his commitment, with great calmness and propriety. He was confined in the Round Tower, near the drawbridge: two wardens were constantly in the room with him, and one at the door; two sentinels were posted at the bottom of the stairs, and one upon the drawbridge, with their bayonets fixed; and from this time the gates were ordered to be shut an hour sooner than usual.

Mrs. Clifford and the four young ladies, who had come up with him from Leicestershire, took a lodging in Tower Street, and for some time a servant was continually passing with letters between them; but afterwards this correspondence was permitted only once a day.

During his confinement he was moderate both in eating and drinking; his breakfast was a half-pint basin of tea, with a small spoonful of brandy in it, and a muffin; with his dinner he generally drank a pint of wine and a pint of water, and another pint of each with his supper. In general his behaviour was decent and quiet, except that he would sometimes suddenly start, tear open his waistcoat, and use other gestures, which showed that his mind was disturbed.

Mrs. Clifford came three times to the Tower to see him, but was not admitted; but his children were suffered to be with him some time.

On the 16th of April, having been a prisoner in the Tower two months and two days, he was brought to his trial, which continued till the 18th, before the House of Lords, assembled for that purpose; Lord Henley, Keeper of the Great Seal, having been created Lord High Steward upon the occasion.

The fact was easily proved, and his lordship, in his defence, examined several witnesses to prove his insanity; none of whom proved such an insanity as made him not accountable for his conduct. His lordship managed his defence himself, in such a manner as showed perfect recollection of mind, and an uncommon understanding; he mentioned the situation of being reduced to the necessity of attempting to prove himself a lunatic, that he might not be deemed a murderer, with the most delicate and affecting sensibility; and, when he found that his plea could not avail him, he confessed that he made it only to gratify his friends; that he was always averse to it himself; and that it had prevented what he had proposed, and what perhaps might have taken off the malignity, at least, of the accusation.

His lordship, immediately upon conviction, received sentence to be hanged on Monday, the 21st of April, and then to be anatomized; but, in consideration of his rank, the execution of this sentence was respited till Monday, the 5th of May.

During this interval he made a will, by which he left one thousand three hundred pounds to Mr. Johnson's children; one thousand pounds to each of his four natural daughters; and sixty pounds a year to Mrs. Clifford for her life. This will, however, being made after his conviction, was not valid; yet it was said that the same, or nearly the same, provision was made for the parties.

In the mean time a scaffold was erected under the gallows at Tyburn, and part of it, about a yard square, was raised about eighteen inches above the rest of the floor, with a contrivance to sink down upon a signal given; and the whole was covered with black baize.

In the morning of the 5th of May, about nine o'clock, his body was demanded of the keeper, at the gates of the Tower, by the sheriffs of London and Middlesex. His lordship, being informed of it, sent a message to the sheriffs, requesting that he might go in his own landau, instead of the mourning coach which had been provided by his friends; and this request being granted, he entered his landau, drawn by six horses, with Mr. Humphries, Chaplain of the Tower, who had been admitted to his lordship that morning, for the first time: the landau was conducted to the outer gate of the Tower by the officers of that fortress, and was there delivered to the sheriffs.

Here Mr. Sheriff Vaillant entered the landau of his lordship, and, expressing his concern at having so melancholy a duty to perform, his lordship said 'He was much obliged to him, and took it kindly that he accompanied him.'

He was dressed in a suit of light-colored clothes, embroidered with silver, said to be his wedding suit; and, soon after Mr. Vaillant came into the landau, he said 'You may, perhaps, Sir, think it strange to see me in this dress; but I have my particular reasons for it.'

The procession then began in the following order:—

A very large body of constables for the county of Middlesex, preceded by one of the high constables.

A party of horse-grenadiers, and a party of foot.

Mr. Sheriff Errington in his chariot, accompanied by his under-sheriff, Mr. Jackson.

The landau, escorted by two other parties of horse-grenadiers and foot.

Mr. Sheriff Vaillant's carriage, in which was his under-sheriff, Mr. Nichols.

A mourning-coach and six, with some of his lordship's friends.

A hearse and six, which was provided for the conveyance of his lordship's corpse from the place of execution to Surgeons' Hall.

The procession moved so slow, that his lordship was two hours and three quarters in his landau; but during the whole time he appeared perfectly easy and composed, though he often expressed his desire to have it over, saying that 'the apparatus of death, and the passing through such crowds of people, were ten times worse than death itself.'

He told the sheriff that he had written to the king to beg 'that he might suffer where his ancestor, the Earl of Essex, had suffered; and was in greater hopes of obtaining that favour, as he had the honour of quartering part of the same arms, and of being allied to his majesty; and that he thought it was hard that he must die at the place appointed for the execution of common felons.'

Mr. Humphries took occasion to observe, that 'the world would naturally be very inquisitive concerning the religion his lordship professed, and asked him if he chose to say any thing upon that subject.' To which his lordship answered, 'That he did not think himself accountable to the world for his sentiments on religion; but that he had always believed in and adored one God, the Maker of all things;—that, whatever his notions were, he had never propagated them, or endeavored to gain any persons over to his persuasion;—that all countries and nations had a form of religion by which the people were governed, and that he looked upon whoever disturbed them in it as an enemy to society.—That he very much blamed Lord Bolingbroke for permitting his sentiments on religion to be published to the world.—That the many facts and disputes which happen about religion have almost turned morality out of doors.—That he never could believe what some sectaries teach, that faith alone will save mankind; so that if a man, just before he dies, should say only "I believe," that *that* alone will save him.'

As to the crime for which he suffered, he declared 'that he was under particular circumstances—that he had met with so many crosses and vexations, he scarce knew what he did': and most solemnly protested 'that he had not the least malice against Mr. Johnson.'

When his lordship had got to that part of Holborn which is near Drury Lane, he said 'he was thirsty, and should be glad of a glass of wine and water'; upon which the sheriffs remonstrating to him, 'that a stop for that purpose would necessarily draw a greater crowd about him, which might possibly disturb and incommode him, yet, if his lordship still desired it, it should be done,' he most readily answered, 'that's true—I say no more—let us by no means stop.'

When they approached near the place of execution, his lordship told the sheriff 'that there was a person waiting in a coach near there, for whom he had a very sincere regard, and of whom he should be glad to take his leave before he died'; to which the sheriff answered, that, 'if his lordship insisted upon it, it should be so; but that he wished his lordship, for his own sake, would decline it, lest the sight of a person, for whom he had such a regard, should unman him, and disarm him of the fortitude he possessed.'—To which his lordship, without the least hesitation, replied, 'Sir, if you think I am wrong, I submit'; and upon the sheriff telling his lordship that if he had any thing to deliver to that person, or any one else, he would faithfully do it, his lordship delivered to him a pocket-book, in which were a bank-note and a ring, and a purse with some guineas, in order to be delivered to that person, which were delivered accordingly.

The landau being now advanced to the place of execution, his lordship alighted from it, and ascended upon the

scaffold with the same composure and fortitude of mind
he had possessed from the time he left the Tower. Soon
after he had mounted the scaffold, Mr. Humphries asked
his lordship if he chose to say prayers; which he declined;
but, upon his asking him 'if he did not choose to join with
him in the Lord's Prayer,' he readily answered 'he would,
for he always thought it a very fine prayer'; upon which
they knelt down together upon two cushions, covered with
black baize; and his lordship, with an audible voice, very
devoutly repeated the Lord's Prayer, and afterwards, with
great energy, the following ejaculation: 'O God, forgive me
all my errors—pardon all my sins!'

His lordship, then rising, took his leave of the sheriff and
the chaplain; and, after thanking them for their many civil-
ities, he presented his watch to Mr. Sheriff Vaillant, which
he desired his acceptance of; and requested that his body
might be buried at Breden or Stanton, in Leicestershire.

His lordship then called for the executioner, who immediately came to him, and asked him forgiveness; upon which
his lordship said 'I freely forgive you, as I do all mankind,
and hope myself to be forgiven.' He then intended to give
the executioner five guineas, but, by mistake, giving it into
the hands of the executioner's assistant, an unreasonable
dispute ensued between these unthinking and unfeeling
wretches, which Mr. Sheriff Vaillant instantly silenced.

The executioner, now proceeded to do his duty, to which
his lordship, with great resignation, submitted. His neck-
cloth being taken off, a white cap, which he had brought
in his pocket, being put upon his head, his arms secured
by three black sash, and the cord put round his neck, he
advanced by three steps to the elevated part of the scaffold, and, standing under the cross-beam which went over
it, which was also covered with black baize, he asked the
executioner: 'Am I right?' Then the cap was drawn over
his face, and, upon a signal given by the sheriff (for his

lordship, upon being before asked, declined to give one himself), that part upon which he stood instantly sank down from beneath his feet, and he was launched into eternity, the 5th of May, 1760.

From the time of his lordship's ascending upon the scaffold, until his execution, was about eight minutes; during which his countenance did not change, nor his tongue falter.

The accustomed time of one hour being past, the coffin was raised up, with the greatest decency, to receive the body; and, being deposited in the hearse, was conveyed by the sheriffs, with the same procession, to Surgeons' Hall, to undergo the remainder of the sentence.

A large incision was made from the neck to the bottom of the breast, and another across the throat; the lower part of the belly was laid open, and the bowels taken away. It was afterwards publicly exposed to view in a room up one pair of stairs at the Hall; and on the evening of Thursday, the 8th of May, it was delivered to his friends for interment.

The following verse is said to have been found in his apartment:

> 'In doubt I liv'd, in doubt I die,
> Yet stand prepared the vast abyss to try,
> And, undismayed, expect eternity.'

MRS. DANIELS BROUGHT HOME INTOXICATED.

THOMAS DANIELS

Condemned for the supposed murder of his wife.

———

———'O Death!
Where art thou?—Death! thou dread of guilt
Thou wash of innocence! affection's friend!
Thou Nature calls thee: come, in mercy, come
And lay me pillow' in eternal rest.'

THIS is an extraordinary hard case, and we think that
every reader must agree in opinion that the accused, so far
from being guilty of murder, had long submitted to the very

worst kind of usage with which a woman can possibly treat a husband.

The whole proof adduced against him was circumstantial; and we hope no jury sitting upon the life of their fellow-creature will again convict a man on such evidence.

That they erred in their judgment, or, at all events, that the Privy Council of the realm differed from them in opinion, is evident, from the unfortunate man immediately receiving the king's pardon.

But, that every one may form a judgment on the case, we shall simply narrate the circumstances drawn from the different publications of the day, including his own confession.

Thomas Daniels was a journeyman carpenter, and about the year 1757, at which time he worked with his father, he became acquainted with Sarah Carridine, a very pretty girl, who was servant at a public house; this girl he was very desirous to marry, but his father and mother would not consent, because she had lived in an alehouse. After consulting with the girl, and the girl's mother, it was agreed they should live together without being married. The mother, therefore, took a lodging for them, to which Daniels removed. His father, however, soon found out what he had done, upon which a quarrel ensued, and he determined to work with his father no longer.

As he was going about seeking employment elsewhere, he met with some of his acquaintance, who had entered on board the Britannia privateer, and they persuaded him to enter also.

When he went home, and told Carridine what he had done, she fell into violent fits of crying, and was, with great difficulty, pacified, by his telling her that the cruise was but for six months, that he hoped he should make his fortune and that he would marry her where he came back, advising her, in the mean time, to go to service.

In this situation she was naturally exposed to great danger. It is probable that her grief was mixed with resentment; that she considered herself as slighted and deserted; and that she doubted whether he would return again, and, if he did, whether he, who could so soon forsake her, would make good his engagement; at the same time, having been already debauched, she was not restrained by the powerful motives from which women resist solicitations to the first fault, and she was under every possible temptation to form another connexion that was likely to be more certain and durable.

Under all these disadvantages she was seduced by one John Jones, a founder, a wretch who had been the intimate acquaintance of Daniels, and professed great friendship for him. This fellow promised to marry her if Daniels did not return; that, if he did, he would continue his kindness to her; and that, if he should die himself, he would leave her all his goods, and all his interest in the capital of a box-club, to which he belonged.

Not long after this connexion became Carridine and Jones, Daniels came home, having been absent about eight months. As soon as he came to London he went to Mr. Archer's, who kept the White Bear, at the corner of Barbican, in Aldersgate Street, whom he called his master, and sent for his father and mother, with whom he spent an agreeable evening. He then inquired of Mrs. Archer after Carridine; and she referred him to Jones. Jones took him over the water to an alehouse near the Bridge-foot, where he saw her. At this time she lived with her mother, and Daniels took a lodging in the same house with Jones, who, pretending great friendship for them both, urged Daniels to marry going every night with him to spend the evening with the girl, and offering to give her away. Daniels, without suspicion of so perfidious and base a conduct, fell into the snare, and fixed upon a day; but, as our laws have laid a tax upon marriage, which other States have encouraged by pecuniary or honorary advantages, Daniels could not be married, because he had not money enough to pay the fees. He would have borrowed a guinea of his master, but his master refused; upon which Jones urged him to raise it by pawning his watch: to this Daniels consented, the watch was pawned for him by Jones himself, and Daniels and Carridine were married.

Daniels, at first, lived in ready-furnished lodgings, till his wife's mother persuaded him to live with her in Catherine-wheel Alley, Whitechapel. While they lived here Daniels frequently found his wife abroad when he came home from work, and when she did come home she was generally in liquor. The mother excused both her absence and her condition by saying she had been to see some young women in Spitalfields, and that a very little matter got into her head. It was not long, however, before Daniels found that she kept company with Jones; and having once followed them to an alehouse, when the mother pretended she was gone to see the young women in Spitalfields, he went to them, and, after some words, sent his wife home. She was then drunk, and, when he went home to her, a violent quarrel ensued, during which the wife and the mother both fell upon him; and the wife afterwards ran out of the house, and was absent all night.

Next day, however, Daniels was persuaded to make it up; and soon after put her into a little shop in the Minories, to sell pork and greens, and other articles. She promised to mind her business, and never go into Jones's company more.

On the next Lord Mayor's Day Daniels attended his master to the hall of his company, and, his master having given him a bottle of wine, he went into the kitchen, and got some bread and meat. He would not, however, touch either the wine or the victuals there, but brought both home, pleasing himself with the thought of enjoying them quietly with his wife. When he came home his wife was out, and soon after he found her and Jones together upon the stairs, Jones having taken the opportunity of Daniels's absence to supply his place, not suspecting that he would leave the good cheer of the hall, and come home so early.

This caused a great quarrel, and Daniels would suffer his wife to keep shop no longer; he also removed from her mother's, and, having got a few goods of his own, took a room in the Little Minories. Here they lived somewhat more quiet for a little while; but, the wife falling again into irregularities, Daniels entered a second time on board the Britannia privateer, as carpenter's mate, and, without acquainting any body with what he had done, went down to the ship at Greenhithe; but in a few days, to his great surprise, he was visited on board by his wife, in company with Jones: they staid on board all night, and, she lamenting and behaving like a mad woman, he was at length persuaded to return home with her.

Soon after he took a house, the corner of Hare Court, Aldersgate Street, and put his wife once more into a shop; but she soon returned to her old ways, kept company with Jones and several other people, and at length ran away and left him.

Notwithstanding this conduct he was persuaded to receive her again, though she acknowledged her criminal intimacy with Jones, upon her promise of amendment; yet she not only contracted other intimacies of an infamous kind, but, when Daniels came home to his meals, she would be abroad, with the key of their room in her pocket, so that he was obliged to eat at an alehouse.

Notwithstanding all this, Daniels seems to have had a strong attachment to her, and to have done every thing in his power to please her, that she might make his home agreeable, and was solicitous to the last to unite his pleasure with hers, in which he was constantly disappointed.

The following instance, among many others, is a remarkable representation of his conduct and her character.

One Sunday, with a view to entertain her, he took her down to Ilford, that they might spend the day agreeably together: they dined at the White Horse there, and after dinner she drank freely. When the reckoning came to be paid she flew into a rage with the landlord, and, upon Daniels endeavoring to moderate matters, she turned all her resentment upon him, and carried it to such a degree, that she declared she would not go home with him, but would go with the first person that asked her, or even with the next man that went by. This threat, extravagant as it was, she made good; for a person dressed like an officer, stopping in a chaise at the door, she asked him to let her ride home with him: he consented, and away they went.

Daniels, though he had offered his wife a place in the stage, now walked home by himself; and, having sat up for his wife till it was very late, he at length gave her over, and went to bed. About two in the morning he was roused by a violent knocking at his door where he found his wife so drunk that she could not stand, attended by her mother; and he quietly let her in, with the mother, whose assistance was absolutely necessary to put her to bed.

The account of what happened immediately before the accident that put an end to her life, and of that accident itself, is added in his own words, the truth of which he has attested upon oath, before a magistrate, since his pardon:—

'The night before this melancholy accident happened, I came home, to be sure, not entirely I sober where, not finding my wife, I went directly to her home where I found her very drunk. It being night, her mother said it not proper to take her home in that condition, and therefore advised me to lie there that night, while she and her girl would go and sleep at my lodging. We did so.

'In the morning, after my wife's mother came back, we all breakfasted together at her lodgings. After breakfast I went to Mr. Clarke, timber-merchant, in St. Mary Axe, to solicit for some India Company's work; from whence I went to the Mansion Home alehouse, and drank a pint of beer. I then intended to go to work at Mr. Perry's, in Noble Street; but it being near dinner-time, I stopped at the Bell, opposite his house, for another pint of beer, where, meeting some acquaintance eating beef steaks I dined with them. As I was eating, in came my wife and her mother; she at first abused me for the alehouse, but they afterwards, with great seeming good humour, drank with me, and, as they wanted money: I gave my wife two shillings, a six-and-nine penny piece, which I had just received in change for half a guinea, from the master of the public house. As the day was now far spent, and as I was pleased with the prospect of working for the East India Company, I thought it not worth while to begin a day's work late: I therefore went to Smithfield, to see how the horse-market went; from thence to Warwick Lane, to see for a young man whom I had promised to get to work for the Company also. I took him to Mr. Clarke, St. Mary Axe, and afterward went with him to two or three places more; the last place was the Nag's Head, in Houndsditch; and about half an hour after nine o'clock went home.

'When I came, there I went in at the back door, which is under the gateway, and which used to be only on a single latch, for the conveniency of my lodgers. I went up to my room-door: but, finding it fast, came down stairs again.

'There was then some disturbance over the way, in Aldersgate street, which I walked over to see the meaning of, imagining my wife might chance to be engaged in it. Not finding her in the crowd, I returned, and went up stairs again: while I was on the stairs I heard my wife cough, by which I knew she was at home. Finding my door still fast, I knocked and called again; still she would not answer: I then said "Sally, I know you are at home, and I desire you will open the door; if you will not I will burst it open." Nobody yet answering, I set my shoulder against the door, and forced it open; upon this she jumped out of bed. I immediately began to undress me, by slipping off my coat and waistcoat, saying, at the same time, "Sally, what makes you use me so? you follow, me wherever I go, to abuse me, and then lock me out of my lodging; I never served you so." On this she flew upon me, called me a scoundrel dog, said she supposed I had been with some of my whores, and, so saying, tore my shirt down from the bosom: on this I pushed her down; she then ran to the chimney-corner, and snatched up several things, which I successively wrested from her, and in the scuffle a table and a screen fell down. At length she struck me several blows with a hand-brush; and, while I was struggling to get it from her, she cried out several times "Indeed, indeed, I will do so no more." When I got the brush from her, which I did with some difficulty, I gave her a blow with it, and then concluded she would be easy. She sat down on the floor, by the cupboard door, tearing her shift from her back, which had been rent in the skirmish: I sat down on the opposite side of the bed, with my back towards her, preparing to go into it; and, seeing her fling the remnants of her shift about in so mad a manner, I said "Sally, you are a silly girl; why don't you be easy?" On that she suddenly rose up, and with something gave me a blow on the head, which struck me down: I fell on the bedstead, with my head against the folding doors of it. I imagined she was then afraid she had killed me, for I heard her cry, two or three times, "O save me, save me!" How she went out of the window it is impossible for me to say, in the condition she left me in; but, from her cries, I supposed her gone that way; and in my consternation, when I arose, I ran down one pair of stairs, where, not knowing how to behave, I went up again, and sat me down on the bed from whence I rose. In this position Mr. Clarke, the constable, and the numbers who followed him, found me. He said "Daniels, you have stabbed your wife, and flung her out at the window." I replied "No, Mr. Clarke, I have not; she threw herself out."

'Mr. Clarke took a candle, and examined all the room in search of blood, but found none; and luckily it was for me that neither of our noses happened to bleed in the fray, though mine was subject to do so on any trifling occasion.

'He then went to the window, where he found a piece of a saucer, and asked me what it was. I told him I did not know, but recollected afterwards that it was what I fed my squirrel in; though I knew not how it came broke; it was whole that day.

'From thence I was taken to the Compter; and the public are already acquainted with the proceedings on my trial, when I was condemned for the supposed fact, September the 21st, 1761.

'I am informed that the next morning they found a pair of small pliers, bloody, in the window, which were then considered as a proof of my guilt. These pliers were what I have mended my squirrel's chain with whenever he broke loose, which was sometimes the case. How they should be bloody, as God is my Saviours, I cannot answer; but, as no wound was perceived on the body, they were not produced as evidence against me. However, when my wife was brought up from the street, it is said she was blooded, and that the basin was put in the window where these pliers were found. It is therefore possible that, in such confusion, a drop or two might accidentally be spilled upon them, more especially when we consider the tumult of a morning's exhibition of a dead body, for penny gratuities, by the unprincipled mother of it.'

The following judicious remarks are added by the person who assisted Daniels in publishing his case, and they seem to confirm the man's declaration of his innocence beyond the possibility of doubt.

The window of Daniels's room has two casements folding against each other, with garden-pots before them. One of these casements only used to be opened, the other being in general kept shut. These casements were each about sixteen or seventeen inches wide, and the window was about a yard and a quarter high. When this accident happened one casement was open, the other shut, as usual; consequently the opening then through the window was about sixteen or seventeen inches wide, and a yard and a quarter high. Through this space a man was to thrust a woman, nearly as strong as himself! If such a thing had been attempted, the following consequences must be incontestably allowed to ensue:

I. The woman would resist the attempt.

II. When persons struggle to avoid imminent danger, and are driven to despair, they are capable of a surprising degree of exertion, beyond their ordinary abilities.

III. This woman would therefore have continued in so narrow a gap a very considerable while before she could have been forced through, and would all that time have uttered cries, entreaties, and exclamations, too expressive of her situation to have been mistaken by the neighbours and spectators.

IV. Her resistance would have overturned the before-mentioned garden-pots, and would have shattered the glass of the casement that was shut, and even forced open, or broke, the casement itself, which obstructed her passage.

V. In breaking the glass of the window her skin must have been greatly scratched and torn, and her limbs, naked as she was, have been otherwise greatly maimed and bruised.

VI. The man who undertook to force her out must have borne some very conspicuous marks of his attempt.

The two first of these propositions will be universally granted.

The third is contradicted by all the evidence, on the trial, who unanimously agree that the moment the woman was seen she came through the window, and was only then heard to use such expressions, which Daniels accounts for better than anyone else.

In reply to the fourth—the pots were not discomposed nor the window broken, except one pane; and it does not appear that even that pane might not have been broken before.

In answer to the fifth—the body, by the evidence of the surgeon, did not appear to have received any other damage than the natural consequences of so great a fall.

As to the last—the man was not seen at the window at all; and, as to any wounds or bruises sustained by him, the constable, when asked whether he saw the blow on his head, which he affirmed to be given him by his wife, declared he did not. But he was not asked whether he looked for it; a question, it may be presumed, he would have answered in the negative.

In such a situation, it is to be concluded, the poor fellow was little heard, and less regarded, concerning whatever he might allege in his own behalf.

A man may be stunned by a blow that might not perhaps exhibit any remarkable appearance; and, had it been seen, his account of it would have weighed but little.

It is not even probable, had he knocked this woman on the head first, that he could have sent the body through the window so completely as, either by fright or design, she accomplished it herself. But that she came there living is past all doubt.

To conclude:—the evidence against this unfortunate man was only presumptive at most, and, upon clear scrutiny, is really productive of *nothing*; so that, as he was discharged by royal authority, so has he also a just claim to an acquittal in the minds of all judicious and candid people.

HANNAH DAGOE RESISTING HER EXECUTION.

HANNAH DAGOE

Executed for robbing a poor woman.

———

WE have adduced many instances of the hardness of heart, and contempt of the commandments of God, in *men* who have undergone the last sentence of the law; but we are of opinion that in this *female* will be found a more relentless heart, in her last moments, than any criminal whom we have yet recorded.

Hannah Dagoe was born in Ireland, and was one of that numerous class of women who ply at Covent Garden Market, to the exclusion of poor Englishwomen.

She became acquainted with a poor and industrious woman of the name of Eleanor Hussey, who lived by herself in a small apartment, in which was some creditable household furniture, the remains of the worldly goods of her deceased husband. Seizing an opportunity, when the owner was from home, this daring woman broke into Hussey's room, and stripped it of every article which it contained.

For this burglary and robbery she was brought to trial at the Old Bailey, found guilty, and sentenced to death.

She was a strong masculine woman, the terror of her fellow-prisoners, and actually stabbed one of the men who had given evidence against her; but the wound happened not to prove dangerous.

On the road to Tyburn she showed little concern at her miserable state, and paid no attention to the exhortations of the Romish priest who attended her.

When the cart in which she was bound was drawn under the gallows she got her hands and arms loose, seized the executioner, struggled with him, and gave him so violent a blow on the breast as nearly knocked him down. She dared him to hang her, and took off her hat, cloak, and other parts of her dress, and disposed of them among the crowd, in despite of him. After much resistance he got the rope about her neck, which she had no sooner found accomplished, than, pulling a handkerchief, bound round her head, over her face, she threw herself out of the cart, before the signal given, with such violence, that she broke her neck, and died instantly, on the 4th of May, 1763.

HARROW, WHILE POUCHING, DISCOVERED BY THE GAMEKEEPER.

WILLIAM HARROW, commonly called the FLYING HIGHWAYMAN

Executed for robbery.

———

THIS malefactor may be said to have galloped to his fate over the beaten road. He commenced his career in idleness, the parent vice; then he became dexterous at throwing at cocks, and in cock-fighting.[6] These cruel and infamous

---

[6] KIND TREATMENT To animals, made for man's use, is a sign of a humane and excellent disposition; while cruelty and barbarity to them show a wicked and diabolical temper. Do not these creatures, when they are bruised and wounded, show an equal sense of pain with ourselves?

acquirements lead to robbery, adultery, and every other deadly sin. Such is the general course of highwaymen; and their goal—the gallows.

He had likewise a propensity to poaching: and the gamekeeper of a gentleman near Hatfield having detected him in a fact of this kind, Harrow threatened his destruction; the consequence of which was, that he was lodged in Hertford gaol; but, before the time of holding the quarter-sessions, he broke out, and made his escape; on which a reward of fifty pounds was offered for taking him into custody.

Made desperate by this circumstance, he took to robbing on the highway. The depredations he committed were very numerous; and he obtained the name of 'The Flying Highwayman' by his horse leaping the several turnpikes, so that he constantly escaped detection.

His career in villainy was, however, happily but short. He laid a scheme for committing a burglary and robbery, for which he and two of his associates forfeited their lives, in company with Thomas Jones, a noted travelling rat-catcher, William Bosford, and another desperate villain. They went to the house of an old farmer, named Thomas Glasscock, who had, by an extraordinary degree of parsimony, accumulated a very considerable sum, of which these

---

Are not their shrieks and mournful cries as so many calls upon their tormentors for pity? And do not their dying pangs, and the painful convulsions of their tortured bodies, cause uneasiness in every humane spectator? To give ease and happiness to them, and to relieve their miseries, would give pleasure to ourselves, provided we are such men as we ought to be. But, if we take any delight in tormenting, or in seeing animals tormented, whom do we resemble but that evil being, who takes pleasure in the misery of man? And how easily may that youth be induced to delight in wounding and murdering his fellow-creatures, who has been trained up in his childhood to exercise cruelty upon poor innocent animals?

abandoned men determined to rob him, under the pretence of being peace-officers, who were come to apprehend some deserters. The old gentleman refused them admittance; on which they forced their way through the window, and, binding Mr. Glasscock and his housekeeper, they searched the house, when, finding a tea-chest which contained three hundred pounds, they seized it, and departed.

Having divided the booty, they separated; and Harrow, taking a girl with him as a companion, travelled into Gloucestershire, and, putting up at an alehouse in a small village, and assuming the character of a sailor, who had brought home prize-money to a considerable amount, he continued for two months without any suspicion arising. At length a quarrel happening between him and some of the customers of the house, a scuffle ensued, and a pistol in one of Harrow's pockets going off, a suspicion arose that he was a highwayman, on which he was carried before a magistrate for examination.

Nothing like proof arising to criminate him, he was dismissed; but, not thinking it prudent to remain any longer, he set out with his girl; but did not tell any one the road that he intended to travel.

Very near the time that he departed, one of the magistrates of Gloucestershire received a letter from Sir John Fielding, requesting that he would order a search for one William Harrow, who stood charged with having committed a variety of robberies in the neighborhood of St. Albans.

Upon this the magistrates sent some persons in pursuit of him, who, having traced him to Worcester, made such inquiries as led them to think he had gone towards Wolverhampton. Taking this road, they found him in bed with his girl, and, having taken him into custody, he was conducted to prison at Gloucester.

By a writ of habeas corpus he was removed to Hertford, where he lay till the assizes, when he was indicted for robbing Mr. Glasscock; and, being convicted on the clearest evidence, was sentenced to die.

A number of clergymen visited him after conviction, and labored to convince him of the necessity of making an immediate preparation for eternity. He was likewise visited by his mother, who burst into tears at the sight of her wretched son.

On the night before his execution he sawed off his irons, with an intent to have made his escape; but he had not quite time enough to effect his purpose. When the gaoler came in the morning, he said he would have saved the hangman his trouble, if he had not come so soon; and threw at him the irons, which he had by this time got from his legs.

Before he was put in the cart, a sermon was preached on the occasion of his fatal exit.

Immense numbers of people attended at the place of execution, to see the last of a man who had made himself dreaded through the country by the enormity of his conduct.

Harrow, Jones, and Bosford, were executed at Hertford, March the 28th, 1763, along with John Wright, for a highway robbery on the Buntingfield road.

The unfortunate Mr. Glasscock seems to have been a devoted prey to robbers. On the 7th of September, 1764, he was attacked in his own fields by a daring villain, at noontime of day, who obliged him to go to his house, and deliver his money. On entering, the robber shut the door, knocked the old man down, and carried off every thing valuable that was left by Harrow and his gang, with which he escaped.

ELIZABETH BROWNRIGG CRUELLY FLOGGING HER APPRENTICE, MARY CLIFFORD.

ELIZABETH BROWNRIGG

Executed for torturing her female apprentices to death.

———

THE long scene of torture in which this inhuman woman kept the innocent object of her remorseless cruelty, ere she finished the long-premeditated murder, engaged the interest of the superior ranks, and roused the indignation of the populace more than any criminal, occurrence in the whole course of our melancholy narratives.

This cruel woman, having passed the early part of her life in the service of private families, was married to James Brownrigg, a plumber, who, after being seven years in

Greenwich, came to London, and took a house in Flower-de-Luce Court, Fleet Street, where he carried on a considerable share of business, and had a little house at Islington for an occasional retreat.

She had been the mother of sixteen children; and, having practised midwifery, was appointed by the overseers of the poor of St. Dunstan's parish to take care of the poor women who were taken in labour in the workhouse, which duty she performed to the entire satisfaction of her employers.

Mary Mitchell, a poor girl, of the precinct of White Friars, was put apprentice to Mrs. Brownrigg in the year 1765; and about the same time Mary Jones, one of the children of the Foundling Hospital, was likewise placed with her in the same capacity; and she had other apprentices.

As Mrs. Brownrigg received pregnant women to lie-in privately, these girls were taken with a view of saving the expense of women servants. At first the poor orphans were treated with some degree of civility; but this was soon changed for the most savage barbarity.

Having laid Mary Jones across two chairs in the kitchen, she whipped her with such wanton cruelty that she was occasionally obliged to desist through mere weariness.

This treatment was frequently repeated; and Mrs. Brownrigg used to throw water on her when she had done whipping her, and sometimes she would dip her head into a pail of water. The room appointed for the girl to sleep in adjoined the passage leading to the street door; and, as she had received many wounds on her head, shoulders, and various parts of her body, she determined not to bear such treatment any longer, if she could effect her escape.

Observing that the key was left in the street door when the family went to bed, she opened it cautiously one morning, and escaped into the street.

Thus freed from her horrid confinement, she repeatedly inquired her way to the Foundling Hospital till she found it, and was admitted after describing in what manner she had been treated, and showing the bruises she had received.

The child having been examined by a surgeon, (who found her wounds to be of a most alarming nature), the governors of the hospital ordered Mr. Plumbtree, their solicitor, to write to James Brownrigg, threatening a prosecution, if he did not give a proper reason for the severities exercised toward the child.

No notice of this having been taken, and the governors of the hospital thinking it imprudent to indict at common law, the girl was discharged, in consequence of an application to the chamberlain of London. The other girl, Mary Mitchell, continued with her mistress for the space of a year, during which she was treated with equal cruelty, and she also resolved to quit her service. Having escaped out of the house, she was met in the street by the younger son of Brownrigg, who forced her to return home, where her sufferings were greatly aggravated on account of her elopement. In the interim, the overseers of the precinct of White Friars bound Mary Clifford to Brownrigg; nor was it long before she experienced similar cruelties to those inflicted on the other poor girls, and possibly still more severe. She was frequently tied up naked, and beaten with a hearthbroom, a horsewhip, or a cane, till she was absolutely speechless. This poor girl having a natural infirmity, the mistress would not permit her to lie in a bed, but placed her on a mat, in a coal-hole that was remarkably cold: however, after sometime, a sack and a quantity of straw formed her bed, instead of the mat. During her confinement in this wretched situation she had nothing to subsist on but bread and water; and her covering, during the night, consisted only of her own clothes, so that she sometime lay almost perished with cold.

On a particular occasion, when she was almost starving with hunger, she broke open a cupboard in search of food, but found it empty; and on another occasion she broke down some boards, in order to procure a draught of water.

Though she was thus pressed for the humblest necessaries of life, Mrs. Brownrigg determined to punish her with rigour for the means she had taken to supply herself with them. On this she caused the girl to strip to the skin, and during the course of a whole day, while she remained naked, she repeatedly beat her with the butt-end of a whip.

In the course of this most inhuman treatment a jack-chain was fixed round her neck, the end of which was fastened to the yard door, and then it was pulled as tight as possible without strangling her.

A day being passed in the practice of these savage barbarities, the girl was remanded to the coal-hole at night, her hands being tied behind her, and the chain still remaining about her neck.

The husband having been obliged to find his wife's apprentices in wearing apparel, they were repeatedly stripped naked, and kept so for whole days, if their garments happened to be torn.

The elder son had frequently the superintendence of these wretched girls; but this was sometimes committed to the apprentice, who declared that she was totally naked one night when he went to tie her up. The two poor girls were frequently so beaten that their heads and shoulders appeared as one general sore; and, when a plaster was applied to their wounds, the skin used to peel away with it.

Sometimes Mrs. Brownrigg, when resolved on uncommon severity, used to tie their hands with a cord, and draw them up to a water-pipe which ran across the ceiling in the kitchen; but that giving way, she desired her husband to fix a hook in the beam, through which a cord was drawn, and, their arms being extended, she used to horsewhip them till she was weary, and till the blood followed at every stroke.

The elder son having one day directed Mary Clifford to put up a half-tester bedstead, the poor girl was unable to do it; on which he beat her till she could no longer support his severity; and at another time, when the mother had been whipping her in the kitchen till she was absolutely tired, the son renewed the savage treatment. Mrs. Brownrigg would sometimes seize the poor girl by the cheeks, and, forcing the skin down violently with her fingers, cause the blood to gush from her eyes.

Mary Clifford, unable to bear these repeated severities, complained of her hard treatment to a French lady who lodged in the house; and she having represented the impropriety of such behaviour to Mrs. Brownrigg, the inhuman monster flew at the girl, and cut her tongue in two places with a pair of scissors.

On the morning of the 13th of July this barbarous woman went into the kitchen, and, after obliging Mary Clifford to strip to the skin, drew her up to the staple, and though her body was an entire sore from former bruises, yet this wretch renewed her cruelties with her accustomed severity.

After whipping her till the blood streamed down her body, she let her down, and made her wash herself in a tub of cold water; Mary Mitchell, the other poor girl, being present during this transaction. While Clifford was washing herself Mrs. Brownrigg struck her on the shoulders, already sore with former bruises, with the butt-end of a whip; and she treated the child in this manner five times in the same day.

The poor girl's wounds now began to show evident signs of mortification. Her mother-in-law, who had resided some time in the country, came about this time to town, and inquired after her. Being informed that she was placed at Brownrigg's, she went thither, but was refused admittance by Mr. Brownrigg, who even threatened to carry her before

the lord mayor if she came there to make further disturbances. Upon this the mother-in-law was going away, when
Mrs. Deacon, wife of Mr. Deacon, baker, at the adjoining
house, called her in, and informed her that she and her family had often heard moanings and groans issue from Brownrigg's house, and that she suspected the apprentices were
treated with unwarrantable severity. This good woman
likewise promised to exert herself to ascertain the truth.

At this juncture Mr. Brownrigg, going to Hampstead on
business, bought a hog, which he sent home. The hog was
put into a covered yard, having a sky-light, which it was
thought necessary to remove, in order to give air to the
animal.

As soon as it was known that the sky-light was removed,
Mr. Deacon ordered his servants to watch, in order, if possible, to discover the girls. Accordingly, one of the maids,
looking from a window, saw one of the girls stooping down,
on which she called her mistress, and she desired the attendance of some of the neighbours, who having been witnesses
of the shocking scene, some men got upon the leads, and
dropped bits of dirt, in order to induce the girl to speak to
them; but she seemed wholly incapable. Mrs. Deacon then
sent to the girl's mother-in-law, who immediately called
upon Mr. Grundy, one of the overseers of St. Dunstan's,
and represented the case. Mr. Grundy and the rest of the
overseers, with the women, went and demanded a sight
of Mary Clifford; but Brownrigg, who had nicknamed her
Nan, told them that he knew no such person; but, if they
wanted to see Mary (meaning Mary Mitchell), they might,
and accordingly produced her. Upon this Mr. Deacon's
servant declared that Mary Mitchell was not the girl they
wanted. Mr. Grundy now sent for a constable, to search the
house, but no discovery was then made.

Mr. Brownrigg threatened highly; but Mr. Grundy, with
the spirit that became the officer of a parish, took Mary

Mitchell with him to the workhouse, where, on the taking off her leathern boddice, it stuck so fast to her wounds that she shrieked with the pain; but, on being treated with great humanity, and told that she should not be sent back to Brownrigg's, she gave an account of the horrid treatment that she and Mary Clifford had sustained, and confessed that she had met the latter on the stairs just before they came to the house. Upon this information Mr. Grundy and some others returned to the house, to make a stricter search; on which Brownrigg sent for a lawyer, in order to intimidate them, and even threatened a prosecution unless they immediately quitted the premises. Unterrified by these threats, Mr. Grundy sent for a coach, to carry Brownrigg to the Compter; on which the latter promised to produce the girl in about half an hour, if the coach was discharged. This being consented to, the girl was produced from a cupboard under a beaufet in the dining-room, after a pair of shoes, which young Brownrigg had in his hand during the proposal, had been put upon her. It is not in language to describe the miserable appearance this poor girl made; almost her whole body was ulcerated.

Being taken to the workhouse, an apothecary was sent for, who pronounced her to be in danger.

Brownrigg was therefore conveyed to Wood Street Compter; but his wife and son made their escape, taking with them a gold watch and some money. Mr. Brownrigg was now carried before Alderman Cross-by, who fully committed him, and ordered the girls to be taken to St. Bartholomew's Hospital, where Mary Clifford died within a few days; and the coroner's inquest, being summoned, found a verdict of Wilful Murder against James and Elizabeth Brownrigg, and John their son.

In the mean time Mrs. Brownrigg and her son shifted from place to place in London, bought clothes in Rag Fair to disguise themselves, and then went to Wandsworth, where they took lodgings in the house of Mr. Dunbar, who kept a chandler's shop.

This chandler, happening to read a newspaper on the 15th of August, saw an advertisement, which so clearly described his lodgers, that he had no doubt but they were the murderers.

On this he went to London the next day, which was Sunday, and, going to church, sent for Mr. Owen, the church warden, to attend him in the vestry, and gave him such a description of the parties that Mr. Owen desired Mr. Deacon and Mr. Wingrave, a constable, to go to Wandsworth, and make the necessary inquiry.

On their arrival at Dunbar's house, they found the wretched mother and son in a room by themselves, who evinced great agitation at this discovery. A coach being procured, they were conveyed to London, without any person in Wandsworth having knowledge of the affair, except Mr. and Mrs. Dunbar.

At the ensuing sessions at the Old Bailey, the father, mother, and son, were indicted; when Elizabeth Brownrigg, after a trial of eleven hours, was found guilty of murder, and ordered for execution; but the man and his son, being acquitted of the higher charge[7], were detained, to take their trials for a misdemeanor, of which they were convicted, and imprisoned for the space of six months.

After sentence of death was passed on Mrs. Brownrigg she was attended by a clergyman, to whom she confessed the enormity of her crime, and acknowledged the justice of the sentence by which she had been condemned. The parting between her and her husband and son, on the morning

---

[7] IT SEEMS THE child was looked upon as the apprentice of the wife, and not the husband; though the husband was obliged to find her apparel: however, accessories in murder are equally guilty, and it is strange that the man and his son should have been acquitted.

of her execution, was affecting beyond description. The son falling on his knees, she bent herself over him and embraced him; while the husband was kneeling on the other side.

On her way to the fatal tree the people expressed their abhorrence of her crime in terms which, though not proper at the moment, testified their detestation of her cruelty. Before her exit, she joined in prayer with the Ordinary of Newgate, whom she desired to declare to the multitude that she confessed her guilt, and acknowledged the justice of her sentence.

After her execution, which took place at Tyburn, September the 14th, 1767, her body was put into a hackney-coach, and conveyed to Surgeons' Hall, where it was dissected, and her skeleton hung up.

That Mrs. Brownrigg, a midwife by profession, and herself the mother of many children, should wantonly murder the offspring of other women, is truly astonishing, and can only be accounted for by that depravity of human nature which philosophers have always disputed, but which true Christians will be ready to allow.

Let her crimes be buried, though her skeleton be exposed; and may no one hereafter be found wicked enough to copy her vile example!

Women who have the care of children from parish workhouse or hospitals should consider themselves at once as mistresses and in mothers; nor ever permit the strictness of the former character to preponderate over the humanity of the latter.

HAWKINS AND THE RIUTERS BEFORE THE MANSION HOUSE.

WILLIAM HAWKINS and JOSEPH WILD

Indicted for rioting.

———

AT the sessions of the Old Bailey for July, 1768, William Hawkins and Joseph Wild were tried for assaulting and wounding two of the servants of the lord mayor of London, and for other unlawful acts against the peace of our sovereign lord the king.

On the part of the prosecution the first witness called was Mr. Way, a gentleman who was accidentally passing on the evening of this riot. He deposed that he saw a crowd of people carrying a gibbet, on which hung a boot and a petticoat, and making a stand at the Mansion House; he saw the lord mayor come out, and rush among the people who carried the gibbet, on which an affray began, and he presently heard the words 'Knock him down, knock him down!' At this instant he saw the prisoner, Hawkins, laying about him with a stick, which he afterwards found was stuck with nails, and he saw him strike one or two people, who proved to be his lordship's servants. They then seized Hawkins, and were dragging him into the Mansion House; but the mob rescued him, and he was making off, when the witness collared him, and, with the assistance of the wounded servants, secured him in the Mansion House.

Philip Pyle swore that, being in waiting upon the lord mayor the night of the riot (the 9th of May, the next day after the outlawry against Wilkes was reversed), he observed a great mob advancing with a gibbet, a boot and a petticoat hanging upon it; and being ordered by his lordship to seize it, he gave it a shake, which obliged the mob to quit it; that he was pulling it along, when a man, whom he believed to be the prisoner Hawkins, caught a flambeau out of his hand, and broke his head with it in several places. Dropping the gibbet, he recovered the flambeau, and made a stroke at the assailants (for there were now two or three striking at him), and was endeavoring to retreat for fear of falling, in which case, he said, he must undoubtedly have been murdered, when he received several blows on his head with a stick stuck full of nails, which happened to fly out of the prisoner's, Hawkins, hand, and his fellow-servant snatched it up. The prisoner then endeavored to defend himself with his hands, but the witness dragged him, in his rage, near twenty yards through the mob; but when he had got him within ten yards of the Mansion House the mob rescued him, and when he was making off Mr. Way collared him, and brought him back.

Thomas Woodward, another servant of the lord mayor, corroborated the evidence of the two former witnesses.

There being no positive proof against the prisoner Wild, he was acquitted; but Hawkins was found guilty, and sentenced to death.

MORGAN AT THE CLUB.

RICHARD MORGAN

Executed for privately stealing.

———

This malefactor was a native of Ellesmere, in Shropshire, descended of poor parents, whose virtuous characters were the greatest part of their possession. They bestowed on him as good an education as their circumstances would admit, and were careful to instruct him in the duties of religion. When he grew towards years of maturity he entered into the service of a farmer in the neighbourhood, with whom he lived near three years with an unblemished reputation.

After this he engaged to serve other farmers in different parts of England, continuing to labour as a husbandman till he became almost two-and-twenty years of age, and then repaired to London, in order to obtain subsistence by his honest endeavours.

He had not been long in town before he entered into the service of Mr. Hotchkin, a capital linen-draper near Smithfield Bars. His principal business was to carry out parcels, and his behaviour was such, for a considerable time, as entitled him to the approbation of his master.

At length he was unfortunate enough to become acquainted with the servant of a distiller in the neighbourhood, who introduced him into a set of company which led to his ruin. Morgan had been hitherto remarkable for his sobriety; but a fatal change soon took place. The distiller's servant was one of a low alehouse club, of which Morgan became a member; and each of the company paid four-pence halfpenny for his evening's expenses in beer and tobacco.

It was in this club that the first taint appears to have been given to Morgan's morals. Some of the company, who were chiefly porters, used to boast how considerably they defrauded their masters, and even mentioned the names of the parties to whom they sold the stolen effects.

For some time Morgan appeared shocked at the idea of obtaining money by such a violation of the laws of duty and integrity, and actually absented himself from the club; but at length the servant of the distiller prevailed on him to rejoin the company, which he did, but with a reserve in his own mind that he would not be concerned in any of their iniquitous transactions.

These good resolutions, however, did not last any considerable time; for his companions, wishing him to enter into their practices, artfully took him to the house of the man who received the stolen goods, where he saw such various articles which porters had stolen from their masters, and remained undetected, that he was but too easily induced to commence the illicit practice.

His mind being thus prepared for acts of dishonesty, he soon began to purloin his master's effects, which he stole in considerable quantities; and as Mr. Hotchkin had a very large stock, and dealt in the wholesale trade, the articles could not be easily missed, so that he had an opportunity of continuing his depredations for a considerable space of time; and, indeed, when the articles were at length missed, no one suspected Morgan to be the thief, as his character had been hitherto irreproachable, and his behaviour such as to entitle him to general respect.

His custom was to convey the stolen goods to a stable in Durham Yard, Chick Lane, where they were deposited till the usual purchaser came, and bought them, and carried them off.

Morgan's practices in this way were so considerable, that his companions of the club began to look on him as a proper agent for disposing of such goods as should be stolen by others; but this plan was defeated almost as soon as it was formed.

Mr. Hotchkin at length discovering that he had been robbed, and that the depredations had been frequently renewed, and observing that not any person had broken into his house, he concluded that the robber must be one who lived in the family.

In consequence hereof a person was appointed to watch the motions of Morgan; and on his going out he was followed to a house, whence he took several parcels to an inn, to be carried by the Birmingham waggon.

Inquiry being made into the affair, it was discovered that Morgan had a considerable quantity of goods destined for the same place; and these, being examined, were found to be the property of Mr. Hotchkin, whose marks were on the several pieces; on which the offender was taken into custody, and carried before a magistrate. On his examination he denied having been guilty of the crime alleged against him; but, as the presumptive evidence of the fact was too strong to allow of his being dismissed, he was committed to Newgate, till the ensuing sessions at the Old Bailey, that his guilt or innocence might abide the award of a jury.

On his trial the evidence against him was so conclusive that no hesitation could be made to find him guilty, and judgment of death passed of course.

After conviction he acknowledged to the Ordinary of Newgate the justice of his sentence, and owned that he had defrauded his master of goods to a considerable amount. He was constant and regular in his devotions, both in the chapel and in his cell; nor did he seem to entertain a hope of that mercy which he had no right to expect.

When he was told that his name was included in the warrant for execution, he received the dreadful news with great composure; and confessed that he had merited the shocking fate that awaited him. He behaved even with pious resignation, and acknowledged that faith in the merits of Christ by which poor sinners are to expect salvation.

He was visited after conviction by a number of people who had known him in the former part of life, and who kindly assisted him in his solemn preparations for eternity.

He received the sacrament on the morning of his death, and repeated the declarations he had formerly made of his guilt. At the fatal tree he addressed himself to the surrounding multitude, earnestly desiring servants not to defraud their employers. He prayed in the most earnest manner, and so audibly as to be heard by great numbers who attended his fatal exit. After the body had hung the customary time it was delivered to his friends, in order to its being buried as they might think proper.

Richard Morgan suffered at Tyburn on the 27th of May, 1772.

From the case of this unfortunate man persons in a dependent situation should principally learn two things; as *viz.* never to injure their masters; and by all means to avoid any connexion with low company at alehouses, as keeping such company may insensibly involve them in expenses which may lead to the commitment of acts of dishonesty.

Honest countrymen are generally too fond of repairing to London, in the vain hope of making that fortune which very few of them ever acquire; and perhaps those who do might be more happy in their native fields, undisturbed with the cares of the busy world.

It is not every man that grows rich that becomes happy of course; and perhaps the contrary is more generally the case.

Upon the whole, we should learn resignation to the will of Providence, and be taught the great doctrine of being content in any station in which we may be placed:—

HILL SETTING FIRE TO THE ROPE-HOUSE IN PORTSMOUTH DOCK-YARD.

JAMES HILL, commonly called
JOHN THE PAINTER

Executed for setting fire to Portsmouth dock-yard.

———

So dangerous an individual to the kingdom as this man perhaps never existed, and whose confession and repentance can hardly soften the abhorrence felt on the contemplation of the extent of his crimes.

James Hill, that universally detested character, during the progress of his public ruin and desolation, had gone by several names—a plan generally adopted in a long course of villainy.

He was once a journeyman to Mr. Golden, a painter, at Titchfield, whence he procured the familiar title of 'John the Painter.' During a residence of some years in America he imbibed principles destructive to the interests of this country. Transported with party zeal, he formed the desperate resolution of committing a most atrocious crime, which he, in some degree, effected. About four o'clock in the afternoon of the 7th of December, 1776, a fire broke out in the round-house of Portsmouth dock, which entirely consumed that building. The fire was wholly attributed to accident; but on the 5th of January three men who were employed in the hemp-house found a tin machine, somewhat resembling a tea-canister, and near the same spot a wooden box, containing various kinds of combustibles. This circumstance being communicated to the commissioner of the dock, and circulated among the public, several vague and indefinite suspicions fell upon Hill, who had been lurking about the dock-yard, whose surname was not known, but who had been distinguished by the appellation of 'John the Painter.'

In consequence of advertisements in the newspapers, offering a reward of fifty pounds for apprehending him, he was secured at Odiham. On the 17th of February the prisoner was examined at Sir John Fielding's office, Bow Street, where John Baldwin, who exercised the trade of a painter in different parts of America, attended, by the direction of Lord Temple. The prisoner's discourse with Baldwin operated very materially towards his conviction, as it was brought in corroboration of a variety of evidence on the trial. He said he had taken a view of most of the dock-yards and fortifications about England, the number of ships in the navy, and observed their weight of metal and their number of men, and had been to France two or three times to inform Silas Dean, the American, of his discoveries; and that Dean gave him bills to the amount of three hundred pounds, and letters of recommendation to a merchant in the city, which he had burnt, lest they should lead to a discovery. He informed Baldwin that he had instructed a tin-man's apprentice at Canterbury to make him a tin canister, which he carried to Portsmouth, where he hired a lodging at one Mrs. Boxall's, and tried his preparations for setting fire to the dock-yard.

After recounting the manner of preparing matches and combustibles, he said that, on the 6th of the preceding December, he got into the hemp-house, and, having placed a candle in a wooden box, and a tin canister over it, and sprinkled turpentine over some of the hemp, he proceeded to the rope-house, where he placed a bottle of turpentine among the loose hemp, which he sprinkled with turpentine; and having laid matches, made of paper painted over with powdered charcoal and gunpowder diluted with water, and other combustibles, about the place, he returned to his lodgings. These matches were so contrived as to continue burning for twenty-four hours, so that by cutting them into proper lengths he provided for his escape, knowing the precise time when the fire would reach the combustibles. He had hired lodgings in two other houses, to which he intended to set fire, that the engines might not be all employed together in quenching the conflagration at the dock. On the 7th he again went to the hemp-house, intending to set it on fire; which he, however, was unable to effect, owing to a halfpenny-worth of common house matches that he had bought not being sufficiently dry. This disappointment, he said, rendered him exceedingly uneasy, and he went from the hemp-house to the rope-house, and set fire to the matches he had placed there. He said his uneasiness was increased because he could not return to his lodging, where he had left a bundle containing an 'Ovid's Metamorphoses,' a 'Treatise on War and making Fire-works,' a 'Justin,' a pistol, and a French passport, in which his real name was inserted.

When he had set fire to the rope-house he proceeded towards London, deeply regretting his failure in attempting to fire the other building, and was strongly inclined to fire into the windows of the women who had sold him the bad matches. He jumped into a cart, and gave the woman who drove it sixpence, to induce her to drive quick; and, when he had passed the sentinels, he observed the fire to have made so rapid a progress that the elements seemed in a blaze. He might have added, with Chaos to the Devil.

'Havoc, and spoil, and ruin, are my gain.'

About ten the next morning he arrived at Kingston, where he remained until the dusk of the evening, and proceeded to London in the stage. Soon after his arrival he waited upon the gentleman in the city, and informed him of having been under the necessity of burning the bills upon, and letters to, him from Silas Dean. The gentleman behaved to him with shyness, but appointed to meet him at a coffee-house. At the coffee-house the gentleman seemed to be doubtful as to the story told by Hill, who there-fore went away displeased, and as soon as he reached Hammersmith wrote to the merchant, saying he was going to Bristol, and that the 'handy works he meant to perform there would be soon known to the public.'[8] A short time after his arrival at Bristol he set fire to several houses, which were all burning with great rapidity at one time, and the flames were not extinguished till damage was sustained to the amount of fifteen thousand pounds. He also set fire to combustibles that he had placed among a number of oil-barrels upon the quay, but happily without effect. He related to Baldwin a great number of other circumstances, which were confirmed by a variety of evidence on his trial, which came on, Thursday, March 6, 1777, at Winchester Castle, when witnesses were produced from different parts of the country, who proved

---

[8] IT IS TO be regretted that this merchant was not apprehended.

the whole of his confession to Baldwin to be true, and gave other proofs of his guilt.

When called upon for his defence, he complained of the newspapers and reports circulated to his prejudice; and observed that it was easy for such a man as Baldwin to feign the story he had told, and for a number of witnesses to be collected to give it support.

He declared that God alone knew whether he was, or was not, the person who set fire to the dock-yard of his Britannic Majesty at Portsmouth; and begged it might be attended to, how far Baldwin ought to be credited: that if he had art enough, by lies, to insinuate any thing out of him, his giving it to the knowledge of others was a breach of confidence; and if he would speak falsely to deceive him, he might also impose upon a jury. Upon this head the prisoner, with some ingenuity, dwelt for some time, and concluded by begging the judge to repeat his defence in proper terms to the jury, as he was not endowed with the gift of oratory, which they might easily perceive.

The prisoner had no counsel.

The jury, after a clear and impartial charge from Baron Hotham, in an instant agreed upon their verdict—'Guilty.'

The learned judge then proceeded to pass the sentence of the law upon the prisoner. He told him that he had a long and fair trial; that he had been found guilty on the fullest and clearest evidence; that he could not have any thing to complain of in the candour of the Court, and that his crime was of a nature so enormous, that it was not in the power of words to aggravate it.

The judge then said that he would not increase the prisoner's present unhappy moments, nor add to his distress, by dwelling upon the horrors attending the crime of which he was convicted; but was sorry to say that he felt, he feared, much more for him than his appearance bespoke him feeling for himself: yet would he earnestly recommend him to consider his case, and prepare to meet his God; for that he was bound—and it was by much the most disagreeable part of his duty—to pass the sentence of the law upon him; and he accordingly adjudged him to be hanged by the neck until he was dead. Further, he said, he thought it right to advise him, that, as his offence was of such a nature as might not only have proved fatal to every person present, but have involved the whole British nation in universal ruin, there was not any probability of his receiving mercy; and concluded by strongly urging the prisoner to repentance, and preparation for that pardon in the world to come which upon earth could not be granted to him.

He was allowed for this purpose four days, and suffered at Portsmouth, March the 10th, 1777, in sight of the ruins which he had occasioned.

His body, for several years, hung in chains on Blockhouse Point, on the opposite side of the harbour to the town.

To these particulars we shall present his confession. On the morning after his condemnation he informed the turnkey, of his own spontaneous accord, that he felt an earnest desire of confessing his crime, and laying the history of his life before the public; and that, by discovering the whole of his unaccountable plots and treasonable practices, he might make some atonement to his most injured country for the wrongs he had done, of which he was now truly sensible, and a repentant sinner.

This request being made known to the Earl of Sandwich, then first lord of the admiralty, that nobleman directed Sir John Fielding to send down proper persons to take and attest his confession.

He began by saying that he was by birth a Scotchman, and had left Scotland in order to embark for America, where he resided the greater part of his life. The diabolical scheme of setting fire to the dock-yards and the shipping, he said, originated in his own wicked mind, on the very breaking out of the rebellion in America; and he had no peace until he proceeded to put it in practice. The more he thought of it, the more practicable it appeared; and with this wicked intent he crossed again the great Atlantic.

He had no sooner landed than he proceeded to take surveys of the different dock-yards; which done, he went to Paris, and had several conferences with Silas Dean, the rebel minister to the court of France.

Dean (as well indeed he might) was astonished at Hill's proposals, which embraced the destruction of the English dock-yards and the shipping,

Finding the projector an enthusiast in the cause of America, and a man of daring spirit, he gradually listened to his schemes; and such was the enmity of the first Congress to the mother country, that Dean supplied this traitor with money, to enable him to carry them into execution; procured him a French passport; and gave him a letter of credit on a merchant in London, who, as we have already observed, escaped detection.

He then confirmed the evidence given against him, and in particular his confessions to Baldwin. He was, he further declared, to have been rewarded by a commission in the American army for setting fire to the dock-yard at Plymouth; and fully admitted the justice of his sentence for a crime so heinous.

ROACH AND HIS COMPANIONS STEALING A LEADEN COFFIN.

GEORGE ROACH, ROBERT ELLIOT, and JONAS PARKER

Convicted of robbing a grave.

———

THE robbing of churches has ever been deemed sacrilegious by all who have professed any veneration for the duties and obligations of religion. The idea of disturbing the ashes of the dead has something in it abhorrent to the feelings of human nature and to the dictates of Christian piety. When the clay-cold body is committed to the tomb, we presume that it is to rest in peace till the final renovation of all things; nor can the surviving friends and relations easily pardon these who violate the mansions of the dead, and make a jest of the type of sepulture.

These men were indicted at the Old Bailey in April, 1778:—the two former for stealing a leaden coffin, of three hundred pounds, weight, value five pounds, the property of William Thornton Anton, Esq.; and Parker for receiving fifty pounds' weight of the lead, value five shillings, knowing the same to have been stolen. The second count in the indictment laid the lead to be the property of the parishioners of Aldermanbury, and stolen by Roach and Elliot; and the third count charged Jonas Parker with receiving it, being the property of the parishioners of Aldermanbury, well knowing it to have been stolen.

William Thornton Anton, Esq. deposed that, on the 1st of January preceding, his brother was interred in a leaden coffin in the church of Aldermanbury; that the coffin was stolen out of the church, and was missed on the 7th of March.

James Gould, who had been admitted an evidence, deposed that Roach, Elliot, and himself, were journeymen carpenters, working under Mr. Augurs in the repair of the church. He said that on Friday, the 6th of March, he and Roach went into the vault, and unscrewed all the screws of Mr. Thornton's coffin except two, after which they returned to the work; and that, afterwards, themselves and Elliot agreed to work again on the coffin.

On the Saturday morning they went to the church, and about five o'clock a watchman followed them in, and desired a door to be planed, which was done by Gould. The accomplices then loosened the other screws, and turned the coffins bottom upwards, taking off the outside coffin, and leaving only the shell. They then cut the leaden coffin in pieces, and, replacing the other coffin on the shell, screwed it down again.

These transactions occupied them till near eight in the morning, when they took the pieces of the coffin, and, having concealed them under the children's gallery, they conferred on selling what they had stolen; when Elliot mentioned Parker, in Grub Street, as a likely purchaser.

The lead being in two pieces, Gould put one of them in a bag, and took it away, and the other was put in a basket, and carried by one of the accomplices. When they got to London Wall, Elliot beckoned Gould, and they went to a shop, where they offered the lead to sale to a person who refused to be the purchaser. They then went to Parker's, who weighed the lead; without asking them any questions; said it was forty-two pounds, and paid them three shillings and sixpence for it, being at the rate of a penny a pound. When they were going away with the empty bag, Mr. Augurs's apprentice came in and seized on Gould, desiring Parker, who was a constable, to assist in conveying him and Elliot to Mr. Augurs's. Parker said, 'You had better go to your master, and try to make the matter up.' They went, and were all charged with the felony. Parker said 'Give them a *trevalle* for it.'

Gould, being asked what he understood, by that term, said he did not exactly know what it meant, but supposed it was a hint to attempt making their escape; on which they made a run for it (to use his own words), and Parker likewise ran away; but they were stopped, and taken into custody, before they had got to any considerable distance.

John Brotherous, apprentice to Mr. Augurs, confirmed so much of the former testimony as related to himself. He said that, passing by London Wall about eight in the morning, he saw Roach coming down Wood Street with a basket on his back; and that Roach, seeing him, crossed over the street. Brotherous demanded what he had with him: he said his tools, and turned round, as if to prevent his looking in his basket; but he did look in, and saw there was lead; on which he seized Roach, and sent for a constable to take him into custody. This was the occasion of his going to the house of Parker, whom he knew to be a constable. On his arrival at Parker's, he met with Gould and Elliot coming out of the house with empty sacks; on which he supposed they had sold something there.

He charged Parker with the prisoners; but he said, 'You had better go to your master quietly, and make the affair up.' Brotherous told his master what had passed; and he caused all the prisoners to be apprehended, who endeavored to make their escape as the proper officer was conveying them to the Compter.

Mr. Reynolds, an undertaker, deposed that he buried Mr. Thornton in a leaden coffin; that he surveyed the vault on the 7th of March, when the coffin was missing; that he compared the pieces that were found at Parker's with the rest of the coffin, that was found under the gallery of the church; and, when all were beaten together into the same form, they made out the shape and quantity of Mr. Thornton's coffin. The plate, with Mr. Thornton's name on it, was found in Roach's chest; the lead, to the weight of fifty-two pounds, was found under the counter in Parker's shop; and this deponent added that it was a sort of lead worked in a fashion peculiar to coffins, and that people in the trade knew very well that it was coffin lead.

Isaac Mather deposed that old lead was worth about thirteen shillings and sixpence the hundred weight, or halfpence the pound.

By way of defence, Roach said that Gould put the lead into his basket, but that he knew nothing of its being stolen. Elliot likewise denied all knowledge of the stealing of the lead, and said he never received any money or other thing on account of it, but was in Parker's shop buying a hinge for his own use, and was astonished when he saw Gould there, and still more at his master's apprentice giving charge of him.

Parker's defence was, that the evidence came into his shop to sell some lead, which he did not know was stolen;—that when he had weighed, and was paying for it, Mr. Augurs's apprentice entered, and gave him charge of the prisoners; and that, when at the master's house, he charged him likewise; but that he immediately mentioned where the two pieces were which he had bought; in consequence of which they were found.

All the prisoners called persons who gave them good characters; but the jury, having fully considered the nature of the evidence, gave a verdict that they were guilty, in consequence of which, at the close of the sessions, Roach and Elliot were sentenced to labour three years on the Thames, and Parker to be imprisoned for a like term.

MR. HACKMAN SHOOTING MISS REAY AND ATTEMPTING SUICIDE.

THE REVEREND JAMES HACKMAN

Executed for murder.

———

THIS shocking and truly lamentable case interested all ranks of people, who pitied the murderer's fate, conceiving him stimulated to commit the horrid crime through love and madness. Pamphlets and poem were written on the occasion, and the crime was long the common topic of conversation.

The object of Mr. Hackman's love renders his case still more singular.

Miss Reay had been the mistress of Lord Sandwich near twenty years, was the mother of nine children, and nearly double the age of Mr. Hackman.

This murder affords a melancholy proof that there is no act so contrary to reason that men will not commit when under the dominion of their passions. In short, it is impossible to convey an idea of the impression it made; and the manner in which it was done created horror and pity in every feeling mind.

The Rev. James Hackman was born at Gosport, in Hampshire, and originally designed for trade; but he was too volatile in disposition to submit to the drudgery of the shop or counting-house. His parents, willing to promote his interest as far as lay in their power, purchased him an ensign's commission in the 68th regiment of foot. He had not been long in the army when he was sent to command a recruiting party; and, being at Huntingdon, he was frequently invited to dine with Lord Sandwich, who had a seat in that neighbourhood. Here it was that he first became acquainted with Miss Reay, who lived under the protection of that nobleman.

The lady was the daughter of a staymaker in Covent Garden, and served her apprenticeship to a mantua-maker in George's Court, St. John's Lane, Clerkenwell. She was bound when only thirteen; and, during her apprenticeship, was taken notice of by the nobleman above mentioned, who took her under his protection, and treated her with every mark of tenderness. No sooner had Mr. Hackman seen her than he became enamoured of her, though she had then lived nineteen years with his lordship. Finding he could not obtain preferment in the army, he turned his thoughts to the church, and entered into orders. Soon after he obtained the living of Wiverton, in Norfolk, which was only about Christmas preceding the shocking deed which cost him his life; so that it may be said he never enjoyed it.

It is probable that Mr. Hackman imagined that there was a mutual passion—that Miss Reay had the same regard for him as he had for her. Love and madness are often little better than synonymous terms; for, had Mr. Hackman not been blinded by a bewitching passion, he could never have imagined that Miss Reay would have left the family of a noble lord at the head of one of the highest departments of the state, in order to live in a humble station. Those who have been long accustomed to affluence, and even profusion, seldom choose to lower their flags. However, he was still tormented by this unhappy, irregular, and ungovernable passion, which, in an unhappy moment, led him to commit the crime for which he suffered.

Miss Reay was extremely fond of music, and, as her noble protector was in a high rank, we need not be surprised to find that frequent concerts were performed both in London and at Hinchinbrook: at the latter place Mr. Hackman was generally of the party, and his attention to her at those times was very great. How long he had been in London previous to this affair is not certainly known, but at that time he lodged in Duke's Court, St. Martin's Lane. On the morning of the 7th of April, 1779, he sat some time in his closet, reading 'Blair's Sermons'; but in the evening he took a walk to the Admiralty, where he saw Miss Reay go into the coach along with Signora Galli, who attended her. The coach drove to Covent Garden Theatre, where she staid to see the performance of 'Love in a Village.' Mr. Hackman went into the theatre at the same time; but, not being able to contain the violence of his passion, returned, and again went to his lodgings, and, having loaded two pistols, went to the playhouse, where he waited till the play was over. Seeing Miss Reay ready to step into the coach, he took a pistol in each hand, one of which he discharged against her, which killed her on the spot, and the other at himself, which, however, did not take effect.

He then beat himself with the butt end on his head, in order to destroy himself, so fully bent was he on the destruction of both. After some struggle he was secured, his wounds dressed, and then he was carried before Sir John Fielding, who committed him to Tothillfields' Bridewell, and next to Newgate, where a person was appointed to attend him, lest he should lay violent hands on himself. In Newgate, as he knew he had no favour to expect, as he prepared himself for the awful change he was about to make. He had dined with his sister on the day the murder was committed; and, in the afternoon, wrote a letter to her husband, Mr. Booth, an eminent attorney, acquainting him of his resolution of destroying himself, desiring him to sell what effects he should leave behind him, to pay a small debt; but this letter was not sent, for it was found in his pocket.

On the trial Mr. Macnamara deposed that, on Wednesday, the 7th day of April, on seeing Miss Reay, with whom he had some little acquaintance, in some difficulties in getting from the playhouse, he offered his assistance to hand her to her coach; and just as they were in the Piazzas, very near the carriage, he heard the report of a pistol, and felt an impression on his right arm, which arm she held with her left, and instantly dropped. He thought at first that the pistol had been fired through wantonness, and that she had fallen from the fright, and therefore fell upon his knees to help her up; but, finding his hands bloody, he then conceived an idea of what had happened, and, by the assistance of a link-boy, got the deceased into the Shakespeare Tavern, where he first saw the prisoner, after he was secured. He asked him some questions relative to the fact and the cause; and his answer was, that neither the time nor place were proper to resolve him. He asked his name, and was told Hackman: he knew a Mr. Booth, in Craven Street, and desired he might be sent for.

He asked to see the lady; to which he (the witness) objected, and had her removed to a private room. From the impression he felt, and the great quantity of blood, about him, he grew sick, and went home; and knew nothing more about it.

Mary Anderson, a fruit-woman, disposed that, just as the play was over, she saw two ladies and a gentleman coming out of the playhouse, and a gentleman in black following them. Lord Sandwich's coach was called. When the carriage came up the gentleman handed the other lady into it. The lady that was shot stood behind, when the gentleman in black came up, laid hold of her gown, and pulled two pistols out of his pocket: the one in his right hand he discharged at the lady, and the other, in his left, he discharged at himself. They fell feet to feet. He beat himself violently over the head with his pistol, and desired somebody would kill him.

Richard Blandy, the constable, swore to the finding of two letters in the prisoner's pocket, which he delivered to Mr. Campbell, the master of the Shakespeare Tavern, in Covent Garden.

Mr. Mahon, an apothecary, corroborated the evidence of the fruit-woman: he wrenched the pistol out of his hand, with which he was beating himself, as he lay on the ground—took him to his house, dressed his wounds, and accompanied him to the Shakespeare.

Denis O'Brian, a surgeon, examined the wound of the deceased, and found it mortal.

Being called upon for his defence, he addressed the Court in the following words:—

'I should not have troubled the Court with the examination of witnesses to support the charge against me, had I not thought that the pleading guilty to the indictment gave an indication of condemning death, not suitable to my present condition, and was, in some measure, being accessory to a second peril of my life; and I likewise thought that the justice of my country ought to be satisfied by suffering my offence to be proved, and the fact established by evidence.

'I stand here this day the most wretched of human beings, and confess myself criminal in a high degree; yet while I acknowledge, with shame and repentance, that my determination against my own life was formal and complete, I protest, with that regard to truth which becomes my situation, that the will to destroy her, who was ever dearer to me than life, was never mine till a momentary frenzy overcame me, and induced me to commit the deed I now deplore. The letter, which I meant for my brother-in-law after my decease, will have its due weight, as to this point, with good men.

'Before this dreadful act, I trust nothing will be found in the tenor of my life which the common charity of mankind will not excuse. I have no wish to avoid the punishment which the laws of my country appoint for my crime; but, being already too unhappy to feel a punishment in death or a satisfaction in life, I submit myself with penitence and patience to the disposal and judgment of Almighty God, and to the consequences of this inquiry into my conduct and intention.'

Then was read the following letter:—

'My dear Frederic,—When this reaches you I shall be no more; but do not let my unhappy fate distress you too much: I have strove against it as long as possible, but it now overpowers me. You well know where my affections were placed: my having by some means or other lost hers (an idea which I could not support) has driven me to madness. The world will condemn me, but your good heart will pity me. God bless you, my dear Frederic! Would I had a sum to leave you, to convince you of my great regard! You was my only friend. I have hid one circumstance from you, which gives me great pain. I owe Mr. Knight, of Gosport, one hundred pounds, for which he has the writings of my houses; but I hope in God, when they are sold, and all other matters collected, there will be nearly enough to settle our account. May Almighty God bless you and yours with comfort and happiness; and may you ever be a stranger to the pangs I now feel! May Heaven protect my beloved woman, and forgive this act, which alone could relieve me from a world of misery I have long endured! Oh! if it should ever be in your power to do her an act of friendship, remember your faithful friend, 'J. HACK MAN.'

The jury immediately returned their fatal verdict. The unhappy man heard the sentence pronounced against him with calm resignation to his fate, and employed the very short time allowed murderers after conviction in repentance and prayer.

During the procession to the fatal tree at Tyburn he seemed much affected, and said but little; and when he arrived at Tyburn, and got out of the coach and mounted the cart, he took leave of Dr. Porter and the Ordinary.

After some time spent in prayer, he was turned off, on April the 19th, 1779; and, having hung the usual time, his body was carried to Surgeons' Hall for dissection.

Such was the end of a young gentleman who might have been an ornament to his country, the delight of his friends, and a comfort to his relations, had he not been led away by the influence of an unhappy passion.

With the following lines, selected from a number of poetical essays on this melancholy subject, we conclude our account of the unfortunate Mr. Hackman:—

'Ill-fated youth! admit this funeral lay,
Which sympathetic friendship weeps to pay;
This heart, alas! the wound of love has known—
This bosom heaved with sorrow like thy own.
Thou wert whate'er is virtuous, gentle, kind;
To sweetest mirth still turned thy artless mind;

Whence hallowed Piety, with humble care,
To yon bright azure wing'd her constant prayer.
Oh! more than this thou wert, till beauty came,
And raised within a far less sacred flame;
Then thy frail feet the paths of fondness trod,
And woman rose—the rival of thy God!
But slighted fondness every comfort stole,
And to mute anguish gave thy wounded soul;
Till madness closed the agonizing strife,
And bade thy spirit burst to nobler life.
For sure nought else that brow with horror hung,
Where smiled fair Peace, and Joy forever young:
Nought else with grief's sad plaints those accents filled,
Whence cheerful Virtue's roseate balm distilled;
Nought else congealed in death that generous blood,
Which flowed for ever for thy country's good.
Yet happier thou had Heav'n-taught Prudence reigned,
And wild Despair's ecstatic act restrained;
Then Love itself had pleaded strong to save,
And charmed thee bending o'er the tempting wave;
For, when the maid thy piteous tale shall hear,
Her softening heart must pour the frequent tear!
Then had thy soul each deed of death forgot,
In painful patience learned to bear its lot,
Hard clasped this truth my sad experience gives,
That hopeless lover suffers most who lives.'

The dreadful effects of this passion—and well may it be termed 'love and madness'—we have found perverting reason in the lower ranks of society.

Thomas Giles, a barber, in the city of Worcester, had been 'crossed in love.' His beloved was a servant girl, who, preferring the suit of a cobbler, the rejected swain, in a fit of frenzy, went to the house of the girl's master, and with one of his razors cut her throat from ear to ear. He then turned the sharp instrument upon himself in the same manner, and both expired.

The coroner's jury brought in their verdict 'Felo de se' respecting himself, and 'Wilful murder' with regard to the girl.

Like all those who kill themselves, his body was buried in a cross road, and a stake driven through it with every mark of ignominy.

RENWICK WILLIAMS STABBING MISS PORTER.

RENWICK WILLIAMS, or
THE MONSTER

Convicted of a brutal and wanton assault on
Miss Anne Porter.

———

SEVERAL months previous to the apprehension of this man, a report put through all ranks of society that young females had been Secretly wounded in different parts of their bodies, in the public streets, and often in the daytime, by a monster who, upon committing the brutal crime, effected his escape.

Sometimes, as reported, the villain presented a nosegay to a young female, wherein was concealed a sharp instrument; and, as he offered them the flowers to smell, stabbed them in the face. Other tales were told, of some being stabbed in the thigh, and behind; in fine, there was universal terror in the female world in London.

At length a man named Renwick Williams was apprehended on the charge of one of the young ladies thus brutally wounded, and his trial came on at the Old Bailey, on the 18th of July, 1790.

The indictment charged, that with force and arms, in the parish of St. James, on the king's highway, Renwick Williams did, unlawfully, wilfully, and maliciously, make an assault upon, maim, and wound, Anne Porter, against the peace, &c. A second count charged the said Renwick Williams, that, on the same day and year, he did unlawfully, wilfully, and maliciously, tear, spoil, cut, and deface, the garments and clothes—to wit, the cloak, gown, petticoat, and shift, of the said Anne Porter, contrary to the statute, and against the peace, &c.

Miss Anne Porter deposed that she had been at St. James's, to see the ball, on the night of the 18th of January, 1790, accompanied by her sister, Miss Sarah Porter, and another lady; that her father had appointed to meet them at twelve o clock, the hour the ball generally breaks up; but that it ended at eleven, and she was therefore under the necessity either of staying where she was, until her father came, or to return home at that time. Her father, she said, lived in St. James's Street, and that he kept a tavern and a cold bath. She agreed to go home with her party.

As they proceeded up St. James's Street her sister appeared much agitated, and called to her to hasten home, which she and her company accordingly did. Her sister was the first to reach the hall door. As the witness turned the corner of the rails, she received a blow on the right hip; she turned round, and saw the prisoner stoop down: she had seen him before several times, on each of which he had followed close behind her, and used language so gross, that the Court did not press on her to relate the particulars.

He did not immediately run away when he struck her, but looked on her face, and she thus had a perfect opportunity of observing him. She had no doubt, she said, of the prisoner being the man that wounded her. She supposed that the wound was inflicted with a sharp instrument, because her clothes were cut, and she was wounded through them.

Miss Porter farther deposed that on the 13th of June last she was walking in St. James's Park, with her mother and her two sisters, and a gentleman of the name of Coleman. The prisoner at the bar met and passed her; she was struck with his person, and knew him; she found he had turned to look after her. Upon appearing agitated, she was questioned, and pointed him out to Mr. Coleman. She said she knew him when he was brought up to the public office at Bow Street.

Her gown, of pink silk, and her shift, which she wore the night she was wounded, were produced in court, and were cut on the right side, a considerable length.

Miss Sarah Porter was next called. She swore that she had seen the prisoner at the bar prior to the 18th of June last, but had no acquaintance with him. He had followed her, and talked to her in language the most shocking and obscene. She had seen him four or five different times. On that night, when her sister was cut, she saw him standing near the bottom of St. James's Street, and, spying her, he exclaimed, 'O ho! are you there' and immediately struck her a violent blow on the side of the head. She then, as well as she was able being almost stunned, called to her sister to make haste, adding, 'Don't you see the wretch behind us? Upon coming to their own door, the prisoner rushed between them, and about the time he struck her sister he also rent the witness's gown. There were lights in the street, and she knew him.

Two more sisters, Miss Rebeces Porter and Miss Martha Porter also bore unequivocal testimony as to the identity of the prisoner, with respect to his having accosted them, in company with their sisters, with the most obscene and indecent language.[9]

Mr. John Coleman was the next witness called. He swore that he was walking with Miss Anne Porter, and the rest of her family, in St. James's Park, on the evening of Sunday, the 13th of June, 1790. That, upon observing Miss Porter much agitated, and inquiring the cause, she pointed out the prisoner at the bar, and said 'the wretch had just passed her.' Having pointed him out, the witness followed him to the house of Mr. Smith, in South Moulton Street, and, upon going into the parlour where he was, expressed his surprise of the prisoner's not resenting the insults he (the witness) had offered him; and demanded his address. Mr. Smith and the prisoner both expressed their surprise at such a demand, without a reason given; he therefore said, that he, the prisoner, had insulted some ladies, who had pointed him out, and that he must have satisfaction. The prisoner denied having offered any insult; but, upon his persisting, they exchanged addresses.

The prisoner's address was produced by the witness. No. 52, Jermyn Street. The witness and the prisoner then mutually recognised each other, as having been in company with each other before, and the witness then departed. On his departure he repented having quitted him and, turning back, he met with him at the top of St. James's Street; he then accosted him again, saying 'I don't think you are the

---

[9] THIS IS A practice among a set of scoundrels of the present day, in the public wherever they find a modest, well-dressed, unprotected female. They not whisper the most abominable bawdry in her chaste ear, but often pinch her on the side or behind, so as to put her in both bodily and mental pain. Such rascals to be whipped at the cart's tail through every street in London.

person I took you for; you had better come with me now, and let the ladies see you.' The prisoner objected, as it was late at night; but, upon his saying it was close by, he went with him.

On his being introduced into the parlour, where the Miss Porters were sitting, two of them, Anne and Sarah, fainted away, exclaiming. 'Oh! my God! that's the wretch!' The prisoner then said, 'The ladies' behaviour is odd; they don't take me for the monster that is advertised. The witness said they did.

The prisoner was there an hour before he was taken away, and in that time said nothing particular.

Mr. Tomkins, surgeon, was next called. By his description the wound must have been made by a very sharp instrument. He had also examined the clothes, and they must have been cut at the same time. The wound itself was, at the beginning, for two or three inches, but skin-deep; about the middle of it, three or four inches deep, and gradually decreasing in depth towards the and. The length of wound, from the hip downwards, was nine or ten inches.

The prisoner, being called upon for his defence, begged the indulgence of the Court, in supplying the deficiency of his memory, upon what he wished to state, from a written paper. He accordingly read as follows:—

'He stood,' he said, 'an object equally demanding the attention and compassion of the Court. That, conscious of his innocence, he was ready to admit the justice of whatever sufferings he had hitherto undergone, arising from suspicion. He had the greatest confidence in the justice and liberality of an English jury, and hoped they would not suffer his fate to be decided by the popular prejudice raised against him. The hope of proving his innocence had hither sustained him.

"He professed himself the warm friend and admirer of that sex whose cause was now asserted, and concluded with solemnly declaring that the whole prosecution was founded on a dreadful mistake, which, he had no doubt, the evidence he was about to call would clear up to the satisfaction of the Court.'

His counsel then proceeded to call his witnesses.

Mr. Mitchell, the first evidence, was an artificial flower-maker, living in Dover Street, Piccadilly. The prisoner had worked for him nine months in all; he had worked with him on the 18th of January, the queen's birth-day, the day on which Miss Porter had been wounded, from nine o'clock in the morning till one o'clock in the day, and from halfpast two till twelve at night he had then supped with the family. He gave the prisoner a good character, as behaving with good nature to the women in the house.

Miss Mitchell, the witness's sister, told the same story.

Two other witnesses, domestics in the same house, like-wise appeared on behalf of the prisoner; but the whole of the evidence, on his part, proved rather contradictory.

Mr. Justice Buller, with great accuracy and ability, went through the whole of this extraordinary business, stating, with great clearness and perspicuity, the parts of the evidence that were most material for the consideration of the jury, with many excellent observations.

He said it had been stated, in various ways, that great outrages had been committed by the prisoner at the bar, and therefore, in defence, he had, very properly, not only applied to the compassion of the jury, to guard against the effect of prejudice, but also to their judgment. It was very proper to do so, and in this he only demanded justice: prejudice often injured, though it could never serve, the cause of justice.

In this the jury would have only to consider what were the facts of which they were to be satisfied, and on which it was their province to decide. This being done by them, and if they should find the prisoner guilty upon the present charge, he would reserve his case for the opinion of the twelve judges of England; and this he should do for several reasons: first, because this was completely and perfectly a new case in itself; and, secondly, because this was the first indictment of the kind that was ever tried. Therefore, although he himself entertained but little doubt upon the first point, yet, as the case was new, it would be right to have a solemn decision upon it. So that hereafter the law, in that particular, may be declared from undoubted authority.

Upon the second point he owned that he entertained some doubts. This indictment was certainly the first of the kind that was ever drawn in this kingdom. It was founded upon the statute of the C George I. Upon this statute it must be proved that it was the intent of the party accused, not only to wound the body, but also cut, tear, and spoil the garment; (here the learned judge read the clause of the act);—one part of this charge was quite clear, namely, that Miss Porter was wounded, and her clothe torn. The first question, therefore, for the consideration of the jury would be, whether this was done wilfully, and with intent to spoil the garment, as well as to wound the body. That was a fact for the jury to decide; and, if they agreed upon this, then, whether the prisoner was the man who did it.

He observed that there might be cases in which the clothes were torn, and yet where this act would not apply; such, for instance, as a scuffle in a quarrel, where clothes might be torn wilfully, but not with that malice and previous intent which this required.

It should be observed, that here was a wound given, with an instrument that was not calculated solely for the purpose of affecting the body, such, for instance, as piercing or stabbing, by making a hole; but here was an actual cutting, and the consequence wound was of a very length, and so was the rent in the clothes. It was for the Jury to decide whether (as both) body and clothes were cut, he who intended the end did also intend the means.

He left it to the jury to say, upon the whole of the case, whether the prisoner was guilty or innocent.

The jury immediately, without hesitation, found the prisoner guilty.

Mr. Justice Buller then ordered the judgment in this case to be arrested, and the recognizances of the persons bound to prosecute to he respited until the December sessions.

The court was crowded with spectators by nine, when this trial began, which ended at five o'clock at night.

All the witnesses were examined separately.

At the commencement of the sessions at the Old Bailey, on the 10th of December, 1790, Judge Ashurst addressed the prisoner nearly in the following terms: 'You have been capitally convicted under the statute of George I, of maliciously tearing, cutting, spoiling, and defacing, the garments of Anne Porter, on the 18th of January last. Judgment has been arrested upon two points—one, that the indictment is informal; the other that the act of parliament does not reach the crime. Upon solemn consideration, the judges are of opinion that both the objections are well founded: but, although you are discharged from this indictment, yet you are within the purview of the common law. You are therefore to be remanded, to be tried for a misdemeanor.'

He was accordingly, on the 13th of the same month, tried at Hicks's Hall for the misdemeanor, in making an assault on Miss Anne Porter.

The trial lasted sixteen hours: there were three counts in the indictment; *viz.* for assaulting with intent to kill, for assaulting and wounding, and for a common assault.

The charge was that he, on the 18th of January, 1790, made an assault on Anne Porter, and, with a certain knife, inflicted on her person a wound nine inches long, and, in the middle part of it, four inches deep.

The same witnesses were then called in support of the charge as appeared on the trial at the Old Bailey: they gave a very clear, correct, and circumstantial evidence, positively swearing to the person of the prisoner.

The facts proved were nearly the same, with very little variation indeed, with those which were given in evidence on his trial for the felony at the Old Bailey; for which reason we forbear to enter more fully on his trial.

The prisoner produced two witnesses, Miss Amet and Mr. Mitchell, who attempted to prove an *alibi,* and the credit of their testimony was not impeached by any contradiction. The question there-fore was, to which the jury would give credit; for the evidence on both sides was equally fair and unexceptionable.

The prisoner was again put to the bar at ten o'clock the next morning, and tried on the remaining indictments, on three of which he was found guilty; when the Court sentenced him two years' imprisonment in Newgate for each, and at the expiration of the time to find security for his good behaviour, himself in two hundred pounds, and two sureties in one hundred pounds each.

Thus ended the case of this man, which had greatly interested every rank of people; but all were by no means satisfied of his guilt, believing that the female witnesses, a circumstance which we have shown too frequently to have happened, mistook the man who wounded and ill treated the prosecutrix. The particulars we have given of the uncommon and brutal attack on the defenceless, by a monster of the stronger sex, with our full report of the trial, will sufficiently prépare our readers to judge for themselves on the case of Renwick Williams, divested of the popular prejudice then strong against him.

WINTERBOTTOM PREACHING SEDITION.

WILLIAM WINTERBOTTOM

Fined and imprisoned for preaching seditious sermons.

———

THIS factious priest was convicted before Mr. Baron Perryn, at the assizes for the county of Devon, for preaching a seditious sermon at Plymouth, on the 5th of November, 1792.

In the course of this discourse the defendant talked a great deal about the Revolution in 1688. He was sorry to see the laws so much abused as they were at present. He also spoke of the French revolution, and he did not doubt but that would open the eyes of every Briton. He asked why the streets were so crowded with vagrants, the workhouses with beggars, and the gaols with thieves? All this, he said, was to be attributed to our oppressive taxes. It was high time for the people of this country to stand forward and assert their rights. He made mention of the national debt— he denied that any part of it was paid off; it was only like taking money out of one pocket, and putting it into another. He said his majesty had no more right to the throne than the Stuarts, if he did not maintain the laws and established rules of the country. He urged that the revolution in France was wisely calculated for spreading the Gospel through twenty-five millions of people.

The defendant was also indicted and convicted, at the same time, for preaching at Plymouth another seditious sermon, on the 18th of November, 1792. He took his text from Romans xiii. 12. *viz.* 'The night is far spent, the day is at hand: let us therefore cast off the works of darkness, and let us put on the armour of light.' In the course of this discourse the defendant introduced several strong observations.

After the evidence on both sides had been heard, the jury, without hesitation, found the defendant guilty.

Judgment having been prayed by the king's counsel, Mr. Justice Ashurst thus addressed the defendant:— 'William Winterbottom, you have been found guilty of preaching two seditious and atrocious sermons. The first act of this daring profligacy you committed on the 5th of November, and the second on the 18th of the same month. It has been stated that you are a dissenting preacher: of what sect of religion you are I know not; but I can collect from your preaching that you are not at all connected with the Christian religion; for the Christian religion, after first regarding the duty to God, teaches and inspires love for, and obedience to, the established government; but the tendency of your doctrine is to overturn all order, religion, morality, and government, and to introduce anarchy and confusion.

'Your doctrine goes to the abuse of that toleration, by which it is meant that every man may be at liberty to reverence God in the way that his conscience may dictate. But your conscience dictates no such principles; therefore the means that you have taken is a double aggravation of your guilt, and merits a two-fold punishment. In one part of your sermon you approve of the revolution in France.

'As to your first proposition, it is sufficient that the pernicious designs intended to have been executed are frustrated.

'As to your second opinion, that the French revolution would open the eyes of the people of England, there I agree with you—it does open the eyes of the people—it has taken the veil from off the hacknied system of liberty and equality.

'All practical equality consists in the affording equal protection. This chimerical project has been tried in a neighbouring nation, the lamentable effects of which will be handed down with sorrow to the latest generation. This system, which has been tried, must press upon the minds of men, and must operate more forcibly than a volume of arguments.

'As to your second proposition, it is impossible to be justified: you have alleged that the present form of government is a scourge on the people; but that the yoke of bondage will be soon broken; that persecution is near its end; and that every man will soon have to boast of *equality*.

'As to your saying that the French revolution will open the eyes of the people, I trust it will also open your eyes, and be a scourge to those who wish to introduce anarchy and confusion.

'This Court, having taken the malignity of your offence into their serious consideration, do consequently order and adjudge that for your first offence you pay a fine of one hundred pounds to the king, and that you be imprisoned in the New Prison, Clerkenwell, in the county of Middlesex, for the term of two years; and that for your second offence you pay a fine of one hundred pounds to the king, and be imprisoned in the New Prison, Clerkenwell, for the term of two years, to be computed after the expiration of your first imprisonment; and that at the end of your Imprisonment you give security for your good behaviour for the term of five years, yourself in five hundred pounds, and two sureties in two hundred and fifty pounds each.'

The defendant then wished to address the Court, but Lord Kenyon said, 'The Court cannot hear you now. It would have been the duty of the Court to have heard you, if you had offered any thing before sentence was passed: notwithstanding, the source of mercy is open to you.'

The defendant was immediately taken into custody.

Itinerant declaimers from the pulpit to ignorant auditors are, when they turn politicians, not only a nuisance to society, but sometimes dangerous to the state. Let preachers of the gospel stick to their creed; when they dare to dabble in politics, with which they have no business, their punishment cannot excite much regret.

HADFIELD SHOOTING AT THE KING.

JAMES HADFIELD

Tried for high treason.

———

The trial of James Hadfield, for shooting at his late majesty at Drury Lane Theatre, on Thursday, the 15th of May, 1800, came on in the Court of King's Bench, on the 26th of June. The prisoner pleaded 'Not Guilty,' and the attorney-general addressed the jury at considerable length.

Mr. Joseph Craig was the first witness examined: he was a musician, and saw Hadfield above all the rest, with a pistol in his hand, pointed at his majesty; it was instantly fired, and dropped down: he assisted at dragging the prisoner over the rails into the music-room. Mr. Sheridan and the Duke of York came in; he said 'God bless your royal highness! I like you very well, you are a good fellow. This is not the worst that is brewing.'

Mr. John Holroyd sat next the prisoner, spoke to him, and remarked he was a pitiable object; saw a pistol presented across his face, and immediately discharged; he assisted in securing him.

Mr. J. Parkinson, a musician, was next examined: he confirmed what the first witness had deposed; and being asked if the situation was a good one for firing at his majesty, he replied that the prisoner could not have chosen a better.

Mr. Wright, the fourth witness, was in the first row next the orchestra; he heard the report of a pistol as his majesty entered his box; turned round, and caught the prisoner by the collar. A young lady, who sat behind, immediately pointed to the ground, where he saw and picked up the pistol, which he produced in court.

Miss Elizabeth Ormeston deposed that she sat on the third row, but could not say whether it was at the first or second bow to the audience from his majesty the pistol was fired; but immediately he threw down the pistol.

Mr. Law, one of the counsel for the prosecution, here desired that the Duke of York might be called; upon which the prisoner, in a paroxysm of enthusiasm, cried out, 'God bless the duke! I love him.' The Court, seeing his agitation, immediately gave directions that he should be permitted to sit down; and Mr. Kirby, the keeper of Newgate, (who all the time sat next to him), told him he had permission of the Court to sit down; which he did, and remained composed during the remainder of the trial.

The Duke of York was present at the examination; remarked at the time that he knew the prisoner; that he had been one of his orderly men. The prisoner said 'He knew his own life was forfeited; he regretted the fate of his wife only; he would be only two days longer from his wife;' said, 'The worst is not come yet.' His royal highness said the prisoner appeared to be perfectly collected. After his majesty had retired, his royal highness directed a search to be made in the king's box, where a hole was discovered, evidently made by the impression of a shot, fourteen inches from his majesty's head. It had perforated the pillar. In searching below, some slugs were found; by the smell, they had been recently fired off. Mr. Erskine asked his royal highness if the most loyal and brave men were not usually selected to be the orderly men. His royal highness answered that the most tried and trusty men were appointed orderly men. When the prisoner was asked what could induce him to commit so atrocious an act, he said he was tired of life, and thought he should have been killed.

The evidence for the prosecution being closed, Mr. Erskine addressed the jury at considerable length.

Major Ryan, of the 15th light dragoons, in which the prisoner was a private, Hercules M'Gill, private in the same regiment, and John Lane, of the Guards, all knew the prisoner, and deposed to different acts of his insanity.

Mr. Cline, surgeon; Dr. Crichton, physician; and Dr. Letherne, surgeon to the 15th regiment, as professional gentlemen, gave testimony to their belief of the prisoner's insanity.

Captain Wilson, and Christopher Lawton, of the 15th light dragoons; David Hadfield, brother to the prisoner; Mary Gore, sister-in-law to the prisoner; Catharine Harison, and Eliabeth Roberts, detailed different acts of insanity, particularly on the day previous to, and on which he committed the crime for which he stood indicted.

The prisoner was found by the jury to be insane.

THE PRETENDED HAMMERSMITH GHOST FRIGHTENING A POOR WOMAN TO DEATH.

FRANCIS SMITH

Condemned to death for the murder of a supposed ghost.

———

SUPERSTITION, in the beginning of the enlightened year 1804, was revived in the vicinity of Hammersmith, near London, where the inhabitants were possessed with an opinion that a ghost haunted their neighbourhood; but the fancied spectre was proved to be composed of human flesh and blood, which were unfortunately mangled and shed unto death by the unhappy man whose case is now before us.

The wanton performer of the pretended spirit merited severe punishment, for, with the frogs to the mischievous boys, who were pelting them with stones, they might truly have said, 'It is *sport* to you, but death to us.' Besides, the poor man who lost his life being mistaken for this mimic ghost, Smith was condemned to die for the murder.

One poor woman in particular, who was far advanced in her pregnancy of a second child, was so much shocked, that she took to her bed, and survived only two days. She had been crossing near the churchyard about ten o'clock at night, when she beheld something, as she described, rise from the tomb-stones. The figure was very tall, and very white! She attempted to run, but the ghost soon overtook her, and, pressing her in his arms, she fainted; in which situation she remained some hours, till discovered by some neighbours, who kindly led her home, when she took to her bed, from which, alas! she never rose.

The ghost had so much alarmed a waggoner belonging to Mr. Russel, driving a team of eight horses, and which had sixteen passengers at the time, that the driver took to his heels, and left the waggon and horses so precipitately, that the whole were greatly endangered.

Neither man, woman, nor child, could pass that way for some time; and the report was, that it was the apparition of a man who had cut his throat in the neighbourhood above a year ago.

Several lay in wait different nights for the ghost; but there were so many by-lanes and paths leading to Hammersmith, that he was always sure of being on that which was unguarded, and every night played off his tricks to the terror of the passengers.

Francis Smith, doubtless incensed at the unknown person who was in the habit of assuming this supernatural character, and thus frightening the superstitious inhabitants of the village, rashly determined on watching for, and shooting, the ghost; when unfortunately he shot a poor innocent man, Thomas Milwood, a bricklayer, who was in a white dress, the usual habiliment of his occupation. This rash act having been judged wilful murder by the coroner's inquest, Smith was accordingly committed to gaol, and took his trial at the ensuing sessions at the Old Bailey, January 13; when Mr. John Locke, wine merchant, living in Hammersmith, stated, that on the 3rd of January, about half past ten in the evening, he met the prisoner, who told him he had shot a man, whom he believed to be the pretended ghost of Hammersmith.

A rumour of a ghost walking about at night had prevailed for a considerable time. He went with the prisoner, in company with Mr. Stowe and a watchman, up Lima kiln Lane, to Blacklion Lane, where the deceased was lying apparently dead.

The witness and Mr. Stowe consulted together upon what was proper to be done, and they directly sent for the high constable. The body had no appearance of life; there was a shot in the left jaw. The prisoner was much agitated, the witness told him the consequence likely to be the result of his conduct. The prisoner replied, that he fired, but did not know the person whom he had shot; he also said that, before he fired, he spoke twice to the deceased, but received no answer.

Mr. Const, for the prisoner, cross-examined this witness. For five weeks previous to this melancholy catastrophe, the ghost had been the subject of general conversation in Hammersmith. He had never seen it. The dress in which the ghost was said to appear corresponded with that worn by the deceased, being white. The deceased had on white trowsers, down to his shoes; a white apron round him, and a flannel jacket on his body. The ghost sometimes appeared in white, and frequently in a calf's skin.

The prisoner was so agitated when the witness met him, that he could hardly speak. The deceased, after the prisoner called out, continued to advance towards him, which augmented his fear so much that he fired. The witness described the evening as very dark: Blacklion Lane was very dark at all times, being between hedges; and on that evening it was so very obscure, that a person on one side of the road could not distinguish an object on the other.

The prisoner, when he first mentioned the accident, expressed to the witness his wish that he would take him into custody, or send for some person to do so. The prisoner was a man mild and humane, and of a generous temper.

William Girdle, the watchman in Hammersmith, after stating that he went to the spot with Mr. Locke, described the posture in which the deceased was found. He was lying on his back, stretched out, and quite dead. His left jaw was broken by a shot. The prisoner came to the witness, and said he had hurt a man, and he was afraid very badly. Previous to this the prisoner told him he was going to look after the ghost. The witness replied that he would join him, after crying the hour, and that they would search the lanes together. They agreed on a watch-word: 'Who comes there?—A friend.—Advance, friend.' The witness went his rounds, and just before he got to Blacklion Lane he heard the report of a gun. He took no notice of that circumstance, as he frequently heard firing in the night. He did not see a gun lying by the deceased. The prisoner offered to deliver himself up.

On his cross-examination, the witness said that he himself was armed with a pistol, as other watchmen are. He had seen the supposed ghost himself on the Thursday before, being the 29th of December. It was covered with a sheet or large table-cloth. He encountered it opposite the four-mile stone, and pursued it, but without success, as the spirit pulled off the sheet and ran. The alarm had been very great for six weeks or two months, and many people had been terribly frightened. He knew the prisoner, and he was nothing like a cruel man.

Anne Milwood, sister to the deceased, was next called. The Lord Chief Baron lamented that any questions relative to this melancholy affair should be put to her, but for the ends of justice they were rendered indispensably necessary. She stated that she lived with her father and mother; between ten and eleven of the evening of the third of January, her brother called; he had been to inquire for his wife, who was at Mr. Smith's, the outrider. The witness and her mother were going to bed, and her mother asked the deceased, whether his wife had come home? He replied, that she had not. She then desired him to sit down, and wait for her half an hour. He sat till the witness heard the clock go eleven. She then desired him to go home; and he got up and went away, wishing the witness a good night. He shut the door behind him, and the witness directly went and opened it, stepped out, and stood on some bricks, looking after him. At that instant she heard a voice exclaim, 'Damn you, who are you, and what are you? I'll shoot you, if you don't speak.' This address was directly followed by the discharge of a gun. The witness, exceedingly alarmed for her brother's safety, called out 'Thomas' three or four times. The witness then went into the house, but she could not persuade either her father, mother, or a gentleman who lodged with them, that any accident had befallen her brother. She went out alone, and found him quite dead. She ran for assistance to a neighbour's house, and in returning from it she saw the prisoner, Mr. Locke, Mr. Stowe, and the watchman.

Her brother was in his usual working-dress, as described by the first witness in his cross-examination. The witness added, that she had heard great talk of a ghost stalking up and down the neighbourhood, all in white, with *horns* and *glass eyes,* but she did not know that any body had ever watched in order to discover and detect the impostor.

Mr. Flower, a surgeon at Hammersmith, saw the body the day following the accident; and on the 6th of January examined it by order of Mr. Hodgson, the coroner. He found that the deceased had received a gun-shot wound on the left lower jaw, with small shot, as he thought, No. 4, which penetrated to the vertebra of the neck, and injured the spinal marrow, which is a continuation of the brain. The face of the deceased was black, and that blackness was occasioned by the discharge of powder from a gun. The wound in the jaw was doubtless the cause of Milwood's death. He knew Smith; he was not a vindictive, but, on the contrary, a remarkably mild man.

A constable then stated that the prisoner had surrendered to him, and that he had been two days in his custody.

This finished the case for the prosecution.

The prisoner, having been called upon for his defence, said he would leave it to his counsel; but, on being told that they could not speak on his behalf, being only allowed to examine his witnesses, he stated that he went out with no bad design or intention; and that, when the unfortunate accident happened, he knew not what he did. He solemnly declared his innocence, and that he had no intention or idea of taking the life of any one.

The prisoner's counsel then called Mrs. Fullbrook, mother-in-law to the deceased: she said that, on the Saturday evening before his death, he told her that two ladies and a gentleman had taken fright at him, as he was coming down the Terrace, thinking he was the ghost. He told them he was no more a ghost than any of them, and asked the gentleman if he wished for a punch in the head. The witness advised the deceased in future to put on a great coat, in order that he might not encounter any danger.

Thomas Groom was called, as it would appear, to prove that some supernatural being actually visited the town of Hammersmith. He said he was servant to Mr. Burgess, a brewer, and that as he and a fellow-servant were going through the churchyard, one night, something, which he did not see, caught hold of him by the throat.

A number of witnesses were then called to the prisoner's character, which they described as mild and gentle in the extreme.

One of these witnesses said he had known the prisoner for fifteen years; and, during that period, his life had been marked by singular acts of humanity and benevolence.

The Lord Chief Baron then proceeded to address the jury. His lordship observed, that nothing which had been stated, or had appeared in this case, could possibly change the nature of the offence from murder. Although malice was necessary to make out the crime of murder, yet it was not necessary, according to law, to prove that the prisoner had known the deceased, or had cherished any malice, or, as was vulgarly called, spite against him. If a man should fire into the hall where he was now sitting, and kill any body at random, such a deed was murder. On the same principle, if a person was killed by design, without any authority, but from a supposition that the person ought to be killed, such an act was also murder, unless the killing was accidental.

If a man went not armed on the highway, intending to shoot robbers, and should decide in his own mind that an individual whom he might see was a robber, and should kill the man who actually was not a robber, such an act would be held as murder.

However disgusted the jury might feel in their own minds with the abominable person guilty of the misdemeanour of terrifying the neighbourhood, still the prisoner had no right to construe such misdemeanour into a capital offence, or to conclude that a man dressed in white was a ghost. It was his own opinion, and was confirmed by those of his learned brethren on the bench, that if the facts stated in evidence were credible, the prisoner had committed murder. In this case there was a deliberate carrying out a loaded gun, which the prisoner concluded he was entitled to fire, but which he really was not; and he did fire it with a rashness which the law does not excuse. In all the circumstances of the case, no man is allowed to kill another rashly.

His lordship here recapitulated the evidence, and commented on the defence made by the prisoner, which he remarked was singular. The prisoner had gone out persuaded that he was to meet a man, and yet when he did encounter him, he was so terrified as to be unconscious of what he did.

The prisoner had received an excellent character; and here his lordship explained the reason why no witness but one could speak to his character farther than two years. The prisoner was an excise-officer, and, as such, liable to be removed and shifted from one situation to another, so that it was a great chance if he remained long in one place.

His lordship was afraid that his good character could not avail, in point of law, in that place, whatever effect it might have in another quarter, which did not become him to conjecture.

The jury retired for above an hour, and returned a verdict 'Guilty of Manslaughter.'

On hearing this verdict, it was stated by the bench, that such a judgment could not be received in this case; for it ought either to be a verdict of *murder*, or of *acquittal*. If the jury believed the facts, there was no extenuation that could be admitted; for supposing that the unfortunate man was the individual really meant to have been shot, the prisoner would have been guilty of murder. Even with respect to civil processes; if an officer of justice uses a deadly weapon, it is murder, if he occasions death by it even although he had a right to apprehend the person he had so killed.

Mr. Justice Rooke.—'The court have no hesitation whatever, with regard to the law, and, therefore, the verdict must be—Guilty of Murder, or A total acquittal from want of evidence.'

Mr. Justice Lawrence.— 'You have heard the opinion of the whole Court is settled as to the law on this point, it is therefore unnecessary for me to state mine in particular. I perfectly agree with the learned judge who stated the law in so clear and able a manner. If an officer kills a person whom he had a right to apprehend, upon suspicion of felony, he is guilty of murder, except in particular cases. Now this man was not even attempting to run away, supposing it had been the very person who was guilty of the misdemeanour; there was, therefore, no excuse for killing him. But though it had been the person who was alarming the neighbourhood, the prisoner had no right to kill him, even if he should attempt an escape, for the crime is only a misdemeanour. Upon every point of view, this case is, in the eye of the law, a murder, if it be proved by the facts. Whether it has or not is for you to determine, and return your verdict accordingly. The law has been thus stated by Justice Foster, and all the most eminent judges.'

Recorder.—'I perfectly agree with the learned judges who have spoken. Gentlemen, consider your verdict again.'

The jury then turned round, and, after a short consultation, returned their verdict 'Guilty.'

Lord Chief Baron.—'The case, gentlemen, shall be reported to his majesty immediately.'

The Recorder then passed sentence of death on the prisoner in the usual form; which was, that he should be executed on Monday next, and his body given to the surgeons to be dissected.

The prisoner, who was dressed in a suit of black clothes, was then twenty-nine years of age, a short but well-made man, with dark hair and eyebrows; and the pallid hue of his countenance, during the whole trial, together with the signs of contrition which he exhibited, commanded the sympathy of every spectator.

Several of the prisoner's relations were present, and apparently in great distress.

The sessions-house was crowded in every part by nine o'clock; and the yard was filled with an anxious multitude, all making inquiry, and interested in the fate of the prisoner; who, affected by shame and remorse, was now and then so seriously agitated, that he could with difficulty support himself. When called upon for his defence, his voice faltered, insomuch that it was not without a considerable effort he could articulate a word. On the retiring of the jury to reflect on his case, and the return of the verdict, he betrayed such apprehensions of real danger, as to deprive him of the power of sustaining himself without the friendly aid of a bye-stander.

When the jury returned, he made a sort of desperate effort—stood up, and endeavoured to attend to the verdict given. When the dreadful word 'Guilty!' was pronounced, he sunk into a state of stupefaction exceeding despair. He at last retired, supported by the servants of Mr. Kirby.

The Lord Chief Baron having told the jury, after they had given their verdict, that he would immediately report the case to his majesty, was so speedy in this humane office, that a 'respite during pleasure' arrived at the Old Bailey, before seven o'clock, and on the 25th he received a pardon, on condition of being imprisoned one year.

MITCHELL CUTTING HIS DAUGHTER'S THROAT.

SAMUEL WILD MITCHELL

Executed for the murder of his infant daughter.

———

In pity to the memory of this wretched old man, we are inclined to hope that a sudden fit of frenzy alone hurried him to the commission of this most unnatural, horrid, and cruel deed, On the very day before he murdered his daughter, a separation had taken place between him and his wife; and the child, Sally, went that night to the lodgings which her mother had taken for herself. On the next morning the little innocent returned, and was employed in quilling (*i. e.* putting silk on a shuttle for her father to weave with, he being a weaver), when the inhuman parent took a razor, and cut the child's throat from one ear to the other: the wound was four inches in length, and two in depth. He then left the house, confessed his guilt to an acquaintance, and wandered about the streets till evening, when he found his way to his son-in-law's house, and was there apprehended. The officers went to his room, where the razor was found open, and covered with blood, within four or five feet of the unfortunate deceased. The prisoner was taken before a magistrate, and voluntarily confessed the whole of this horrid transaction.

His trial came on at the Sessions House in the Old Bailey, January 11, 1805, before Sir Archibald Macdonald, Knight, Lord Chief Baron. The appearance of the prisoner, when brought to the bar, was wretched in the extreme: his hair was grey, and his head was covered with an old miserable nightcap.

William Godby deposed that he had been married to a daughter of the prisoner for more than eight years; that the prisoner lived, on the 18th of December, 1804, in Wheeler Street, Spitalfields; that he was a married man, and lodged in the top room of the house; his wife, and his child, Sally, the deceased, had lived with him, but he and his wife had been separated the day before this horrid transaction. The prisoner at the bar was a weaver, and Sally, the deceased, used to be employed in winding quills for her father. He saw the prisoner at nine o'clock in the morning of this transaction, and did not see him again on that day till about ten at night: he saw the prisoner at the house where he, the witness, lodged, and he told him he should not come into his room. About half past twelve on the same day, after he had been to the warehouse with his work, he went up to see him; and, when he came into his room, he saw the child, Sally, lying in her blood, but did not notice the wound, he was so alarmed: he went down to the room under the prisoner's, and told Mrs. Nicholls, who lived in that room; he then went away: he had some of his master's property about him, and that he carried home: he returned a second time, and went into the room again, and saw Mr. Kennedy, the officer, there.

Mrs. Nicholls said that she lived in the room immediately under the prisoner; that she was at home on the 18th of December, and said that the prisoner's wife had been with him that morning; that she had a light of her (to light his fire) before eleven o'clock; and that she heard Sally, the deceased, go up stairs, on her return from Spitalfields' charity-school, about twelve o'clock; she knew it was the little girl by the step, and that when she got into her father's room, she heard the quill-wheel go, and the prisoner's loom make a noise, which it usually did when he was weaving; shortly after she heard a woman go down stairs, and after that a man's foot, but did not see either of them; that the prisoner had previously called out to her, a little before twelve, to know what o'clock it was; and that Godby, the former witness, came to her in about half an hour after she heard the quill-wheel go, and the noise of the prisoner's loom when he was weaving: that she went up with him and saw Sally, the deceased, lying in her gore of blood; that she saw nothing of the wound, was afraid of going into the room, and called out, to the landlord, 'Murder!' upon which he came up.

William Byron deposed that he was, on the 18th of December, the landlord of the house, No. 24, Wheeler Street, but had since removed, and that the prisoner, at that time, lodged in the garret. That, on the alarm of murder, he went up stairs, and took the child up by the waist, when her head fell back, and the gash appeared to him; he then gave the alarm, that her throat was cut, and desired them to go for a surgeon, and for her father, who he supposed was at the Elder Tree public house, just by: he then looked round the room, to see if he could find any instrument, but could not. He observed the quill-wheel was bloody, and the track of blood about the room.

Edward Dellafour, a journeyman broad-silk weaver, saw the prisoner on the 18th, between the hours of twelve and one, at his apartments, No. 26, Skinner Street, Shoreditch. He was at work, and the prisoner knocked at his door, upon which he let him in. The prisoner asked him to go down stairs with him, as he had something particular to communicate. He refused to leave his work, unless he would tell him his business; the prisoner then said something had happened that day which never had happened before, and that he should go to Newgate. Seeing him in a violent perturbation of mind, he reluctantly left his work; the prisoner having gone down stairs, and, anxious to know the cause of it, he followed, and found him at the street door; they went about fifty yards from the witness's door; the prisoner then, with a countenance full of grief, turned round to him, and said, 'Ned, I shall die!' The witness asked him what had happened, or what was the matter with him; the prisoner replied, 'I have killed my Sally.' The witness asked him if the child was dead; the prisoner said 'Yes, I have cut her head half off.' It was a very severe morning, and the prisoner was shivering with cold; he desired the witness to go with him into a public house, that he might warm himself, and have something to drink; they went into the first public house they came to, which was the Cock and Magpie, in Worship Street, and had a pot of beer; the prisoner called for it, and a pipe of tobacco. There were three men and a woman there, entire strangers to the witness. The prisoner then said to the witness in the tap-room, 'Sit down, I have something to say to you.' Seeing the strangers in the room, the witness thought it imprudent to speak before them, and desired the prisoner not to say it there: in about a quarter of an hour they went out. The witness asked the prisoner where he was going, and what he meant to do with himself. He said he was going to Shadwell to see two friends of his who were rope-makers, who would, when he was in prison, allow him a shilling or two: he then asked when the sessions would begin; the witness told him; he said he would give himself up to justice, and suffer, with this remark—'It would make no odds to him if they cut him in a thousand pieces, for that when he went hundreds would go at the same minute.' The witness told him he should not have killed his child. The prisoner looked him in the face, and said, 'I know that—do not you retort on me now it is done.' The witness accompanied him as far as Whitechapel Church, then shook him by the hand, and saw him no more till at the office; the witness said the magistrate sent for him, and he gave the same account at that time as now. When in the public house he observed a small quantity of blood on one of his hands.

Thomas Grice, a watchman, of Bethnal Green, apprehended the prisoner, who said he was the man that was guilty of the murder, and resigned himself up.

James Kennedy, an officer of Worship Street, received information of the murder about one o'clock in the afternoon, and went with Bishop into the prisoner's room, and there saw the deceased lying with her head towards the door, with no cap on, and her throat cut quite through the windpipe; she had done bleeding when the witness saw her, but the blood lying on the floor was warm. On the block of the quill-wheel there was a quantity of blood, and a track of blood from the wheel to where the body lay. Near the quill-wheel there was a low stool, and at the side of it he found a razor open. It was covered with fresh blood at that time. [This he produced in court, and a cap of the deceased, stained with blood, that had fallen from her head.] About twelve at night they received information that he was in Spitalfields' watch-house. Armstrong and he went there, and saw the prisoner sitting by the watch-house fire. He turned his head round, and said, 'Kennedy, I have given you much trouble to-day in searching after me.' Armstrong said to him, 'What do you mean by that? Is your name Mitchell?' He said it was. Armstrong again asked him did he know he was charged with murdering his own daughter; and said he had found a cap and a razor in his room. The prisoner then answered, with that razor he had often shaved himself, and with that razor he committed the horrid deed.

Joseph Moser, Esq. the magistrate of Worship Street office, stated that the prisoner was brought before him to be examined on Wednesday, the 19th of December: he took down the confession of the prisoner in writing, telling him the consequences in every point of view, and the use that would be made of it after he had signed it: he repeated it over to him several times, said it was true what he had signed, and signed it in the magistrate's presence.

The prisoner's examination was as follows:—

'*Public Office, Worship Street.*
'The voluntary confession of Samuel Mitchell, weaver, for the wilful murder of his child, aged nine years, taken by Joseph Moser, Esq. December 19, 1801.

'I, Samuel Wild Mitchell, weaver, late of the parish of Christ Church, Middlesex, now standing at the bar of the public office, Worship Street, being fully apprized of the nature of my situation by the magistrate, and through him made perfectly sensible of the nature of this acknowledgment, do make this free and unbiassed confession, which is taken by my own desire:—That I had a daughter named Sally, and my wife had a daughter named Elizabeth, who at one time did live with me, but whom I afterwards took to my apartment, where I instructed her in the art of weaving, and we lived all together: this said daughter of my wife's caused some uneasiness, as I thought; and I thought my wife was more indulgent to her faults, and favoured her more than she ought, which was the reason of our separation on the 17th of December last; my wife also took with her Sarah Mitchell, whom I loved with the most ardent affection, which vexed me a great deal, as I saw there would be a continual dispute. I could not bear the little girl coming to see me, as coming on a visit. I resolved that neither my wife nor me should possess her. I seized the moment of the mother going away; the child was sitting by the fire, winding quills. I took the razor from the drawer; my affection made me almost lay it down again, but my resolution overcame that. I turned round, and cut her throat. I was too resolute to make a faint attempt; the child was dead in a moment; she neither made noise nor resistance. When I had done the deed, the child fell. As I went out I saw her blood; then I ran down stairs. After this act was done to my child, Sarah Mitchell, I went to a man named Bell, where I had lived, and left word for him to run and secure my master's work; then I went to Mr. Dellafour, and my friends at Wapping. This acknowledgment is free, and made by my own desire.

(Signed)
'SAMUEL WILD MITCHELL.
'JOSEPH MOSER.'

'Dec. 19, 1804.'

The prisoner having been now called on for his defence, the wretched man addressed the Court and jury in a manner above his rank or appearance. His defence was nearly as follows:—

'My Lord, and Gentlemen of the Jury,—I stand in this place to-day, an awful spectacle of guilt and disgrace; but I will endeavour to be as collected in my reason as possible, though at certain times and seasons I am particularly under heavy pressure of mind, which my wife well knows, and was well aware of: that I have committed the horrid deed laid to my charge I have no wish to deny, any more than I have to avoid the dreadful punishment that awaits my guilt; to that I am resigned; nor was it my wish from the unfortunate moment of my crime to evade justice; but that I committed the deed maliciously against my poor child, who was the victim of my fatal passion, I solemnly deny. Malice I had none. I declare in the presence of God, before whom I stand, and make this declaration, and before whose awful tribunal I must shortly appear, instead of bearing to her malice, I loved her most tenderly. I had kind love to the child, and wished her not to be from me; and to that love, strange and perverse as it may seem, is owing chiefly the sad cause that brings me here this day. I am married to a second wife, by whom this child was my only daughter; we had long known each other before our marriage, when I was in better days, and when she and I were the wife and husband of others. I thought I could be happy with her; but I found her temper incompatible with my happiness or her own. I found the friends and the family with which she was connected thought her marriage with me degrading to her. Disputes and controversy, for ten years, frequently took place between us; in which, unhappily, both were in fault, too much so; those disputes were often carried to a pitch of fury (and may this sad spectacle that I now stand be a warning to others, that if they meet with double families to have more love to their duty); and what tended still more to exasperate me and aggravate our dissensions was, that those she called her friends always sided with her in every thing, whether right or wrong; and many of them, I am sorry to say, who were strenuous supporters of religious principles, were always more ready to lend a hand to the creating of mischief than to the promotion of charity and peace:—May the Lord forgive them, and take me to himself! Our disputes at last ended in a mutual agreement to separate, and the child I so tenderly loved was to go with her mother: this my unhappy temper and feeling could not bear, which led me to the fatal resolution that neither she nor I should have the child, by committing the horrid deed, by putting an end to her life in the manner I have done! I pray God Almighty to forgive me, and to direct you in your decision upon me this day; and though here I stand an object of sin and misery, yet I hope my unhappy fate will prove an awful example to those who form second marriages, with children on both sides, against giving way to intemperate disputes, that may lead them, as they have done me, to acts of desperation and vengeance, beyond the control of reason or reflection. If my wife was present, she could vouch and prove that it was impossible I could ever have deliberately executed such an act. She could testify that my disposition was not cruel; and that, when I have been the most resolute to good purposes, unfortunately, under agitations of mind or provocations of temper, such has been my weakness, I am not always the same man: and, under such circumstances, I have very frequently been led into excesses of frenzy, which, in cool moments, have astonished me. Once, in particular, urged by distress, when I had no work, I applied for relief at my parish work-house. I had come too late in the day, when, wound up by disappointment to madness, I broke as many windows as cost the parish four pounds for the repair; and yet the par-ish officers, though they might have punished me, did not, knowing that my act was the result of a mind deranged.— May the Lord forgive me, and take me to himself! I must die a spectacle of sin and horror!'

The learned judge observed to the jury, 'That the fact of a person's being overcome by any sudden paroxysm of passion to commit a deed of so flagitious a nature operated as no justification of the crime. If God afflicted any man with a temporary or occasional want of reason, that was a different question. There, from the mere occasional suspension of the reasoning faculties, the crime might have been committed; but such could by no means be compared to the case where the dereliction of the reasoning faculties had been occasioned, either by the contemplation of a circumstance, by which alone the mind was affected, or by which, after its completion, the mind could be supposed capable of being agitated. Here a strange mixture of affection was discernible amidst the cruelty which had prompted the perpetration of the deed; but he could see nothing in the case to induce him to point out to the jury any distinction between this case and the various other cases of a similar kind which presented themselves.'

After the Lord Chief Baron had made his remarks, the prisoner requested permission to speak again, which was granted immediately by the Court.

'There is one single point I have to say, which my wife could attest, if she was here, as she was well acquainted with my misery, as well as my mother's, who would frequently go into the same way: she was a very sensible woman; she would frequently ask me to cut her hair, for, unless her hair was kept cut in a very particular close manner, her weakness was upon her. So it has been with me.'

The jury having found him guilty, the prisoner was asked what he had to say for himself, why sentence of death should not be passed according to law? The prisoner distinctly replied, 'I have nothing to say.'

The awful sentence, that he was to be hanged the succeeding Monday, and his body afterwards dissected and anatomized, was immediately pronounced by the recorder; which the prisoner heard without any visible emotion. The court was crowded in almost every part, and particularly with ladies; and not only the women, but even the jury, the counsel, and nearly all present, were melted into tears. During the whole trial the prisoner appeared calm, but not insensible. He was very attentive to the evidence, and appeared frequently to utter a low ejaculation.

On the morning after his trial, this unhappy man expressed a desire to see his wife, that they might exchange forgiveness. The day following (Sunday) she came to visit him in Newgate, but was so ill that she was obliged to be brought in a hackney-coach, supported between two friends. As soon as the distressing interview was over, he applied himself devoutly to prayer, in which he continued nearly the whole of the day. On that day he was extremely solicitous to obtain Dr. Ford's promise to publish to the world that he died in the faith of the Church of England; as it had been generally understood that he belonged to the sect denominated Methodists. At half past six o'clock Mitchell's cell was unlocked, and the Ordinary attended him to the chapel to prayers; which being concluded, he returned to the Press-yard, and there walked for some time, holding two friends by the arms; meanwhile his mind was occupied with his unhappy situation: he begged of all around him to pray with him. He first put up a prayer to Heaven for his own soul; next invoked a blessing on his wife, his two daughters by a former marriage, his son and daughter-in-law, in the most pathetic manner. The unhappy man blessed the memory of his murdered child, and trusted the sacrifice he was about to make would, in some degree, expiate his crime in Heaven, which he did not despair to see. Then, in language which would have done credit to the pulpit or the bar, he besought God to grant the king health and long life; and to endue his ministers with wisdom, that it might be applied to the happiness and prosperity of his country.

His last petition was to the sheriffs, to request that, after the surgeons had practised upon his body, his mangled remains might be given to his daughter, for burial; which request the sheriffs promised should be complied with.

On Monday, January the 14th, at a very early hour, every avenue leading to the Old Bailey was crowded by persons of various descriptions, all eager and anxious to witness the last moments of this unhappy man; indeed a greater crowd was seldom seen on any similar occasion.

Mitchell seemed to attend with much earnestness and fervour to the clergyman, and he was seen to clasp his hands together the instant the rope was fixed. After the drop fell he appeared to feel great pain, as he swung round twice, which was occasioned by the violence of the convulsive struggles he sustained.

He suffered before Newgate, January the 14th, 1805, and, after hanging the usual time, was taken to St. Bartholomew's Hospital for dissection.

THE DISTRACTION OF ONE OF MORRIS'S WIVES ON HIS CONVICTION.

HENRY MORRIS

Transported for bigamy.

———

'FRAILTY, thy name is Woman,' says Shakespeare. The
immortal bard is right; or how could we find them, in spite
of precept and example, still the victims of the dissolute
and designing; clinging to their destroyers with a devotional tenacity, which, like their beauty, almost makes us
pardon their indiscretion; so accustomed are we to expect
virtue where appearances promise all that is commendable.
But, if we must lament the infatuation of the frailer sex,
in what terms can we express our detestation of the villain

who calculates on their weakness and simplicity; and, like the veiled prophet of Korassan, exhibits not the hideousness of his natural character until the victim is secured? But, alas! not even then has infatuated woman resolution enough to evince the dignity of insulted virtue; for we too often find them, as in the present instance, become more attached, as their destroyer becomes more worthless.

Henry Morris, in 1813, was indicted at Green Street, Dublin, for marrying Mary Anne Murphy, on the 15th of May, 1811, having previously been married to Maria Fontaine, on the 7th of August, 1805, who was alive at the time of his second marriage.

Both marriages being proved, Dennis Murphy, the afflicted father of the last of the prisoner's wives, (for he had several), came forward, and detailed a narrative of wrongs, that sensibly affected the Court. He first knew the prisoner on the 15th of October twelvemonth, at a billiard-room, in Dame Street. He told him of his being deeply in love with his daughter, who was then only fifteen years of age; and represented himself as a teacher, of great respectability. Morris was then introduced to Mr. Murphy's family, and continued his visits for five or six months; at the expiration of which period he persuaded the credulous girl to elope with him.

Two months after, the villain Morris wrote the unfortunate father a letter; expressed much contrition for what had occurred; and attributed it to the violence of his love, 'which would not brook delay.' He begged God's and Murphy's pardon; and requested a meeting. A meeting accordingly took place; the parties were reconciled; and Morris and Miss Murphy were legally married. But, before the wounded feelings of the father had been healed, he accidentally acquired information which caused them to bleed afresh. He learned, too surely, that his hopeful son-in-law had several wives; and that he had abandoned four young girls whom he had successively married. The poor man, with tears which bespoke the anguish of his heart, here mentioned that Maria Fontaine had died of a broken heart three weeks before the trial"; and said that his unfortunate daughter still continued so attached to her destroyer, that she spent the whole of her time with him in Newgate, coming home occasionally for support, which was given to her; for the unhappy parents could not bring themselves to desert their poor child, under any circumstance; and, if they were to do so, would consider themselves accountable in the eye of Heaven for the crimes she should fall into; as, in case of being turned from the paternal door, she had no alternative but street prostitution.

This wretched girl, lovely as unfortunate, was in court during the trial, and remained close to the prisoner. When the verdict was pronounced, she burst into the most outrageous expressions of grief; cried out most violently to save him; tore her hair, and clung round his neck, declaring that she would not be separated from him. The judges, however, ordered her to be removed, but directed that it should be done as gently as possible; and she was accordingly carried out of court in a state of utter distraction. Morris was then sentenced to transportation for seven years; the judge remarking that he had often ordered a man to be hanged for an offence much less heinous.

We cannot omit this opportunity of saying a few words respecting the virtue of prudence, which may be called the guardian of all the other domestic virtues. Without expatiating on its general importance, perhaps, it may be sufficient to remark that the affliction of Murphy's family, and the ruin of his miserable child, proceeded directly from the total absence of prudence in the old man. He introduces a stranger; encourages his addresses to his daughter, only fifteen years of age; and then permits them to go out alone; for under pretence of going to prayers they had eloped!

Surely he who took such little precaution to guard his child from error deserved to suffer for that child's impropriety. This case, however, we hope will not be unproductive of public benefit. Parents may learn from it to guard their children from the arts of strangers; and young women may be taught that to trust their ears to the tongue of men, whose character they know not, is to invite the seducer to spread his snares for their ruin.

THE SUPERSTITIOUS APPLICATION OF THE DEAD HAND OF HOLLINGS.

W. H. HOLLINGS

Executed for the murder of Elizabeth Pitcher.

———

THIS man's conduct was at once infamous and extravagant. He had been in the excise, where he became acquainted with one Pitcher, also an excise-officer, who on his death-bed recommended his wife and daughter, Elizabeth, to the care and protection of his friend Hollings.

The friend of the father was caressed by the mother and daughter. The latter lived servant with Mr. Cartwright, in Lower Grosvenor Street, where Hollings had been in the habit of calling on her. Notwithstanding that he had a wife of his own, who did not live with him, and was fifty years of age, without any personal recommendation whatever, he had the infamous audacity to annoy this poor girl with his fulsome addresses, which she appears to have rejected altogether, as an honest and virtuous young woman should do.

For refusing to entertain his abominable passion, Hollings meditated the ruin of this unfortunate girl, who was only in her twentieth year. On July the 4th he went in the evening to the house of her master, and asked for Betsy; she came out to him, and closed the door after her; they had continued together for a few minutes when the report of a pistol was heard, and the butler, running out, saw Hollings supporting the poor girl who had been shot through the heart, a wound of immense size being made in her side, from which flowed a copious discharge of blood.

Hollings did not attempt to escape. He held another pistol in his hand, which was found loaded to the muzzle, and the other had burst into a thousand pieces, having been similarly charged. On the steps lay a broken phial, containing arsenic and water, which Hollings thought to have taken, but the explosion of the pistol had shattered it out of his hands. When the patrol came up, he said, 'Don't seize me; I shall not attempt to go away.' He also asked 'if Elizabeth was dead, and if he might be permitted to kiss her cold lips.'

When taken to the watch-house, he said that he was in love with the deceased; and that he had sacrificed her for refusing to comply with his wishes. Being asked what those wishes were, he refused to give any explanation. During the night he drank four or five quarts of water, and vomited very much, occasioned by the poison he had taken, which, not being sufficient to cause death, only made him sick. His intention was, having shot the unfortunate girl, to poison himself; but the explosion of the pistol defeated his intentions.

On Friday, September the 16th, he was indicted at the Old Bailey, and tried, after the diabolical murderer, Mitchell.

The facts of the murder having been proved, several witnesses deposed to various acts of insanity committed by the prisoner, during the last twelve months. He had been discharged from the excise in consequence of his strange conduct; and certainly there appeared sufficient evidence to lead to an opinion that he was under the dominion of occasional insanity. But his whole conduct, with regard to the murder, was atrociously consistent. He had loaded the pistols on purpose, provided the poison, and procured the presence of his victim, by pretending that he had a message for her. All these, taken into account, left no room to doubt but that at the time of the horrid deed he was perfectly sane. He was accordingly found Guilty; after which Hollings addressed the Court. He acknowledged that he had been fairly tried, and justly convicted. He hoped his fate would be a warning to all who heard his case against the indulgence of violent passions: he had loved—fervently loved—the unhappy girl whose life he had taken away. His offence was great; but he hoped for mercy, through the Saviour of mankind.

On Monday morning, September 19th, 1814, Mitchell and Hollings were executed in front of Newgate. So great was the public curiosity to see the unfortunate malefactors, that, at seven o'clock on Monday morning the Old Bailey and Giltspur Street were crowded to a degree almost unprecedented. Much money was given for indifferent seats at the top of the houses opposite the debtors' door; and carts, waggons, and other vehicles, were all in requisition. It appears that Mitchell had entertained some hopes of acquittal, as he was often heard to say, 'There was no corroborating proof of his having fired the pistol.' At a quarter before eight the prisoners were introduced to the Press Yard, for the purpose of having their irons knocked off, accompanied by the Reverend Mr. Cotton and the Reverend Mr. Frere, the latter of whom sat up in constant prayer all the night with Hollings, who joined most fervently in the devotion.

Mitchell, who was dressed in black, was first brought out from the cell; he looked pale, and maintained a deportment of sullen resignation; he did not say a word, nor did he betray the slightest symptoms of feeling at his awful situation. He appeared regardless of any earthly transaction. The irons being knocked off, and the usual awful ceremony of tying the hands being executed, he lifted his hands as far as he was permitted, and, looking up, bowed, and appeared to be in prayer. Hollings stepped forward to the block with an activity which at first reminded us of the unhappy man, Ashton. He was, however, very tranquil; and, upon being disencumbered of his irons, addressed the persons around him in nearly the following words: 'Here, you see, I stand, a victim to passion and barbarity: my crime is great; and I acknowledge the justice of my sentence. But oh! the unfortunate girl I loved, I adored, as one of my own. I have made contrition, and prayed for forgiveness; I resign myself, under an impression that Almighty God has heard my prayers, and will forgive me: may you and the world take warning by my example; and here I confess the justice of my fate—receive my soul, O God!' At the last expression his feelings overcame him, and he wept.

The whole of the awful arrangements being complete, they were ushered to the fatal scaffold. Mitchell was until this time firm and unconcerned: he was prayed to by Mr. Cotton. He became much agitated, and the horrors of death were strongly portrayed in his countenance. Hollings shook hands with the officers of justice, declared to Mr. Frere that he was quite happy, and mounted the scaffold with great firmness and resignation. The clergymen continued to pray to them until the fatal signal was given, when the drop fell. Mitchell continued in the strongest convulsions for several minutes, and appeared to die very hard.

After they had hung some time, three females were introduced, for the application of the 'dead man's hand,' supposed to remove marks, wens, &c. The first was a young woman of interesting appearance, who was so much affected by the ceremony that she was obliged to be supported.

At nine the bodies were cut down, and sent to St. Bartholomew's Hospital for dissection.

THE ABDUCTION OF MISS CROCKATT.

SAMUEL DICK

Convicted of an abduction and rape.

———

THE barbarous practice of forcibly carrying off females prevails in Ireland to a shameful extent. Dishonoured women are too often induced to bestow their hand on the ravisher, and thus the success of one villain stimulates the lust and avarice of twenty. The law, which visits this crime with death, has not been sufficient to abolish so base and abominable a practice, as the Irish newspapers are, from time to time, filled with details of cases of abduction.

The robber may plead necessity, and the murderer provocation; but the wretch who deliberately invades the chastity of a female whom he wishes to make his wife, is not only without any excuse whatever, but betrays such a total absence of manly feeling that we know not any offender whose crime deserves a more speedy and capital punishment. Such a monster should be hurried, with a fearful precipitancy, out of society; for he has given proof that he is unfit for the company of virtuous and honourable men, by deliberately attempting to debase what all the world regards as sanctified and pure. Among the lower orders in Ireland, and sometimes among those of a higher rank, this practice is not looked on in the light it deserves. Indelicate and gross minds can see no moral turpitude in an abduction which terminates in marriage; but, as female purity is the vital essence of morality in society, whoever invades that source of all our virtues, and all our happiness, should be hunted down as a monster that preyed upon the dearest interests of man. Besides, it is a crime fearful, not only in its consequences, but in its commission. Family anguish must proclaim its commencement; virgin screams announce its completion; and protracted grief seal its guilt; for how can that woman, though a wife, feel happy, who is liable to have the 'slow unmoving finger of scorn' pointed at her, as one that had been dishonoured among men?

Samuel Dick was one of those contemptible wretches, who would arrive at wealth through the charnel-house of Inst, where his own sister stood the officiating goddess. His case is one of revolting indelicacy and deep-laid villainy. We shall give it in the words of the counsel retained to prosecute him at the Carrickfergus assizes, March the 21st, 1818.

'The prisoner, Samuel Dick, stands indicted for the forcible abduction and subsequent defilement of Elizabeth Crockatt, the prosecutrix. She is a young woman of respectable family in Derry; and upon the death of her father she became possessed of about two thousand six hundred pounds: this property, her youth, being scarcely seventeen,

and her personal attractions, had been the causes of two different atrocious outrages, for the purpose of obtaining possession of them. In August last, upon the Sabbath day, while
returning from the meeting, she was forcibly carried off, and
taken to Ballymena, where she was rescued by her brother
and her uncle. On their return home, her mother, alarmed
for her safety, sent her for some time to reside within a few
miles of Stewartstown, with a Mr. Matthew Fairservice. On
the night of the 3rd of November, Mr. Fairservice's family
were invited to spend the evening at Mr. Henry's, where
the prosecutrix met Miss Jane Dick, sister to the prisoner,
and who is related to the prosecutrix. The prosecutrix, with
Mr. Robert Fairservice, his sister, and Miss Dick, then went
from Mr. Henry's upon the car to a ball at a Mr. Park's,
where she danced the greater part of the night. While at
Mr. Park's, Miss Dick invited prosecutrix to Stewartstown,
which she declined. When they had got on the car, Robert
Fairservice drove rapidly towards Stewartstown, without
paying any attention to the remonstrances of the prosecutrix; when in Stewartstown, they drove to the prisoner's
house, where she saw the prisoner: after breakfast Miss
Dick asked Miss Fairservice and the prosecutrix to go to
Dungannon with her, as she wished to make some pur-
chases. She was prevailed upon, and did go into Dungannon; remained shopping there until the evening; returned
to Stewartstown, dined in the prisoner's house; and about
nine or ten o'clock the prosecutrix was asked by Miss
Dick to go out to the next door to assist her in purchas-
ing some thread; and the distance being so trifling, she did
not think even of putting on her bonnet. When out of the
hall-door, she was forcibly seized by some person, and put
into a chaise in which was the prisoner, who caught her
by the arm; when in the carriage, she found her cloak and
bonnet had been previously placed there, which was sufficient proof of the pre-concerted plan. The prosecutrix, the

prisoner, with Miss Dick, and the other person, were driven to Lurgan, a distance of twenty miles, before day-light in the morning, the prisoner Dick guarding the prosecutrix with a pistol! After some time she was again put into the chaise, and driven to the house of a person named Swayne, where, after having wept and fasted the whole day, she was prevailed upon to go to bed with Miss Dick. From the fatigue she had suffered the two preceding nights, joined to the anxiety of mind she had undergone, she fell asleep; and found, on awaking, that in place of Miss Dick being her bed-fellow, the prisoner at the bar was. The next morning the prisoner attempted to soothe the prosecutrix by promises of marriage, and went to Dr. Cupples, of Lisburn, to procure a license, leaving his sister and the other person to watch over her till his return: in spite of them, she contrived to escape to the house of a Mr. English, where she was protected until delivered into the hands of her uncle.'

This statement being supported by the evidence, the jury without hesitation found the prisoner guilty—Death.